SOLDIER PRIEST

by

John J. Morrett

Old Rugged Cross Press

Copyright © 1993 by John J. Morrett

No part of this book may be reproduced in any form or by any means. Published in the United States of America by Old Rugged Cross Press.
Inquiries should be addressed to:
Editor, Old Rugged Cross Press
1160 Alpharetta Street
Suite H,
Roswell, GA 30075

ISBN: 1-882270-01-0

Library of Congress Catalog Number:
92-83986

SOLDIER-PRIEST

Dedicated to my Christian parents

George Daniel and Mary Cecilia Morrett

Acknowledgments

I wish to thank the Rev. Dr. Charles H. Long, Director and Editor of Forward Movement Publications who gave me considerable guidance in strengthening the manuscript for publication. Mr. Robert A. Hite provided an excellent critique early in the writing of the original manuscript.

Elizabeth K. McCreary and her mother, Mrs Florence Kendall, also gave many suggestions and worked on the manuscript for correct grammar, helpful ideas on detail and, in certain places proposed revisions. My sister, Mary Jane McGregor, helped with family information and gave me constant affirmation while I wrote an often difficult story. I wish to thank Jan Ellison and Iris Fujii —who typed the manuscript— and Mr. M.L. Jones of the Living Faith Literary Agency who encouraged me throughout the lengthy process toward publication.

The World War II material was written soon after my escape from the Japanese as a prisoner of war. It was dictated to my father's secretary, but was never organized into full manuscript form until after my retirement in 1982. Date books, travel logs, diaries, letters and notes have been valuable resources in an effort to provide accurate information and to write even in the face of difficult experiences leaving unhappy memories. It is with satisfaction that I have fulfilled a promise to my battalion commanding officer, Lt. Col. William Ray, that some day I would tell our part in the Battle of Bataan.

ABOUT THE AUTHOR

The Reverend John J. Morrett was born in Springfield, Ohio, September 21, 1916. He graduated from Ohio State University in 1939 receiving a BS. degree and commissioned as a 2nd Lt. in the United States Army Reserve Corps. From 1939-1941 he attended the Episcopal Theological School in Cambridge, Massachusetts. At the outbreak of WW II, he was serving with the 2nd Bn. 88th Field Artillery, Philippine Scouts. He was captured on Bataan in April, 1942. After making the "Death March" he endured four Japanese prison camps and finally escaped from a prison ship September 7, 1944. In 1946 he was discharged from the Army and returned to his seminary, graduating in June, 1947.

In the fall of that year, he went to China as a missionary and later was ordered out of China with the impending fall of the Kuo Ming Tang government to the Communists. In 1949, he started a mission church in an abandoned dairy barn on the outskirts of Honolulu, Hawaii. The church was named Holy Nativity and he became its first Rector. In 1962 he was called to be the Rector of St. Andrew's Cathedral, Honolulu. In 1970, he was called to be Rector of St. Alban's Church, Columbus, Ohio and retired from this parish in 1981.

Since his retirement, he has served as "interim" in five different churches, including 2 1/2 years as Vicar of Christ Church, Bangkok, Thailand. He did extensive work on the Thai-Burmese border helping refugees with rice, blankets, medicine and the establishment of churches, schools and one orphanage. At the present time, he is Interim Vicar of St. Augustine's Church, Kapaau, Hawaii.

Prologue

As a soldier, I went willingly to war; I lived as a prisoner for two and a half years. I escaped to freedom.

I joined the military voluntarily, believing it was my duty to serve my country in a time of need. I saw the horrors of war on the battlefield, I survived the Bataan Death March, suffered agony, sickness, physical deterioration and despair as a prisoner of war; and swam, under fire, from a sinking ship and away from captivity.

Through it all, my overwhelming faith in God sustained me and overflowed to help others in their times of greatest need. I ministered to those on the brink of death and to others as they let go their fragile hold on life.

I was not yet the priest I had set out to be (and would later become), but my ministry had begun on the battlefield and in prison camps. There my Christian ministry reached out to men of many faiths.

After the war and in the ministry, I had many opportunities to travel worldwide. Through first hand experiences with different cultures and religions, I learned to appreciate and respect the spiritual depths of religions other than Christianity and observed that many non-Christians were seeking God, too. In most places around the world there is religious tolerance. But one of the great tragedies of human life is that most wars are basically religious wars. Spiritual beliefs should bind us together — but man-made differences tear nations apart or pit nations against one another.

Consequently, I have seen conflict on this planet during three quarters of a century. Kampuchia (Cambodia) is one of the most pathetic of nations — full of internal strife; yet at the beginning of this century it was one of the most peaceful countries in the world. Arabs and Jews are in constant strife in and near Israel. We are polarized in the Middle East between Iraq and most of the rest of the world. Christian Karen and Buddhist Burmans have been fighting each other for over forty years. Religious and ideological differences have divided Europe. One of the darkest moments in this century was the erection of the Berlin wall; one of the brightest the moment it came down.

War is wrong, but oppression, inhumane treatment, and torture by tyrannical governments are also wrong. As long as these wrongs exist, there will be armies to oppose them. The soldier in me fought. The priest in me longs for peace.

For the priest in me there is a constant focus on "faith, hope and love." There is "hunger and thirst after righteousness." With these came for me an insatiable need to renew and replenish my faith throughout my ministry. My need was great for over fifty years while ministering to others. I attempted to fulfill it through daily prayer and meditation, but I also needed to be bolstered by help from others and this frequently came from studies at respected religious centers in Europe as well as America.

But my greatest source of strength has been in the Bible, "from whence cometh my help" through the words of wisdom, comfort and guidance—and above all from God's love through the teachings of His Son, Jesus Christ and His Holy Spirit.

1

STANDING AT A CROSSROADS

With the impending U. S. participation in WW II, a seminary classmate and I felt apart from the rest of the class. We had feelings of separateness. Both of us held reserve commissions in the United States Army while the others were mainly pacifists.

My training for the priesthood in the Episcopal Church began in the Fall of 1939 following graduation from Ohio State University. During the second year at the Episcopal Theological School in Cambridge, Massachusetts, I began to frequent St. John's Chapel late in the evenings for private prayer and meditation. At the time, newspapers were full of war news. In 1939 Germany had invaded Poland and the next year the Nazis had invaded Denmark, Norway, the Netherlands, Belgium and Luxembourg. Belgium surrendered as I was returning home for summer vacation in June, 1940, and before the end of the month the Germans had occupied Paris. Italy was now in the war and the United States was beginning to conscript men for military service.

One day in Dean Angus Dun's theology class we listened to Bishop Appleton Lawrence lecture on pacifism. At the end he asked for comments and questions, so I said that under the circumstances, particularly in Europe at the present time, I could not agree with him. My question on pacifism was how could grown men allow their countries to be invaded, families killed and wounded and not try to stop the aggression? It seemed strange disagreeing with a bishop of the church, but I stood my ground. As the discussion developed I felt somewhat separate and alone in my thinking.

Soon after January, 1941, Dean Angus Dun asked me to come to his office for a conference. He opened the conversation with a reference to my commission in the U.S. Army Reserves. After some discussion he recommended that I resign the commission since I was now over half way through seminary. I told him I could not do that since I had worked out the issue of receiving a commission with Colonel G.L. Townsend, Commandant of the Reserve Officers Training Cadet Program at Ohio State University. At that time all male students had to take compulsory military education for two years, and those who so desired could continue two more years of advanced training. Upon graduation, if properly qualified, a man could receive a Second Lieutenant's commission in the U.S. Army Reserves. Before receiving my commission I had gone to see Colonel Townsend and we discussed the matter of war and peace and the need of a standing army for defense. When our discussion was over it seemed logical for me to receive the commission, and, in several years following graduation from seminary, I could transfer to the Chaplain's Corps.

I said to Dean Dun I would be willing to request a deferment until ordination and he agreed that was a good idea. After that discussion the matter was dropped as far as the school was concerned. Without delay I wrote to the Reserve Officer's Headquarters in Dayton, Ohio, and explained my position as a second year seminary student with only one more year to complete my training for the ministry. I indicated that if I could be granted a deferment, I would like to join the Chaplain's Corps following a few years in a parish situation. In a matter of a few days I received a negative reply. It went something like this:

"Due to hostilities in Europe at the present time, no deferments are being granted. If there is any change in world conditions we will consider your request at a later date."

I told a close friend, Charles Braidwood, about the conversation with the Dean and my correspondence with the Reserve Officer's Headquarters in Dayton. He said, "Oh Jack, I can help you with this. I have an important friend in Washington and I'm sure it can be arranged that you will not be ordered to active duty while you are in seminary." Charlie was an avowed pacifist. I replied, "No, that is not what I feel should be done. I will stay with my commitment to the Army. If war breaks out while I am in seminary, I will probably have to go on active duty as a combat officer. To be sure, I do not want to kill anybody, but I am not a pacifist and will fight if I have to."

Because of these series of events the matter of war was weighing heavily on my mind, so after the conversation I went to the chapel around ten o'clock one evening following some study time in the seminary library. The chapel was completely dark except for a spotlight shining down on the white stone altar. The wood paneling, the high back carved choir stalls, the quietness of the chapel served to create a special atmosphere for prayer and meditation. The altar seemed to be shrouded in a mystical quality of light surrounded by darkness. Over the main doorway entering from Brattle Street, there hung a large American flag. Students and faculty during services always sat in their academic robes in the choir stalls, and in time, everyone in the school had a permanent place. I went to my customary section of the choir and started praying to God about my situation as a student surrounded by so many others holding a different point of view.

Finally, I sat back in the pew to simply be quiet and reflect on the situation. I thought of Klaus Freedburg, my roommate in my senior year at the university who was a student in Veterinary Medicine from Germany, and who thought so much of Adolph Hitler. We lived together in the International House for a year. My reflections also went to Joe Kail, my two year roommate in the Beta Theta Pi House, who had decided with me to take advanced R.O.T.C. training. Then

I reflected on my parents, George and Mary Morrett who had brought me up in a Christian home and were active members of Christ Episcopal Church in Springfield, Ohio. My parents always seemed to be lingering in the back of my mind since they were the two people who had brought me into the world and molded my character to a large extent.

For many years, Dad had been manager of Mass Foos and Company, a manufacturing firm that made riding lawn-mowers. He was small in stature but a bundle of energy and with a practical frame of mind. He loved to tell jokes and tease young women and was on friendly terms with everyone. His closest friends affectionately called him "Morty", and as a Boy Scout Master at the church he was affectionately called "Danny" by the scouts, some of whom were taller than he was. They had picked up the nickname from his middle name, "Daniel." To my mind he had an unusual gift of objectivity which seemed to have come out of a life of practical experience. It was easy to call him "Daddy" as a child and "Dad" after I got to be a teenager. He taught me the twelve scout laws, the scout oath and motto which molded my morality. But most of all I enjoyed camping trips with him and learning how to rough it in the woods. I also enjoyed walking through the factory with him, asking questions about the foundry or the machinery. My sense of practicality and love of nature came from a father I always knew I could count on.

I thought also now of my mother who in high heel shoes, was a little taller than my father. She was a beautiful woman with a lovely full smile and had a warm and gentle way with people, but she could be direct when she wanted to get things done, especially by my older brother and sister who silently felt I was my mother's favorite. We children thought her cooking superb, especially her butterscotch pie. She would become embarrassed by my father's jokes and would say, "Oh, Morty, you shouldn't have told that story!" She was loved and admired by church friends and the community, where she was active in the D.A.R. and in a bridge club. When it came to serious family matters she would always defer decisions to my father as head of the household. With friends, she was a lovely hostess with a gift of reaching out to people to make them feel comfortable and appreciated. Consequently, everyone loved her.

But above all her personal characteristics, mother seemed naturally spiritual. She often attended the quiet mid-week communion services at the church, knew the Book of Common Prayer practically by heart and would sometimes speak of the beauty of the words of the hymns which were as important to her as the tunes.

Alone in the chapel my thoughts traveled beyond my parents to a young people's conference in Piqua, Ohio, when I was deeply moved by a sermon preached by Dr. Francis Cho Ming Wei, President of Central China College. He called for young people to give their lives to China as missionaries. Several nights later I had a religious experience in my bedroom when I felt God's presence in a light mist that seemed to fill the room. God seemed right there with me and called me to surrender to Him, which I did. I wanted to tell mother about the experience, but then decided it was my secret and it wasn't the time to disclose my interest in becoming a missionary. But the feeling of wanting to respond to God's call wouldn't stop with this incident.

At Ohio State I tried to take business courses in the College of Commerce but they were not a challenge. Dr. Allen Cooke, my minister and a former missionary in Japan, sent me a letter suggesting I attend a conference on the ministry at Bexley Hall, Gambier, Ohio. I attended and had a second religious experience which seemed to confirm my original call to go into the missionary field. With that I changed courses from business to social administration.

But now I seemed to be at a crossroad of uncertainty. Dad had some real doubts about my going into the ministry; thinking of poor salaries, difficulties with vestries, and certainly not far off China as a missionary! Mother never outwardly expressed herself. When I told them of my decision she must have sensed some kind of spiritual direction within me for a long time. Now I felt caught in confused circumstances. Manchuria and China had been occupied by the Japanese, there was the awful rape of Nanking, and Chinese armies had retreated to the western provinces. Europe was dominated by the Axis powers led by Hitler and Mussolini, our country was beginning to conscript men for the army, and yet my seminary seemed out of touch with what was really going on in the world.

After a period of time I decided I would have to leave all my predicament up to God and simply go to bed. I stood up and began walking to the crossing of the chapel between the nave and the choir. As I approached the big American flag hanging over the entrance from the street, I stopped. I seemed caught between two powerful loyalties — the flag representing my country and the altar representing the sacrificed Christ, the Son of God. I stretched out my arms to each of them. Tears came to my eyes. I said half aloud to myself, "If I am to be called into the Army, I will give my life for my country, but I will always keep my eyes on the cross." A definite polarization had taken place inside of me and I didn't seem released from either commitment.

I returned to Springfield in June, having completed my second year at seminary. In several days a letter arrived from Charles Braidwood, my pacifist friend, informing me he had intervened in my behalf and I was not to be called to active duty under any circumstances, so I could relax and finish my seminary training. His letter was full of excitement for me. He wrote that he had contacted his friend in Washington explaining my situation as a theological student who had finished his second year. The friend replied that a deferment was being arranged so I could finish theological school the following year.

I was furious. In the same mail came a mimeographed letter from Fort Hayes, Columbus, Ohio, requesting reserve officers to volunteer for active duty in the Panama Canal Zone,

Hawaii, Alaska and the Philippine Islands. I checked on a reply form for Hawaii, signed my name and put the reply form in the post box across the street. Mother said, "Don't you think you ought to wait until your father comes home from work and discuss this with him?" I said, "No mother, this is my decision and I don't like someone interfering in my life this way." I was determined to let the U.S. Army know I was available for active duty. Within two days a telegram arrived from Fort Hayes ordering me to immediate active duty in the Philippine Islands.

2

OFF TO THE PHILIPPINES

The day was charged with electricity I had never felt before; it was a day of intense anticipation. Monday morning, June 25, 1941, and a date I will never forget, I drove to Columbus, Ohio to report to active duty pending, of course, the clearance of a physical examination. At Fort Hayes, draftees and reservists were being inducted into the Army by the hundreds. Lines of men were taking physicals, signing papers, collecting clothing and equipment. Military orders were being issued for various parts of the country and overseas. Within the day, I was given orders to go to Fort Stotsenburg, Philippines Islands, but was allowed several days leave to clear up personal affairs and say good-bye to my family. My parents were mystified by this rapid turn of events in their son's life; a week ago a student in a theological school, now a second lieutenant in the Army.

My big problem was how to deal with Pat Taylor, who had been wearing my Beta pin for around a year. We had given some thought to marriage. Against the strong objection of her parents, I gave her a small engagement ring, financed by my brother-in-law, John McGregor. We went to the Community Church in Arlington and were betrothed in a private ceremony before the minister.

The next day I was on a train to San Francisco with

sixteen other reserve officers from Akron, Dayton, Springfield, Cincinnati and Columbus. We were all trained in the field artillery and looking half civilian and half military in brand new uniforms. Friendships were made quickly, all of us knowing we had embarked on an adventure of a lifetime. The train seemed to be rushing to the West Coast to take us to a distant land. I reflected that I had become something of a chameleon, having changed my outer life in a very short space of time from being a serious theological student to a carefree soldier and world adventurer. I was still the same person, but my direction in life was now entirely different.

There was a lightheartedness about our small group en route to the Philippines. We were pleased, upon arrival in San Francisco, to be booked into the Palace Hotel. For the next several days and nights we had fun together eating cracked crab at Fisherman's Wharf and experiencing the night life of this wonderful port city, going to the "Top of the Mark" Hopkins, the Forbidden City, Pinochios and the Patent Leather Room in the Palace Bar.

On the morning of July 15th, we boarded the President Coolidge, a 21,936 ton passenger liner operated by the American President Lines. It was a handsome vessel chartered by the War Shipping Administration of the U.S. Government for the use of the Army. Except for a few State Department personnel, the ship was loaded with Army men going to Hawaii and the Philippine Islands. No changes had been made to accommodate officers except that there were three persons to a cabin instead of two. We ate all of our meals in the main dining room as if we were first class civilian passengers. However, below decks hundreds of tiers of bunks had been constructed for enlisted personnel. I sent a telegram home without delay:

"Dear Mother and Dad, sailing at five p.m.

Love,
Jack

For two weeks our group from Ohio played deck tennis, shuffle board, sunbathed, and read books from the ship's library. During a short stop in Honolulu, several of us hired a taxi and drove around the island of Oahu returning by way of Pearl Harbor to see many battleships tied up at the docking facilities.

The ship's newspaper, *News Flashes*, carried a series of articles both on the war in Europe and in the Far East.

"London — July 18 (UP) The Admiralty reports British Submarines have sunk 7 Axis transports in the Mediterranean—."

"Berlin — July 18 (UP) Berlin spokesman says that German forces have reached the region of Leningrad—."

"Washington, D.C. — July 18 (UP) President Roosevelt today reiterated that it is the unwavering policy of the United States to protect the sea lanes to Iceland and other outlying defense bases against any attack, or any threat of attack—."

"Tokyo—July 18 (UP) A new highly militaristic Cabinet has taken over control of Japan. The major shift in the new ministry is the appointment of Admiral Toyoda as Foreign Minister to succeed Yosuke Matsuoka, who made agreements with both Germany and Russia — ."

Things looked ominous for our country even though we were not yet at war. As we neared the Philippines we began to hear broadcasts in Filipino. The strange conversation and the totally different kind of music than we were use to made us realize a whole new world was ahead of us. We began to pick up information about the Philippine Islands, a series of islands lying entirely within the tropics. In large measure they are mountain peaks rising out of the sea. The larger islands had 5,000 — 9,000 foot mountains, some with active volcanoes. On the plains, rice and sugar cane were grown and there were valuable gold mining operations in Northern Luzon. The Spanish had ruled the islands for three hundred years and then in 1889 they sold them to the United States for $20,000,000. With U.S. guidance the islands progressed toward self-government. Under the Jones Act of 1916 the United States specifically promised independence at some undisclosed time. In 1935, the Philippine Commonwealth was established which practically gave the Filipinos self government except for a High Commissioner, appointed by the President, who had an advisory function. I discovered he was Francis B. Sayre, the father of one of my fellow students at the Episcopal Theological School, Frank Sayre. I had hopes of meeting him sometime during my tour of duty.

As we neared the Philippines, the daily news flashes were getting worse.

"Moscow—July 28 (UP) An official Russian spokesman claims that the entire 1800 mile Soviet Battle Line is holding firm. The spokesman described the military operations along the Russo-German front as a gigantic Verdun. The Russians are said to be on the verge of an important success in the Smolensk area, 235 miles from Moscow, where the Russians have held up the Nazis for two weeks."

"Rome — July 28 (UP) The leading Fascist Party newspaper declares that the Rome, Berlin, Tokyo Alliance has been transformed from a diplomatic instrument to a war reality—."

On August 1st, the President Coolidge made its way into Manila Bay. Weather during the past fourteen days had been beautiful — clear skies, warm breezes and a calm sea. But now we had reached the Philippines during the rainy season. In spite of some mist, it was clear enough for us to see little fishing canoes (which I learned later were called "boncas") dotting the harbor. Filled with miscellaneous ships, presumably from all over the world, the harbor was a lovely sight, even though visibility was poor because of a light rain and the cloudy mist overhead. Our beautiful, self-contained ocean liner gave us a feeling of orderliness, peace and security. I wanted to forever capture this scene of Manila Bay, one of the most beautiful harbors of the Orient, for the moment shrouded in a light blanket of mystery. So, this was the Far East! Already I knew it to be different, peculiar to my Western eyes, and romantic in contrast to our organized, mechanical, practical world. A strange excited feeling of anticipation began to pass through me as we reached this distant land we had been waiting to see for the past month.

Suddenly, we saw a little boat rushing toward us. On it was the pilot who would bring our large ship into port. Following the pilot's boat came a motor launch with customs officials, health inspectors and Army officers who quickly boarded our ship, which helped to calm us. Our anxiety about possible delays to get ashore were allayed. The officers were called into the main lounge on "A" deck and divided into groups according to our branch of service. A Major Virgil Kerr introduced himself to the collection of Field Artillerymen. He was a small man with bright, sparkling eyes and a lot of enthusiasm. He quickly placed orders in our hands with specific instructions about debarkation.

By the time the ship docked we were crowded into the forays and companion ways, ready to leave. A great deal of noise on the pier, the blustering exhaust of large trucks, the exciting sound of an Army band playing some sprightly march and a continuous chatter of many voices in a foreign tongue created an excitement for everyone. Suddenly, we began moving quickly, almost running down the gangway, and entered onto a gigantic pier. We were immediately hustled past crowds of people into waiting Army vehicles and taken to the delightful Army Navy Club which looked out on the harbor. There, some congenial Field Artillery Officers welcomed us with scotch and sodas, rum and cokes, and gin highballs. Lt. Col. Joe Tracey, a warm affable man, moved among the crowd introducing himself and other officers as our senior host. We had a splendid time consuming piles of sandwiches, drinking highballs and asking all kinds of questions.

In a short while we were loaded into command cars, jeeps and trucks. With a motorcycle escort, our convoy moved swiftly through the city of Manila giving us little time to observe the surroundings. But we couldn't help noticing small ponies pulling elaborately decorated buggies and carriages (which I later learned were called "corretelas" and "carromatas"). Despite the din and noise of this heavily populated city, I could hear the constant clack, clack, clack of the tiny horseshoes gaily tripping along the streets. Mingling with the coarse sounds of the extremely heavy city traffic were tinkling bells attached to the harnesses of these delightful little animals.

Many people were dressed in western clothing, but there were also many in native attire, men in cool-looking transparent shirts made from light pineapple fiber called "pinia cloth" and women in long graceful skirts and sheer colorful blouses with high puffy shoulders.

The buildings were constructed mostly of wood and the architecture reminiscent of the days of Spanish occupation. Although the streets were paved there were many potholes. Trolley cars added some western flavor, but blended with an almost indescribable mixture of traffic; bicycles, automobiles, trucks, carromata carriages, queer looking Willys taxicabs and even odd looking water buffalo (carabao) pulling heavily laden wooden carts. Horns on cars driven by Filipinos were constantly in use and the drivers swerved in and out of traffic like men gone wild.

By the time our convoy reached the countryside, the rain had stopped. Water dripped from banana trees and a wide variety of other lush green foliage. Little bamboo huts with corrugated iron roofs, clucking chickens, skinny dogs, pigs with sagging bellies, and naked children stood around the huts. As we passed, many held up their fingers giving us the "V" sign of victory and even a few little boys stood at an exaggerated attention and saluted. The beautiful rice fields (called paddies) were cut into well planned squares and rectangles which created an orderly appearing countryside. Workers in the fields driving their lumbering carabao, wore shorts and had on wide brimmed hats to shade them from the bright, hot sun. I was thrilled with the whole scene.

Roughly two hours later we reached Ft. Stotsenburg. It was an old Army post with the officer's quarters and the officer's club situated along two sides of a large rectangular parade ground. At one end was the Provisional Field Artillery Brigade Headquarters and at the other the base hospital and chapel. Back toward the mountains, which sloped down toward the post, were barracks for the enlisted men. Beyond these were the sheds for the trucks and guns. To one side of Stotsenburg was a large series of horse barns because the post included the 26th Cavalry of approximately one thousand horses and a mule pack battery of light artillery pieces which belonged to the field artillery brigade.

Adjacent to the post was Clark Field, our United States Air Force Base in the Philippines. Upon arrival we were taken to previously assigned quarters, lovely old wooden houses surrounded by sweet-smelling gardenia bushes which were especially fragrant. After the rain the scent was strong. Large trees provided shade for the neat row of houses whose screened-in porches looked out upon the parade ground. Since it was Friday, we had time to relax over the weekend and become familiar with the post. From the officers already there, we learned that military dependents had been returned to the United States in June because of a strong feeling that war could break out at anytime. We learned that no officer was to leave the post for more than six hours except when on maneuvers. Troops were taken into the field daily. Saturday was reserved for time to clean and inspect equipment and Sunday for church services and rest.

On Monday morning I went to my assigned field artillery battery: Battery B, First Battalion, 88th Field Artillery, Philippine Scouts. Captain Carl Baehr was the Battery Commander, First Lieutenant Keith George, Reconnaissance Officer, Second Lieutenant John J. Murphy Executive Officer and myself as Supply Officer. Our troops were the Philippine Scouts, a component of the United States Army consisting of American officers and Filipino enlisted men. These men were carefully chosen from applicants all over the Islands and tended to stay in the Scouts until retirement. They were, in fact, professional mercenary soldiers. Equipment was of World War I vintage. Helmets, uniforms, small arms, and the Dodge trucks were long outmoded. To even an inexperienced man like myself it was obvious that this equipment and the WWI 75mm guns should have been replaced a long time ago.

Capt. Baehr, Lt. Murphy and Master Sgt. Agpoon were helpful and kind to me in the face of my limitations as an active duty officer. Lt. George was a reservist like myself, so he too had a lot to learn. Soon we were both burning the midnight oil studying basic training manuals to prepare for battery exercises the next day. The Scouts were dedicated soldiers, proud of their batteries and anxious to do well. I soon learned, however, that there was a basic communication problem because many Scouts spoke only a limited amount of English. "Speak English" signs were posted in all the barracks. Nevertheless, officers had to go through a three step process: 1) We gave a command, 2) We checked to see that it was being carried out, 3) We made a point of seeing that the command was completed properly. The Scouts were good soldiers, but they had difficulty in saying, "Sir, I do not understand." To make things more complicated, they spoke in different dialects so they even had difficulty in talking with one another. Some from the cities were very knowledgeable, others from the villages (barrios) knew very little about the mechanized world of machinery and armaments.

Soon after arrival, a meeting was held at the Provisional Headquarters for the new officers. Commanding Officer of the Brigade, Col. Louis R. Dougherty, explained a war plan known as WPO3. He made it clear that our forces were now facing a critical situation. In the event of a war alert the gun batteries were to go immediately to Aparri on the northern tip of Luzon, or, as an alternative, to Lingayen Gulf, another possible landing site. WPO3 called only for defensive delaying tactics; all troops would withdraw into the Bataan peninsula, close to Corregidor until reinforcements would come with the help of the Navy. Batangas, located south of Manila, was also another possible attack point. Our artillery was to be accompanied by the 26th Cavalry Regiment and the regular infantry regiments which were stationed at Ft. McKinley, just outside of Manila. One 155mm gun battery was already stationed to the north at Lingayen and another south at Batangas.

There was a good deal of discussion about the merits of the war plan with one opinion being that our forces should fight a guerrilla warfare operation so we wouldn't face the danger of getting bottled up on Bataan. A lot of talk also centered around two concerns: 1) How well could the Philippine Army and the Philippine Constabulary (Police) hold up and support the American forces in case of an invasion, and 2) If our forces ended up on Bataan, how soon could we count on American help?

Despite these uncertainties in the first several months I found the weekends relaxing, especially since some of us would ride the 26th Cavalry horses into the mountains behind Ft. Stotsenburg on Saturday afternoons. We would see little Negrito people peeking out at us from behind bushes and trees. They were pygmies, under five feet tall, had fuzzy hair, and distinct negroid features. Children were generally naked, the men wore loin cloths, the women's breasts were uncovered and they had on simple, wrap-around skirts. They were always very dirty looking because they lived in simple lean-tos in the jungle. Their food consisted of roots, snakes, lizards and small animals which they would kill with primitive bows and arrows and spears.

Saturday evenings were often spent at the post theater, and on Sunday mornings some of us would attend the post chapel service. On several occasions a small group of us went to Manila where I visited the Episcopal Cathedral. One of the American missionaries agreed to help me continue my theological education on a tutorial basis.

During the month I was with Capt. Baehr I found him

to be a good role model. He was conscientious and always the last to leave the battery when we had finished a full day of maneuvers in the area around Stotsenburg. He was polite and kind to the Scouts and considerate of my shortcomings and inexperience. He would back me up before the troops, but would correct me privately when I had made a mistake. I could not have been assigned to a finer officer at the time. Early in September the Philippine Division held a maneuver at Fort McKinley involving the Field Artillery Brigade and the three combat infantry regiments. General Jonathan Wainwright was in command. When it was over all the officers gathered in an auditorium to receive a critique of the operation and to meet our Commanding Officer. The exercise was viewed as a success but we realized we were extremely limited in the number of our forces.

In the latter part of September, the 200th Coast Artillery New Mexico National Guard arrived at the post under the command of Colonel Charles Sage. By October, the 192nd and 194th National Guard Tank Battalions arrived from the U.S. Immediately, changes took place in the quiet old military post. The guardsmen appeared in the Post Exchange in fatigues or in khaki uniforms without ties, a freedom never allowed the Philippine Scouts. The American troops seemed loud and lacking in military bearing. There seemed to be an over-familiarity between the officers and enlisted men. Nevertheless, we were glad to see these reinforcements. I soon became acquainted with Chaplain Frederick Howden, whose father at one time had been Bishop of the Diocese of New Mexico. He was a quiet-spoken man, tall and thin, around 6'5", and who looked strange towering over the small Filipinos. In time we became fast friends.

In the early part of November a large number of field grade officers arrived on the post, majors and above. Because a number of them were over-age for combat duty, they were sent to the Philippine Army to serve as instructors. Several times a week a few non-commissioned officers with guns, trucks, and drivers were sent to Fort Dau, a Philippine Army Camp to allow them to use our equipment. Many of their infantry units were being trained with wooden guns. It became obvious to us that the Philippine Army, just being fully mobilized, lacked even the basic equipment to become a fighting force in case the Japanese attacked the Islands.

Among the newly arriving officers in November was Captain Howard Batson, who was given command of Battery B. Captain Carl Baehr was transferred to Battalion Headquarters to serve on the staff. Lieutenant George continued as Reconnaissance Officer and, since Lt. Murphy had been transferred to the Philippine Army, I was made Executive Officer. 105mm howitzers were brought in from Manila and our 75mm guns went to the Philippine Army. We heard that a lot of new equipment, including new guns, was about to arrive, and as supply officer for the battery I was now bogged down in paperwork, turning in our present equipment and supplies. We also learned at this time that General Douglas MacArthur was given command of a newly designated force, the United States Army in the Far East — USAFE. It was quite evident that big military changes were taking place in the Philippines right before our eyes. We had the impression at Fort Stotsenburg that the WPO3 plan had been scrapped and that our armed forces would make a major effort to defend all of the Philippine Islands against a major invasion.

However, in the early days of December confusion was evident about the strength of our defense. Captain Batson was ordered to take one hundred 75mm guns to the expanded Philippine Army. Had they enough time for training to use them? Fifty half-track combat vehicles appeared suddenly on the post but without gun sights, supporting trucks, or equipment and men to operate them. Our Scouts were sent to the area where the vehicles were parked to clean the protective grease from the guns. Some of the men, including those on our survey team, did not return to serve in the battery again. We never did learn what happened to them, but presumably they were assigned to whatever this unit was to be. Our own gun batteries began to be depleted of essential non-commissioned officers to the point that our battery was understrengthed by fifty men and one officer.

On Sunday night, December 7th, Captain Batson was assigned as Officer of the Day for the Post and I was assigned as Officer of the Guard. At three o'clock in the morning, leaving the guard house, I inspected the guard posts, chewed out an enlisted man who was sitting on the ground with his back to a tree, probably one of our newest recruits, and then returned to the guard house. At about four o'clock a.m., the telephones rang at the desk where I was sitting. I answered, "Second Lieutenant Morrett speaking, Officer of the Guard." Then I heard an excited voice say, "Sir, this is the communications shack, we have just heard that Pearl Harbor has been bombed and we are at war with Japan."

There was a click and then a terrible silence. I said to myself, "Well it has finally come!" A strange sensation ran through me. War was no longer in the imagination, it was real, and all the horror of it would soon be experienced.

Without delay I telephoned the Military Police Officer of the post and told him the news. In a casual voice he said, "Don't get upset, I will be over in about an hour." Following some alert instructions, I went into the barracks room behind the office and began waking up the M.P'.s who were on permanent duty, all of them Americans. I was excited, but no one else seemed to be. I then called Capt. Batson and, in contrast to the other responses, he said he would come over to the guard post office immediately. He told me to call out the Army Post Band and exchange them for our artillery men on guard duty. Our combat troops needed to get to the barracks and gun park to receive orders. The band members, probably trained to act quickly in such a situation, arrived shortly and I began to drive them to our Battery B guards located around the post. Soon it was daylight with all sorts of commotion going on. When I finished the posting of the band I went to the barracks for instructions. The battery area was filled with excitement. I was told that the whole brigade was ordered out of the post immediately. This included our trucks and guns, along with our many 26th Cavalry horses and the cavalry trucks which hauled the animals from place to place. The war had begun thousands of miles from the United States and how little we were prepared for it in spite of what must have been frantic efforts on the part of the War Department to give us last minute reinforcements before hostilities began.

3

WITHDRAWAL INTO BATAAN

With a quick response to the situation, the Brigade's gun batteries dispersed into the foothills behind the post. Having been up all night, I was suddenly very tired and hungry. Mess Sergeant Jose' Calugas said, "Sir, you look tired, let me give you some lunch." He pulled out a small field table and set up a chair for me. "Thanks so much Sergeant, I'm exhausted," I said. I sat down and ate a few mouthfuls when I heard in the distance a muffled roar. One of the Scouts pointed up toward the sky and shouted, "Look!" Far above us we saw a perfect formation of what appeared to be a big flight of ducks coming our way. I counted 27 planes of what appeared to be medium bombers. Air raid sirens began sounding a frightening wail, and then the planes dropped their bombs on Clark Field, just adjacent to Ft. Stotsenburg. The impact of the bombs made a terrible pounding sound and clouds of dust and dirt bellowed toward the sky. I could not see the airfield from where I stood behind the post, but it was obvious that buildings, hangers and many planes on the field must have been destroyed. The 200th Coast Artillery had been dug in around the post on alert for several weeks. Their guns began firing. I could see puffs of their anti-aircraft fire bursting around the planes. Immediately after the bombers had passed the field, Japanese Zeros came zooming around strafing back and forth. One came zooming near us, so close to where Sgt. Calugas and I were crouched in a gravel pit that I could see the pilot in his helmet and goggles. Calugas stood up, completely exposing himself, shook his fist at the plane and shouted, "We're not afraid, we'll fight you. Goddamn you Japs!" It seemed to me that the strafing lasted about twenty minutes, but by now I had lost all conception of time. The raid, we learned later, had destroyed the vast majority of B17's, P-40's and old B-10 and B-18 medium bombers. We also learned that only seven Japanese fighter aircraft were lost. This was a devastating blow to the defense of the Philippines.

Shortly, a scout from battalion headquarters came looking for me. He said I was to report to Lt. Col. William Ray. Ray was an older officer who had served in WWI and had just arrived from the U.S. within the past few weeks. He was now in command of the battalion. When I reached him he told me I was to be relieved of my position in the gun battery and now serve as Ammunition and Supply Officer. Up until this time the battalion did not have such a person on the staff or even a Supply Battery, which an operational Field Artillery Battalion normally has. I was given one corporal and ten privates immediately. The corporal and his men were already there with Col. Ray when we went to the Brigade Motor Park. We began to receive commandeered civilian trucks and automobiles which were being taken off the roads by the military police. With the help of my Corporal, who served as my interpreter, I began sending the vehicles to Lt. Arthur Derby who was waiting at the ammunition depot. There they were loaded with boxes of shells. I had no training whatsoever in ammunition and supplies. The situation could have been laughable were it not so serious.

Drivers and trucks of all descriptions — old, new, large, small — were coming into the motor park with their loads. Most of the drivers did not speak any English and none of them had ever been in the Army. By 6:00 p.m. I had formed a convoy of 16 two and a half-ton to four ton trucks and six civilian automobiles loaded with ammunition and food supplies. A messenger came to me from Capt. Baehr ordering our new ammunition and supply train to go to Saipang Biabias, a small barrio some 20 kilometers north of the post and off the main road to Bagio five kilometers. It was a place where I had never been, but with the help of my corporal, who knew the location, our strange variety of vehicles moved out after dark in complete blackout. By this time the road was jammed with 200 Coast Artillery vehicles and guns going south to Manila and other big four ton quartermaster trucks coming into the post from Manila. The moon was not yet out, and since it was the dry season dust filled the air and no one seemed sure where they were going. I was sorry for our civilian drivers who were concerned for their families, who must have wondered where they were. I was in the lead truck while my corporal, Art Derby, and a driver occupied the last truck in our convoy. Our privates were dispersed among the other vehicles.

Around 3:30 a.m. we arrived in Saipang Biabias. The day had been a harrowing, exhausting experience. Sgt. Calugas, from my old Battery B assignment, was awake and got me some food again. I hadn't eaten since the air raid. After all the vehicles were dispersed I lay down on some hard sacks of rice in back of a pickup truck and tried to sleep. I found I was still keyed up over the events of the day. I realized that the big war had begun and I was in the middle of it. I got up and began walking around in the moonlight looking at my strange array of vehicles and wondering how on earth I ever arrived in this strange place. What was my family thinking, what was going on in the peaceful old seminary in Cambridge, what was my fiancée thinking?

Around five o'clock, when the sun was coming up, the roosters began crowing, the chickens clucked, the pigs grunted with their noses in the mud, caribao let out an occasional snort and the calm Filipino women began putting wood on their cooking fires. The smell of the barrio was particularly pungent of wood smoke, decay and excrement from the variety of life there. Large trees, graceful bamboo thickets, and scattered nipa shacks with straw roofs made me realize I was in the Asian world and would be living there for sometime to come.

Several hours after daybreak I was sent back into Ft. Stotsenburg with several empty trucks to pick up rations at the quartermaster depot, uniforms for the civilian truck drivers and more ammunition. More air raids devastated Clark Field. I could see the bombs falling from the planes like small black pellets. I did not get back to the barrio until after dark. That night after some chow, I fell exhausted on some hard rice sacks and, with an automatic pistol in my hand, I fell asleep. We had heard that the Japanese had landed at Linguyen Gulf and were already breaking through our lines. It was a false rumor, but we couldn't be sure of anything after the air attack on Ft. Stotsenburg.

The next day, in a civilian car followed by several more trucks, I went back into Stotsenburg for more rations and supplies. The post was now almost deserted and seemed ghost-like. The empty buildings and sheds made for a strange, foreboding atmosphere. When I returned to Saipang Biabias in the afternoon, our ammunition and supply train had orders to go into Bataan. The gun batteries and the Headquarters Battery were already on the road. Some of the civilian trucks were old, had flat tires and one had a dead battery. I sent most of the convoy ahead with Lt. Derby. I was the last to leave at nightfall with a final truck. I expected at any moment the Japanese would surround us, so I took off my officer's insignia. However, in several hours we caught up with the convoy which had to stop while Lt. Derby helped repair a broken down truck on the side of the road at daybreak. We made it to Hermosa, a town just inside Bataan. The trucks and automobiles were camouflaged with branches and dispersed under trees.

We stayed in Hermosa a week. Lt. Derby and I found an empty room on the second floor of a house at the edge of town, sleeping on the floor in our sleeping bags. Daily, I went scrounging for more rations and supplies. The Ammunition and Supply Train became a part of the Service Battery which repaired the trucks and guns. A Captain Hix Meyer was sent to the battalion from the 86th F.A. to serve as Battery Commander since he knew a lot about the upkeep and repair of vehicles. Lt. Derby was transferred to the battalion staff as the Forward Observer for the gun batteries and I continued as Ammunition and Supply Officer for the battalion. Shortly thereafter, a Second Lieutenant, Bill Miller, who had worked as a civilian with the Pambusco Bus Company in San Fernando, was sent to us as the assistant Ammunition and Supply Officer. I placed him in charge of distributing rations and supplies and keeping track of ammunition, since I felt procurement was my most important job at this time. Top non-commissioned officers were given "bamboo commissions" in the field to fill many vacancies created by shifts of officers at the outset of hostilities.

On December 10th we learned that the Japanese had landed at Aparri on the northern tip of Luzon and at Vigan on the northwest coast. Twelve days later they made landings at Linguyen Gulf and southwest of Manila at Lagaspi. The Japanese had now bracketed Luzon Island. They seemed to be driving toward Manila, but news of what was happening was sketchy.

As the Japanese made their landings, I began to see Philippine Army soldiers being hauled north in civilian trucks and buses. Then a few days later individuals and small groups were seen trudging south. Their coconut fiber hats, thin blue denim uniforms and brown tennis shoes made them look like anything but combat soldiers. They were a sorry sight, having been taken out of the rice and sugar cane fields and inducted into the Army only a short time before the invasion. They were afraid, and had a right to be. In all likelihood, most of them had never fired a rifle before the war broke out. Many were retreating from the Japanese invasion and either going to Manila or to their small barrios scattered around Luzon. We knew that the two National Guard tank battalions, the 26th Cavalry and the 86th Field Artillery, with their 155mm guns, were up north to support the Philippine Army Infantry in an effort to delay the Japanese advance, but there would be no driving the enemy back into the sea. One day I ran into a 26th Cavalry supply officer who told me their horses were slaughtered when the Regiment went into action at Rosario, Damortio, Banany and Pazarrubia, all near Linguyen Gulf. I felt sad about this. They had no chance against invading tanks.

Each day I would take several trucks back into Stotsenburg and haul out food (or what was left), signal supplies, truck parts, ammunition and clothing. I would start out early in the morning with the trucks and arrive at the post about ten o'clock, which gave me several hours to search the warehouses. Every noon the Japanese would fly over Clark Field and Stotsenburg and drop bombs. We would hide our vehicles under large trees and look for foxholes where we could hide until the raid was over, then we would scavenge a few more hours. I could not understand why the quartermaster corps was not in evidence to empty the warehouses in the face of our retreat. In any case, we supply officers were getting what we felt we needed. On my last trip into the post I could see fighting at the Bambam River, not two miles away. As the crack of small arms fire came nearer, I felt I had done all I could, so I went into Manila to see what I could finally get there. The city was a mess. There were smoking buildings from recent bombings, debris lay all over the streets and it would seem that a large number of people had abandoned their homes. The Japanese had free access to the skies and bombed at will.

On Christmas Eve I passed around the word in the Service Battery that after nightfall I would hold a simple Christian service honoring the birth of our Lord. However, as the sun began to go down our battalion was ordered out of Hermosa to go north to Mexico in Pampanga Province. How strange to substitute fighting for the worship of our Lord's precious birth!

That night the gun batteries went into position to meet the Japanese. Our own forces had been retreating from Tarlac, further north about 20 kilometers.

The next day we learned that Manila had been declared an "open city." This simply meant that our forces declared to the enemy that it would not be defended.

We waited four days without any contact with the Japanese. I talked with some Signal Corps men who said our troops were beginning to hold a little, which was good news. I also talked with Lt. Col. Fowler who said, spitting and chewing tobacco through his teeth, "You know, Johnny, the way I get those scared Filipino boys to fight for me? I just put on one of those God damned paper hats and walk up and down the firing line so they can see me. I showed them I wasn't afraid of those slant-eyed sons-of-bitches, and they weren't either."

Nevertheless, most Americans felt uneasy. It was obvious our green troops were failing to block the Japanese drive. True, we were supposed to fight a delaying action, but our inexperienced forces weren't even doing that. As the Filipino Army or Constabulary came down the road I would occasionally ask someone what was happening up north. The same answer came from each of them, "But Sir, I was firing at the Japs and turned around to find I was all alone, so I went to look for my companions. When I found them, we couldn't find our officers, so we are going this way to find them!" Needless to say, it was foolish to ask where their rifles were.

On December 29th, still without going into action, our gun batteries were pulled back to Samal on the eastern coast of Bataan to bivouac for a day in a small barrio. The Japanese were now relentlessly bombing the barrios and towns to the north. On December 30th the gun batteries were moved to the Olongapo Road and went into a firing position waiting for the approach of the enemy. The 31st American Infantry was out in front of us. One day during this period I went into Hermosa and asked a Filipino woman about a barber. I hadn't shaved for three days. She took me to one who sat me down and, without soap or water, he began shaving my face with a razor. That might have been ok with a Filipino face, but the pull on my beard was terrible. Soon after that ordeal I went north toward

San Fernando to pick up our rations from the Quartermaster supply depot at Lubao. The barrio was in ruins, nipa shacks burning to the ground and frightened civilians running in every direction. As I approached San Fernando, clouds of smoke came up from the burning city. I was told by an infantry officer that a bridge had been blown up just a kilometer away. I had my first sinking feeling about the war because we were now getting our backs to the wall, trapped in the Bataan peninsula.

The next morning I started out in a truck with food for the gun batteries on the Olongapo Road. I came to a barrio called Dinalupilian. Suddenly, from the sky came three Japanese planes. They dropped their bombs over the huts and then flew away. The little village immediately went up in flames. I was in a station wagon with a supply truck following me. When I had heard the sound of the planes I had stopped our two vehicles and hidden under a large tree not far away. Continuing the trip into the barrio, we found dead and wounded civilians scattered around on the ground. I called for my men and we started loading the wounded into the food trucks. A 31st Infantry corpsman came up to me with some cotton and gauze bandages and we tried to control the bleeding of these poor people who had gone into shock. I soon had blood up to my elbows. Without wasting any time, I had my driver follow the truck in the station wagon while I tried to hold together the gaping wound of a Filipino woman. We returned to Hermosa where there was a 200th Coast Artillery aid station. Upon our arrival a corpsman looked at the wounded and simply said they were in too bad shape for him to be of any help. I would have to take them to the Provincial Hospital at Balanga. This was my first experience with any blood in the war and I was horrified by it. Chaplain Howden who was standing nearby, gave me a strange look, then he said, "War is terrible!" All the way to the hospital I held the ragged buttocks of the old woman to the rest of her body. I kept thinking, "why should these poor, simple peasants be killed and wounded in this awful conflict of power politics?" I became very angry, but also very sad.

After I had left the patients at the hospital and returned to the gun batteries, the executive officer was angry at me for being so late with our daily rations, but I did not care. It was bad enough seeing wounded soldiers, but when the war hurt innocent civilians, the situation smacked of some kind of living hell.

On January 5th, our gun batteries moved to Layac Junction, just north of our present position. We were still in support of the 31st Infantry. To our left was the 26th Cavalry up in the hills — but no longer using horses — and to our right the 71 st Philippine Army Infantry. At this time Lt. Col Ray ordered the Service Battery, with the ammunition and supply train, to move back into Bataan, around two kilometers up the Demaloug Trail. In the middle of the second day, I was ordered to bring up six truck loads of ammunition. Just outside of Hermosa I stopped the trucks because in front of us were some dusty tanks parked alongside the road. One of the tank drivers said there had been fierce fighting on our front since morning. Not knowing what the conditions might be this close to the battle line, I left the ammunition trucks alongside the road and went ahead in my civilian car. By this time it was beginning to get dark. I made my way through a barrio which was nothing but charred ruins, still smoking, and arrived at the gun batteries. Stepping out of the car, several officers rushed up to me. One of them said, "My God, Johnny, what a day we have had! We started firing early in the morning and it has been an artillery duel until our guns were knocked out. That crazy "exec" even put one battery on a forward slope!" Just then someone shouted, "Hit the dirt!" I saw the flash of enemy guns and heard the whistle of shells pass over us. There was a loud explosion about 200 yards to our rear. After the firing quieted down, I began to hear what had happened during the day. I was told we had some very easy targets at daylight, but these lasted for only a short space of time. Then the Japanese opened up with their 105mm guns. We had tried counter battery firing but it was useless. Two of our guns from one battery were destroyed and their crews killed or wounded. The 23rd Artillery Battalion to our right supporting the 70th Infantry, was completely destroyed. The Philippine Army artillery on our left, up in the hills, did a good job but now were knocked out, too. Our own artillery now seemed a remnant of gun support. Apparently, there had been little infantry action and the troops on the front lines simply watched from their foxholes with shells going over their heads.

I had made a wise decision not to go forward to the gun batteries with the ammunition. Now that it was dark, the gun batteries were ordered to withdraw to the rear. Since I was familiar with the area, I led the column back to their new positions.

The withdrawal was a strange retreat to behold. A bren gun carrier was burning on the Hermosa road and the light from it silhouetted every big truck and gun as we passed over the knoll of a hill. Our trucks were on the road with their engines running, ready for an attack at anytime. After we had placed the batteries into a new position, I went back to the main road to find a tank officer shouting some orders. There were exhausted Philippine Army infantry lying in small groups. It was obvious these inexperienced, poorly trained men had had a tough day on the firing lines. The tank officer told me that the Japs were out-flanking the 21st Infantry and we would again have to withdraw immediately. I rushed back to the gun batteries to tell them, but they had already received orders and were beginning to retreat.

The battalion returned to our rear eschelon area on the Demaloug Trail and used all the next day to get reorganized. Two more guns were brought in, along with men and supplies from the 23rd Battalion which had been practically destroyed the previous day — six guns out of eight lost. Our troops were badly shaken up with their first baptism of fire against stronger artillery at Layac Junction.

Peoples' reactions are so very interesting under tense

situations. I learned that Mess Sergeant Calagus was back in his kitchen truck about two kilometers behind the lines when he heard all the artillery firing. He became worried and on his own went to the front to see what he could do. A battery had already been under fire when he arrived and a gunman had been killed. He immediately went to the gunner's seat and manned a gun until more heavy shelling drove him into a foxhole. For this action he was recommended for the Congressional Medal of Honor.

4

DEFENSE OF BATAAN

On January 9th our gun batteries moved north again to the newly established Abucay line in support of the 41st Infantry, Philippine Army. I waved to our Scouts as they pulled out of the rear echelon and they grinned and waved back, acknowledging my shouts of encouragement. I was proud of these men who now had real combat experience. But inwardly I felt uncomfortable. Our gun batteries had taken such a beating at Layac Junction. It was hard to believe that someone I didn't know and who did not know me would try and kill me. I would never forget that first moment of being fired upon, realizing my life was at stake in this war and that all our forces could be killed in the days ahead.

From the 9th to the 23rd of January we held a strong position. Our batteries fired hundreds of shells into the Japanese lines, and yet this time our positions were not hit. The guns were dug into the side of a ravine, giving them plenty of protection, and there was foliage along the stream bank to provide natural camouflage. Nevertheless, the Japanese planes flew over every day, bombing our front lines. The enemy artillery also kept busy firing at us. I would travel with our ammunition trucks at night, bringing to the batteries crates of shells, except that on a number of occasions I had to take the risk and go to the batteries in the daytime.

General MacArthur's headquarters from Corregidor sent a memorandum to all troops stating that we would soon have help: hundreds of guns, tons of ammunition, food and supplies. Our spirits soared! Then one day we saw an American plane fly over. It was one of the six P-40's on Bataan. The Scouts jumped out of their foxholes, yelling and waving their hands in wild enthusiasm, but we never saw an American plane again.

By the middle of January the supply situation had become critical. A general order came out from headquarters that from now on troops would be on half rations — two meals a day. I was glad I had made all those trips into Ft. Stotsenburg early in the war to bring out food. I was receiving from the Quartermaster a sack and a half of rice a day along with other food for 350 men. I would supplement this with a sack and a half of rice from our own battalion stores. To get more rice, I began going out at night with around 60 men. We would harvest the mature rice in the fields not far from our front lines. The Filipino boys would catch the loose carabao and thresh the palay (unpolished rice grains) during the dark hours. It did not make any difference that the guns would fire over our heads all night long. We would laugh and sing the favorite Filipino song, "Planting Rice." In the evening we would also go to the fish ponds just behind Alucay and bring back fresh fish. There wasn't much time for sleep but by now I had learned to sleep whenever I could, whether it was night or day. For a short space of time it seemed fun fighting in a war. I had become close to my Filipino men and there was now a helping, caring feeling in our group, which numbered 35 in the ammunition and supply train. Days were full of things to do distributing food, clothing, ammunition, gasoline, signal supplies, etc. It seemed that all services except for the Engineers were in short supply. Consequently, our Service Battery improvised, scavengered or did without. My civilian truck drivers were not complaining, although one came to me sharing his anxiety over his family. I was happy when they were inducted into the Philippine Scouts, proudly standing at attention in their new uniforms during a simple swearing-in ceremony. We trained them in the use of rifle and military etiquette, although there was little of that under combat conditions.

One day a Lt. Colonel from the Quartermaster Corps came by our rear echelon with a pickup truck saying he was collecting food from the private stores of the battalions. Regardless of his rank, I spoke my piece about what I had seen at Stotsenburg and said quite frankly that we did not want to give up anything. After some arguing we did turn over some canned goods, but I knew he felt my anger and seemed reluctant to push, although he was firm in expressing the need to share at this point. Still, while our troops were on the firing line I wanted them fed as well as possible.

Activity on the front lines became sporadic. The Japanese were constantly sending out patrols to find some weakness in our defenses. Nevertheless, our infantry, with good support from the artillery, held fast so it appeared we had stabilized a holding position. The Scouts were now used to the shelling from the enemy and would laugh about "Charlie", the Japanese observation plane that flew over our lines every day to observe our gun fire. One day outside the battalion command post, some of the young lieutenants, Jimmie English, Frank Stehr and myself, were eating some roasted camotes (native sweet potatoes). It was a beautiful day, pleasantly warm, with lovely white clouds overhead. As we were kidding each other and Jimmie English, who always had a great sense of humor, a shell burst about 100 yards away. We began laughing and someone said, "Those Nips couldn't hit the broadside of a barn." Col. Ray, who was in a bunker became furious and ordered us into the log dugout for protection. We went in rather sheepishly, realizing our sense of security was youthful fantasy.

For around ten days the Japanese artillery pounded the 41st (and 51st) Philippine Infantry Divisions in front of us. It was so bad that the Filipinos could not get out of their foxholes until after dark to get their chow. Finally, after a lot of softening up, the Japanese made a strong penetration and the front line broke. Immediately, the 31st Infantry American and the 57th Infantry Filipino Scouts were sent up to fill in the gap. They drove hard, but the Japanese had already gained the high ground. On the 21st of January we changed our position and relocated near a large Spanish looking hacienda down the main road about two kilometers. Our new gun positions were in a sugar cane field with no terrain protection and poor camouflage. The entire day the Japanese pounded our new position. That night I was bringing ammunition to our two gun batteries. At this point they were firing in three directions: to the north, to the east, and to the west. There appeared to be at least five gun batteries within a number of yards of each other. The next morning a battery of self-propelled 75mm guns opened up on the enemy. "Charlie," the Japanese air observer, sighted his position. He must have radioed his own artillery and they laid down a barrage for him. The shells struck one of our ammunition trucks, exposing our position. The half-tracks quickly moved out. Since our batteries were dug in, we couldn't move as quickly. Consequently, the Japanese shelled our location for the rest of the day. Two of my favorite Scouts, St. Paz and Cpl. Sarmento were killed along with other men. The Japanese artillery hit some of our guns and ten trucks. I was heartsick, more over the death of the Scouts than over the severe loss of guns and vehicles.

All during this onslaught I was back at the rear echelon. Around three o'clock a runner came dashing in with a message that the gun batteries were being shot to pieces. Col. Ray ordered all the kitchen and supply trucks to be brought to the front to pull out what was left of our gun batteries.

Capt. Meyer and Lt. Miller returned with the runner to the front. I stayed behind and furiously began ordering our men to remove the kitchen supplies and equipment from the needed vehicles. Just after dark I pulled eight trucks into the battery positions. Shells were still coming over but the heavy firing had subsided. The battalion Chaplain, Father Curran, was loading our dead on a truck to take the bodies to the Limay Cemetery. The men loaded up what remained of the ammunition, coupled up the guns and once again we moved to the rear. Major Batson (recently promoted) constructed a six-gun artillery battery instead of the normal four and took up a holding position on the Balanga Cadre Road. He was piecing things together as best he could. Japanese flares shot up around us, indicating they were infiltrating our lines. I got into a 2 1/2 ton prime mover, hooked to it a damaged 1 1/2 ton pickup truck, and behind that hooked a damaged gun and took off to the rear. In spite of the confusion, Major Batson organized our remnant of guns to provide an artillery defense as we made another retreat. Once at the rear echelon, some men simply fell on the ground exhausted and slept.

The following day the guns took up another position at the Kapitangan barrio along the Marivales Road. On January 30th the entire battalion came back to the rear echelon at kilometer post 153 to reorganize, to receive repaired guns from Ordinance and to go into position on the Orion line supporting the 31st Infantry Philippine Army. During the following two months in I Corps, on the eastern side of Bataan, a stalemate developed. We fired very little except for interdiction firing to let the enemy know we were on the alert.

However, we knew there was a good deal of action across the mountains at II Corps on the western half of the peninsula. The Japanese penetrated our lines and created pockets as much as 2000 yards deep. Gradually our forces closed the pockets so the enemy tried another strategy. They began making landings on the west coast of Bataan where the extremely heavy jungle provided the Japanese snipers the opportunity to fire from the trees. The regular 45th and 57th Infantry Philippine Scouts had to be brought in to clear out the Japanese and relieve the Marines and some Navy personnel under Comdr. Frances J. Bridget. When the Scouts arrived they grinned at the marines and sailors. One said simply, but with confidence, "We'll take over, Joe."

I went to visit our 2nd Battalion, 88FA(PS) at the time and watched the guns being fired on the Japanese, who were making forced landings at various points. The fighting had become fierce. There must have been as many as 2000 Japanese who died as a result of these assault efforts. I saw them stacked up ready to be hauled away. The Scouts would come back from the firing line laughing. One said, "Well Sir, I got eight that time," but added sorrowfully, "Santiago, my companion was killed." Our Scouts paid a heavy price for their heroic effort.

In spite of our successes in fighting off the Japanese in the pockets in II Corps and crushing their landings on the Coast, circumstances were not good. In the middle of February rations were cut again by the Quartermaster Corps, and so by March we were down to a third of a normal ration a day. I went to an area where animals were slaughtered and saw peculiar looking quarters on arrival. The hair was brown, white and black. I asked the corporal in charge about the meat and he said we were now consuming what was left of our horses and mules. I took my share to the battalion kitchen. When I arrived there was a moment of silence and then someone let out a loud "whinnying" sound which was followed by bursts of laughter.

There were other ways in which we tried to meet the increasing food shortage. At night we dynamited fish in the bay, which was really fun. I must say it furnished some amusement as well as food. It was at these times that I became very close to my men.

Our rear echelon had one other food source which was special. On our withdrawal we had gathered 13 pigs, 1 goat, 2 carabao, 6 ducks, a number of chickens, a horse and a dog. Knowing the Brigade was slaughtering horses, I requisitioned three live ones from the Brigade supply officer. Consequently, we always had some live animals in reserve. Much to my surprise the battalion received three of General Wainwright's personal horses. They were thin and needed shoeing, but still a welcome contribution for travel.

During the lull in the fighting I made several trips to Correigador since there was a daily messenger boat going to the island from Marvelis. On my first trip I sought out High Commissioner Francis B. Sayre and Mrs. Sayre. We had a pleasant time talking about their son Frank Sayre, a fellow seminary student at the Episcopal Theological School. When I left, Mrs. Sayre showed great concern over our forces on Bataan and kindly gave me a number of new toothbrushes, tubes of toothpaste and combs. She said, "Now, these are only for the men on the front lines."

Not far away from our rear echelon was a battery of the 200th Coast Artillery Anti-Aircraft commanded by Capt. Fred Sherman. These National Guardsmen were doing a fine job keeping Japanese planes away from our single small airstrip. The Jap planes came regularly over Bataan in the late afternoon. Sometimes Lt. Miller and I would go over to the firing director and watch as if we were watching a baseball game!

To add to the amusement, some men at the rear echelon began shaving their heads. My Orderly had his shaved and came to me for inspection. When he turned around, I saw that the back of his head was completely bald except for the word "Victory." He stood there grinning, waiting for my reaction. I broke out laughing.

During the month of March, while there was a lull in the fighting at I Corps, we discovered another enemy to combat — the malaria mosquito. Quinine was running short and many men were sick with chills and fever. Finally, we had to establish a small malaria hospital for our own cases. Due to the malaria and lack of a sufficient diet our men were getting thin and weak. They kept asking me, "Sir, when will our help arrive?" I had to conceal my fears and with a smile and an optimistic remark say, "Help is coming, so be patient." However, this question always made me feel sad. For years these loyal Scouts had believed in the American Army and the superiority of the United States over other world powers. But it had become evident we were letting them down. The matter of American aid was discussed daily among the officers, with the big question on everyone's mind, "Had we the right to possess the Philippine Islands if we could not defend them? If we were being let down, who was at fault: the President, the Congress, the military, the general public?"

Regardless of our feelings and fears, the war went on day after day. We could see the heavy raids on Correigador, and to our own rear we heard the heavy bombing of the Quartermaster and Ordinance areas. Our hospital was hit several times, even though it was well identified. The lack of food, the increase of malaria, and the sense of being trapped caused both irritation and anger. From Mt. Samat, a mountain to the rear of our front lines, we could see the Japanese bringing in large reinforcements and supplies. On April 3rd they laid down a heavy mortar barrage and aerial bombardment in the center of our main defense line. We had been expecting a beach landing on the east coast, but this supposition was wrong. The Philippine Army troops were now too weak to hold their position. Planes seemed to be coming from everywhere. Wherever I drove around with supplies there was bombing. One missed my jeep by seconds as it exploded in front of the vehicle. The gun batteries were not having trouble, but it was clear we were being softened up for a big attack. With the bombing of our rear installations, it was now I Corps that was in trouble. The Japanese may have felt the western sector had too much jungle and rugged terrain to penetrate, so they were getting set to make a major attack on our eastern position.

On April 4th, the 42nd and 43rd Infantry were overrun by the enemy. Word filtered back that the weakened Filipino Army could not hold out any longer. The 45th Infantry (PS) was sent in with the support of a few tanks that had been brought over from the west coast. They fought up to the main line of resistance on the right, but the Japanese apparently were pouring through a gap in the center of the front line. On the morning of the 6th of April the men of the 57th Infantry (PS) came up a trail, fighting their way around Mt. Samat. With both flanks exposed, they were cut to shreds. In the afternoon the 31st Infantry American, accompanied by some self-propelled artillery, tried to shore up our defense positions. But no matter how hard our regular Army reinforcements fought, a big gap developed in the line!

At the time I was not aware of all these troop movements, but the very air was electric with combat activity. On the night of April 5th, I was settling down on my cot to get some much needed rest when a runner rushed up and said the Japanese were making a landing on the beach just below us. Immediately, Capt. Meyer, Lt. Miller and I jumped up. We routed out our men, divided them into two platoons, and with our small arms ran to the beach. We contacted the Beach Commander who told us to stay there. He said the Japanese had been towing a barge up near our beach and were shelling it. I did not get any sleep that night!

The following afternoon, on the 6th, we received a note by another runner informing us that the 2nd Battalion 88th FA (PS) was coming over from No. II Corps to help back up our sagging line. Their trucks and guns began pouring into our rear echelon area about four o'clock in the afternoon. I became concerned about this. We had a motor pool right next to us on the side of the main road, and on the other side a 200th Coast Artillery Searchlight Battery. Just 200 yards up the hill was Battery C of the 200th Anti-Aircraft. Before the night was over we had so many vehicles and guns crowded into our area that if the Japanese had dropped a bomb any place within the vicinity they would have hit something.

Orders came from Col. Ray that we must pull out immediately and that the gun batteries needed a truckload of ammunition. For the first time I did not take the ammunition myself but sent the truck with someone else. Instead, I went south on the Marivales Road to find another rear echelon position. That night our own gun batteries pulled into our evacuated position, even though it was already crowded with other units.

I went down the road in the dark doing my best to try and find a bivouac area for the service battery and my ammunition and supply train. We needed considerable tree cover because the Japanese had full access by air for their bombing. At last I found a spot. There were some trees and a lot of scrub bushes. By this time the Marivales Road was filled with retreating trucks, men and equipment. Vehicles were bumper to bumper with infantrymen walking south on both sides of the road. Finally, Capt. Meyer showed up with our convoy followed by Lt. Miller, who came along with the Battalion mess truck. We dispersed our vehicles as best we could. As I was standing beside the road looking at the confusion of men and vehicles go by, along came old Corporal Yari, one of our Moro Scouts from the big island of Mindanao, riding on one of the three Wainwright horses he was bringing along. Yari had served with General (Black Jack) Pershing years ago. For some unknown reason he had been attached to our Services Battery from the outset of the war. He wasn't very intelligent, but he was faithful. The picture of this old Scout with a piece of red cloth wrapped around his forehead brought tears to my eyes. I yelled at him, "Gosh, I'm glad to see you, you old son of a gun! " He laughed and pulled the three horses into the bivouac area. Not far behind Yari was a sight to behold! My orderly came riding our female carabao which was pulling our rickety cart to which was tied the carabao's calf. Following them were honking trucks and yelling drivers. I had told my men that they mustn't leave anything behind when we moved to a new position and so they were doing their best to follow orders. By now I was absolutely exhausted, having had no sleep the night before. The road began to clear a bit; it could have been 2:30 or 3:00 a.m. I told my orderly to set up my cot and I decided to lie down and get some sleep.

I had just stretched out on the cot and said my prayers when one of the kitchen crew came up and said the kitchen truck had brought in a wounded Philippine Army soldier.

Apparently, he had been lying on the side of the road all day. I went over to a miserable looking little soldier. The front part of his foot had been shot off, but was fairly well bandaged. It was unfair to ask someone in the kitchen crew to take him to our main hospital ten kilometers down the road. They, too, were worn out from trying to supply food to the gun batteries during all the confusion of the past several days. I had our men put the soldier on a stretcher and load it onto the jeep. As we drove down the road there was never a word from the Filipino, although he was conscious and must have been in considerable pain.

As we approached the hospital, I drove down a winding dark road beneath thick clusters of bamboo trees and stopped back of a line of ambulances. I asked the soldier how he was, and he said, "All right, Sir." I walked over to a large receiving tent where there were stretchers of wounded waiting to be taken inside. When I raised the flap I saw what seemed like a sea of torn bodies. Doctors and nurses were working frantically dressing wounds. I heard someone crying out, "God damn it, give me a corpsman. I need a corpsman!" I waited awhile, but the hospital staff was so busy I returned to the jeep. I saw an ambulance driver and asked him to help me unload the stretcher. We laid the wounded man down with the rest of the stretcher cases. I knelt down and asked if there was anything else I could do. The soldier said he hadn't had a drink all day. I rushed back to the jeep, got a bottle of raisin-jack wine which I had thrown in the jeep just before we had abandoned our last main bivouac area. Two wounded officers who were recuperating at the rear echelon had made home-made wine from raisins and sugar. I went to the little fellow, put my arm under his head and gave him the wine to drink. That was his holy communion. I said, "So long soldier, best of luck." I got back into my jeep and started back to the bivouac area.

A full moon was out and it was beautiful against the soft, pale blue sky. I looked far across the bay toward Manila, where I could see some lights. Manila was now totally under Japanese control. In spite of this terrible war, I felt a momentary inner peace . . . tranquillity, despite the fact that this part of God's world was tumbling down. What a contrast — momentarily so beautiful, in the midst of such chaos.

The following morning the rout was on again. At daybreak the Marivales Road filled up again with retreating trucks, guns and soldiers. Lt. Miller took the battalion kitchen truck up to the gun batteries and returned to report that they had been heavily bombed. Some Scouts were killed or badly wounded. While bivouacked for several months in the area, Capt. Meyer had dug a tunnel for supplies which now saved some lives. During the day we once again tried to consolidate our position and even make plans to defend the beach nearby. But about five o'clock in the afternoon an order came from Col. Ray to again withdraw to the rear since the gun batteries were also pulling back. I jumped into my jeep and went whizzing down the road toward Marivales, located at the very tip of Bataan. For a bivouac area, I had in mind the 12th Ordinance Depot, feeling pretty sure their personnel must have already pulled out. As I drove down the road I could hear rifle fire to the right of the men strung along the road, having no doubt in my mind that the Japanese were penetrating our rear. Just as I arrived at the Twelfth Ordinance Depot, their trucks were rapidly pulling out. In about fifteen minutes our strange array of civilian trucks began pulling in. Almost immediately to the left of me, off the road about 150 feet, a shell burst. One truck with a trailer behind got twisted on the road and was having difficulty turning because it was in a jackknife position. No doubt the frightened driver was unable to handle his vehicle properly. I don't know how I did it, but I picked up the coupling holding the trailer to the truck, released it and the trailer rolled into the ditch at the side of the road. Lt. Miller had come up in the lead truck, so I shouted to him to keep the convoy going because it was impossible to stay here. I told him I would drive on ahead and pull in at Little Baguio where there was a motor pool. When I arrived there I found the place had been abandoned. In a short while our convoy began pulling in. It was beginning to get dark and so, once again, the Marivales Road filled up with our retreating Army. There was evident confusion, and many frightened Filipino Army soldiers ran past us, not knowing where they should go or what they should do. Soon, a column of what looked like the 57th Infantry Philippine Scouts walked past. The men were in single file on each side of the road, led by an American officer. They had their rifles and packs on their backs, walking in an orderly fashion and at a normal pace. There was no fear or confusion. Instead they gave the impression of men determined to fight on. Their jaws were set in a grim, stern manner. There was evidence of a strong discipline as a result of years of training and preparation for battle. What a contrast to others! If the Philippine Army had had more time for training, possibly this American outpost could have been saved. But the facts were now clear, we had lost the Battle of Bataan.

The trees at Little Baguio were tall and there was a lot of thick underbrush. When all our trucks of the Service Battery were under cover, Capt. Meyer, Lt. Miller and I located some Class C rations and coffee in the motor pool command post. While we were eating, Lt. Cabriedo from the battalion staff rushed up and said the Philippine Ordinance Depot was going to be blown up adjacent to our area. I had a sinking feeling in the pit of my stomach. I had located some of our vehicles near the ammunition bodegas and now our men were endangered. I rushed out to move the trucks but Lt. Cabriedo yelled at me to stop. He said the warehouses were to be blown up immediately and I should come back under cover. We crouched in a dugout and in several minutes there began loud explosions as one warehouse after another was blown up. That night tons of ammunition and ordinance supplies were destroyed since this was our main ordinance depot for the Far East. It was not to be turned over to the Japanese.

I was very confused and fearful about what happened to our men and trucks. Lt. Cabriedo informed me that he had told the Service Battery to move out when he received the message about the demolition. The only thing that remained of the Ammunition and Supply Train were our three horses, tied up and still alive! They had not been near a bodega that was destroyed. I was so grateful for this good news about the horses I could hardly express myself. Lt. Cabriedo was a small man with a lovely face. He had been the Sgt. Major of the battalion before he was given his "bamboo" commission at the outset of hostilities. What a hero of Bataan he was!

After the explosion we decided to look for our men and vehicles. Lt. Miller said he would hunt for them and left in one of our deteriorated civilian cars. Shortly, he returned with Lt. Ladao, a Philippine Army officer who had become attached to our battalion. On his own initiative he had led the Service Battery Convoy to safety ten kilometers down the Marivales Road. The two officers had brought a number of cases of Class C field rations and we then began searching for fresh water to take to our gun batteries. It was now daylight and Japanese planes were overhead bombing and strafing the road. A runner from the firing batteries came to us panting and covered with dust. He carried a message from the battalion commander:

"We are ordered to surrender at twelve noon today. Destroy all of your equipment and vehicles and, if possible, bring food to the firing batteries. All our personnel will surrender on the front lines." What a sad message after all we had been through to defend Bataan! All I had to destroy were three beautiful horses but this I could not bring myself to do.

Trying to fulfill my job as Ammunition and Supply Officer, I said to the others that I would take the food to the gun batteries and they could destroy the Service Battery and come up later. Lt. Miller said he wanted to take the food, so Capt. Meyer told Lt. Cabriedo to pick a number between one and ten. Lt. Miller and I both guessed a number and I won. The runner and I loaded up the cases of Class C rations in my jeep (a modified open taxicab) and tore down the dusty Marivales

Road. Japanese planes were overhead, the road was full of bomb craters and branches of torn trees. Since it was the dry season a thick layer of dust lay on the road. Amidst the turmoil, tears started trickling down my cheeks and I was wild with anger. Why did our struggle to fight off the invading Japanese have to end this way? I was determined to get the food to the gun batteries, even if it cost my life. We reached our destination safely, twenty to thirty minutes later. Men rushed out to greet us with signs of relief on their faces. The guns had been blown up, tires were flat on the trucks, wheels were off. Lt. Jimmie English said it really hurt when he had to destroy his transit that he had used to direct the firing of the guns. The cases of Class C rations were immediately opened and cans distributed to lines of waiting men. I sensed the underlying feeling of depression. There was little time to talk because the Japanese began bombing the area. Japanese observers must have seen the destroyed guns out in the open and a bomb hit squarely on one of them. We were hugging the trees because there were no foxholes around.

I soon learned what had happened the night before. Under General Clifford Bluemel's command a fragmentary line was hastily established at the little Cabcaban Airfield. The 200th Anti-aircraft battery, having destroyed their own guns and equipment, turned to their rifles and under the command of Col. C.G. Sage established a firing line. Along with them were remnants of the 31st Infantry American, 57th Infantry (PS), 26th Cavalry (PS), 31st Infantry Philippine Army, and what few were left of the Philippine Army Divisions still willing to fight. Our 1st Battalion 88th Field Artillery, and the 24th Field Artillery (PS) under Lt. Col. Tom Wilson placed their guns right on the Cabcaban Airfield and fired every round they had. Empty shell cases literally covered the field. They were firing into Lamao just up the road a few kilometers. The General was apparently trying to stop the Japanese advance from slaughtering us completely in a last stand. When the ammunition was all gone the artillery pulled back to kilometer post 167, our present location.

By the middle of the morning the bombing stopped and a stillness came like a soft blanket over the battle area. We were wondering what would happen next? Would the Japanese dash at us through the woods with fixed bayonets and kill us? Would we be machine gunned down? How exactly was our surrender to take place?

At twelve noon we heard Japanese tanks coming down the road. The lead tank approached with machine guns firing on either side of the road. Shortly, another tank came along with the turret down but it was not firing. Then a third tank followed. Its turret was open and a dust-covered Japanese with a pistol in his hand was yelling and motioning back toward the Japanese lines. Then, white flags began to appear. Some of our soldiers stood up and began walking onto the road past the tank. Col. Ives, now C.O. of the Field Artillery Brigade was near me. He said "Come on boys, I guess our time is up." I had taken apart my 45 automatic pistol and thrown the parts around through the underbrush. Jimmie English said, "Johnny, you had better take this rifle to show you are surrendering and keep the muzzle down." So I took it, walked up to the road and threw it down as hard as I could.

Many of the Scouts begged the American officers to go with them into the mountains, but we had our orders to surrender from General Ned King and so accepted the fact that the fighting was over. I had with me only one small bag with some extra clothing and my little pocket *Book of Common Prayer*. The mixture of God and country had brought me to a surrender I never could have imagined. The third tank, which had stopped near us, kept its motor running. The menacing, unshaven, dusty Japanese in the gun turret looked like a man from Mars. Here was no love or peace or goodwill, or friendship; all those attributes we talked so much about in seminary — only hatred and a will to fight to the death.

5

THE LONG MARCH

Once on the Marivales Road we began walking north toward the Japanese front line. It was April 9th in the Philippines, a date I will never forget. We were exhausted; I had had no sleep for three nights. Between fatigue and the surrender, we were broken in spirit. For four months we had held the Bataan Peninsula. We had been promised reinforcements that never came. We were out-gunned, struck down by malaria, at the point of starvation, wounded, and many had been killed.

A small group of artillery officers stayed together as we walked down the road. We had nothing but the clothes on our backs: no toilet articles, no personal effects, except a bag or bundle of extra things we collected at the last moment. After a while we stopped and were herded into an open area where the Japanese infantry searched everyone, taking watches, rings, fountain pens, money and anything else of value. The Japanese were dressed in dirty, sweat-stained uniforms. They too were unshaven, beards were grimy with dust and they grinned at us through gold filled teeth as they took us captive. We could tell they took great delight in having defeated the Americans and Filipinos, but especially the Americans.

Our small group of artillery officers was singled out and taken up a trail to the top of a hill. Lt. Col. Leinback, C.O. of the 24th Field Artillery Battalion was directed to a well camouflaged command post. He asked a Japanese officer inside the tent what was going to be done about evacuating the surrendered forces. Since the Japanese did not speak English, his remarks were unintelligible and there was an obvious indifference to our pathetic situation. No doubt the officer was curious about what Americans looked like and we were curious about the Japanese. It was clear that we were in a precarious situation. In the midst of all this, something very unexpected happened. As we walked down the hill from the Japanese Command Post a Filipino Scout from Headquarters Battery, Tech Sgt. Harris, slipped me a can of condensed milk and a can of Class C ration. This was a most generous gift since we had no idea when we might eat again.

After reaching the main road we continued to walk north for several more kilometers, at which time Japanese soldiers directed us to sit down under a large mango tree. There were not many Japanese soldiers, but they were on the alert with fixed bayonets on their rifles in case anyone made an aggressive move. Crowds of men began to collect in the general area. Someone using sign language went up to a Japanese Sergeant who seemed to be in charge of the privates guarding us to ask if we could go to a nearby stream to fill our canteens. At first he refused, but after being approached several more times, he allowed small groups to go at intervals to get the much needed water. April falls in the dry season, when it is extremely hot in the Philippines. Lt. Virgil Kerr who had a small bottle of iodine urged men to put a drop in their canteens for purification. Some men were getting almost out of control because of thirst.

After several hours we were directed to leave the collecting point at the big mango tree and move on. As we walked down the road we met up with some of the 200th Coast Artillery National Guard. The Japanese began separating civilians who were among the soldiers and trucking them away. At another clearing we were stopped for the night. It was dusk and we had run out of drinking water. I saw a few Filipino soldiers sneaking off into the woods and followed them. I came to a bivouac area which at one point had belonged to the 200th C.A. There, with the Filipinos, I found a big can of fresh water and so we filled our canteens. I also rummaged around in a truck and found a can of corned beef. There were empty canteens around, so I filled them, stuffed two musette bags with clothing and returned to our small group of artillery men in the collecting area. A Japanese soldier watched me return, but seemed indifferent or reluctant to walk into a group of prisoners, especially at nightfall.

The next morning just at daybreak, I sneaked out to the area again where I had found the truck the night before and discovered a full case of Class C rations. I dumped the cans into a blue barracks bag and toted the lucky find back to our group. The chow was passed around so that everyone got two cans. A medical officer from the 200th C.A. gave me some powdered chlorine to purify the water in my canteen and this was shared with other members in our group. All of us had a strong feeling we had to stand together in this tight situation.

That afternoon the Japanese guarding us motioned us to form a column on the road and start moving north. Soon, we started passing through the combat zone. The stench was terrible. A horrible, sinking feeling came over me as I passed by the decomposing bodies. The many shell holes, the destroyed vehicles and guns, and a flattened body on the road made me sick to my stomach.

When we arrived at another collecting point we again slept on the ground, this time near a ravine with a small stream running through it. Men began to fill their canteens with water, disregarding the warning not to do so. We could see dead bodies in the water, but, nevertheless some of the men insisted they had to have water. I still had some of the powdered chlorine which I passed around with the warning to wait half an hour before drinking. Some would not listen. (They probably died of dysentery during the following months.) We lay on the ground, exhausted, and fell asleep.

Early in the morning, Japanese soldiers began shouting, directing us to form a column and start marching down the road. When we reached the barrio of Lamao we were allowed to fill our canteens from an artesian well, and with little delay we were forced to march on. This was on the 11th of April. Disaster for me came at this point in the march. The sun was terrifically hot. Japanese infantry and horse cavalry were coming down the road at a trot, some running. At the artesian well they pushed the Americans aside to fill their own canteens and water their horses. We, the defeated soldiers, stood there by the hundreds waiting at this one well for water. Our water situation had become critical. As our small group stood in a ditch beside the road, a fat American dropped unconscious beside us. Assuming he suffered from heat prostration, someone tried to feed him a salt tablet. A Japanese soldier walking with four or five others came over to me and motioned for my canteen. He took the top off, drank of my precious water and then walked away. He kept my canteen in his hand as he began talking to his companions and they began laughing. I was horrified and began going toward the man to get my canteen back. Then someone shouted, "Johnny, don't be a damn fool!" I returned to our group, very upset. Almost immediately the column of prisoners began moving down the road. Someone who saw the incident and understood my plight, gave me an empty quinine bottle with some of the quinine powder still stuck in the bottom of it. At Lamay I was able to fill it with water. On the road I found some old twine which I tied around the bottle top. The water tasted terrible, but it was still precious water.

When our column reached Balanga it stopped and the Japanese told us through an interpreter that the Field Officers and Captains would be trucked on ahead of the column. We lieutenants simply piled in the trucks with the higher grade officers and nothing was said. Even though feeling some guilt because of my precarious water situation, I needed all the help

I could get. On arrival at Balanga about 20 kilometers away, officers were told to get out of the trucks, completely undress, and display all personal belongings. All valuables were confiscated. We dressed and were permitted to fill our canteens. We marched another twenty-five kilometers to Orani and it was during this march that the twine around the neck of the quinine bottle broke and the bottle of precious water crashed on the road. By now I was almost panic-stricken over the need for water. If we were to walk the 250 kilometers to Manila, my chances of getting there were poor. I told Col. Ray that someday one of us would tell our story.

We arrived at Orani well after dark and were herded into a barbed wire enclosure already congested with Filipinos and Americans. At daylight on the 12th I could see that the compound was a filthy place. The latrine was nothing but a large ditch over in one corner, full of crawling maggots. Dirty old rags and paper were strewn around everywhere. The Japanese were allowing some men to leave the barbed wire fencing and fill up their canteens from a nearby artesian well. Since this was being done in small groups and there were many standing in line, a man was lucky if there was time enough to fill a canteen. About ten o'clock the Japanese brought in some large containers of steamed rice and a sack of rock salt. These were distributed, everyone getting a small portion, but our first cooked food tasted good. During the day Major Brook Maury tried to organize an effort to clean up the filthy litter and so some of us began picking up the rubbish and throwing it into one corner of the compound. Late in the afternoon the Japanese brought in another ration of steamed rice and salt. It wasn't much, but we were grateful.

Before long we were ordered to form columns of four on the road and start marching north. We walked steadily all night except for one time, when for some unknown reason trucks up ahead blocked the road. At this point we lay down on the hard surface, exhausted, while a light rain began to fall. We laughed in joyful thanksgiving for the cool water that wet our faces, but in a matter of minutes the rain stopped. We trudged along again toward an unknown destination. The Japanese rode up and down the column on bicycles, urging us to keep moving. Once I heard an awful moan from the side of the road, and on another occasion I heard some Filipino boys run through the bushes. I could hardly think, but I knew I must force myself to keep putting one foot in front of the other. Dawn came up on the 13th without a cloud in the sky. Unfortunately, I had lost my hat the previous night and so covered my head with an old towel. Maybe it was stolen, because a head covering was very important.

The sun began to beat down and by midday we walked in a daze with sweat dripping from us. I had found an old beer bottle back in the compound at Orani. It was full of water when we started out but now it was empty. About two in the afternoon I could see the smoke-stacks of the sugar mill at San Fernando. At this moment I felt something like Jesus must have felt on the road to Calvary. Suddenly, I became sick to my stomach and my head began spinning, the ground started to weave, twist and turn. Finally, the Japanese guards stopped the column and I fell exhausted on the road. Chaplain Howden who was walking near me, pulled me to the side of the road and gave me some water from his canteen and wet my face. He ripped open one of my Class "C" rations and stuffed some food down my throat. Then the Japanese started the column moving again so he grabbed me under the armpits and got me to my feet. A young Air Corps officer took my musette bag and with both men holding me up we started down the road. After a few steps I determined to walk on my own and said that I was ok to go on by myself. The water and food gave me renewed strength. Near San Fernando the three of us stopped to rest for a few minutes in front of a Filipino house. The column began to dwindle down to stragglers and as the end of the column appeared, I saw Japanese soldiers with long bamboo poles beating men who had fallen to the pavement. Then some shots rang out. The three of us got to our feet immediately and began walking.

When we reached San Fernando the column moved into another dirty compound enclosed by a high barbed wire fence. I went toward a shade tree and crumpled to the ground, unconscious. Sometime in the night someone wakened me, gave me a few pieces of banana and milk in a mess kit, and then I went to sleep again. My guess was that it was Chaplain Howden who had fed me.

On the morning of April 14th, without being fed, we were lined up in the compound in groups of 100 and marched to a railroad station where we were crowded into small box cars. From the San Fernando Railroad Station we proceeded north to the small town of Capas some 80 kilometers away. As we passed over the Bambam River, Filipino workmen on the bridge threw their lunches to us through the open doors of the box cars.

The train arrived in Capas around noon. We were marched from the train to the middle of town and told to sit down in the square. Filipino women crowded on the sidewalk with baskets of fruit on their heads, mangos, oranges, bananas, and papaya. They began throwing the fruit to us and some women stepped in among us to give us water. The Japanese guards, seeing the situation was getting out of their control, began forcing the women back, striking them with the butts of their rifles. This made us angry almost to a fighting pitch. The women refused to leave and started tossing cigarettes to us when the guards were not looking. When the women first appeared among us, I asked one for a water container. She dashed off and I didn't expect to see her again. But when we were ordered to line up in a column of fours and start marching, the little woman dashed toward me. She thrust into my hand a square gin bottle filled with water and a strong piece of twine tied around it's neck. I was so grateful I almost cried.

We trudged along to Camp O'Donnell some thirteen kilometers away, marching as best we could in a column of fours. It had been a Philippine Army Camp, but now it was completely surrounded by a high barbed wire fence with guard towers at intervals around it. We marched through a well-guarded entrance in our groups of 100. The groups were told to sit down in front of an American major; beside him stood a small Japanese captain. The major welcomed us to O'Donnell and gave us some directions about barracks assignments and times for chow. Then the Japanese captain stood on a box. He wore black boots and looked very haughty. He started shouting in broken English:

"We hate you! You are our enemies. If you try and escape we will kill you! Because you have surrendered you must do everything we tell you. You are not prisoners of war, but our captives."

That short but direct speech set the tone for our life at O'Donnell.

6

O'DONNELL — THE DARKEST DAYS

Following the speech by the Japanese captain I kept asking myself "What will become of us captives, what will become of us?"

The American major led us to our barracks, a series of long rectangular buildings constructed of bamboo and woven palm fronds. Inside each barrack was a long corridor passing completely through the building, with a raised platform on either side. We stretched out side-by-side in long rows, glad to be out of the hot sun and to rest. We were issued one blanket apiece and several thin towels. I had a mess kit and cup but no utensils, so after a while I went outside to find some pieces of bamboo with the idea of making chopsticks. I had learned to use them while living at the International House at Ohio State.

At five o'clock we were called out for chow, lining up before a nipa shack kitchen where we were each given a canteen cup of "lugao." This was boiled rice with some camotes (Philippine potatoes) in it. To add some taste we were given a half teaspoon of rock salt. The lugao had a scorched taste, making it very unappetizing. In a few days it created severe problems of diarrhea so that at night the slit trenches above the barracks were over-run by men in need of relief. Lights came on around the barbed wire fence at dusk, and the compound became deathly quiet.

I was grateful to be able to say my prayers, the old faithful ones I'd said in the past and the Lord's Prayer. The fact that I was now a captive of the Japanese seemed like an impossible turn of events. How was I to survive? What was ahead in terms of confinement in such a place? Was there any remote possibility help would come from the United States in the next few months? What could my family and fiancée be thinking after the fall of Bataan? Would they be wondering whether I was dead or alive? I still felt sick from the sun stroke, but continued to be grateful to the little Filipino woman who brought me the gin bottle filled with water and twine tied around the neck. Where would I be without some kind of water container in this hot, dry season? I knew I would never forget that kindness.

The next day I still felt nauseated. I could get my breakfast ration of lugao and salt without difficulty. But in order to get my chow at noon, when the hot sun was blasting down, I had to walk close to the side of the barracks under the eaves to keep in the shade. If I stepped into the sun I wanted to vomit. Getting water was another problem. The Japanese only allowed us to fill our canteens every other hour. Several of my fellow artillery men brought me water, so I did nothing but rest in the barracks for several days.

During the daylight hours heavy Japanese bombers flew over us in the direction of Correigador. We knew the "Rock" was really getting blasted, so it was only a matter of time until the remainder of our forces would have to surrender. Would it be a matter of a month, two months, three months? That was a burning question on our minds. Also, we wondered if and when Correigador surrendered would our status change from "captives" to "prisoners of war"? We felt the Japanese were angry because our forces on Bataan had held out so long.

After several days I began to feel a little better, and to gain strength I ate a precious can of Class "C" rations.

In a few days one of the battalion officers came to me and said that Col. Ray was in terrible shape. He asked if I had any

Class "C" rations left and I gave him my last can. I later went to see the Lt. Colonel, who was lying on the floor of the half constructed hospital. There were no beds, bed pans, bandages, or medicines. Here and there were men lying in their own waste with flies circling around them. The stench was terrible. Lt. Col. Ray was very weak, but still showed a good spirit. It was obvious the long march, along with the lack of nourishing food, had been too much for him, and so his reserves were gone. We had a nice personal talk and I told him I would still write our story some day. All around him were men in a dazed condition: hungry, thirsty, and more than anything else, exhausted and ready to die. An average of 20 Americans were dying each day from dehydration, diarrhea, malaria, and just plain despondency. It would seem they just gave up.

Sometime later the Japanese Camp Commander came through the hospital with two doctors to inspect the facilities. We were told they walked through the corridors in silence. As they left the commander simply said to the American doctor in charge, "Clean it up!" He then turned around and with the Japanese doctors walked out of the gate. The question on the mind of our doctors was how? Where was the water, soap, disinfectant, mops and brooms to clean it up? I had not had a bath in weeks except out of a canteen cup. What about our sick who could not take care of themselves? These had to be our darkest days.

After two weeks the food situation began to improve slightly. We received some brown sugar for the lugao, also margarine, flour (with weevils in it), squash, onions, and about a dozen goats for some meat. The latter would provide precious little protein for an estimated 9,000 Americans. Col. John C. Olsen's excellent book, *O'Donnell, Andersonville of the Pacific*, records 1,508 American deaths at O'Donnell through July, 1992. There were an estimated 50,000 Filipinos separated from the Americans, but at the same camp. It is estimated 20,000—25,000 died.

An enlisted-man detail was organized to go to work on

the wrecked vehicles in Bataan, and to repair roads and blown-up bridges. Another detail was sent to Baguio to carry food and supplies on their backs to Japanese combat units in the mountains. Some were anxious to go but out of the 300 men on the Baguio detail only 100 returned to O'Donnell. When men returned from the outside details they were fighting malaria, dysentery and physical exhaustion.

The Japanese made no effort to contact us except to seek out men who might have some information about Correigador. Lt. Bert Schwarz, who was in the Air Force, was called to report to the Japanese Headquarters. He told us about an interesting interview. On his shirt he had pinned his Air Corps wings. The interrogating officer asked for them so Bert gave up his wings. But as he did so he said he had promised them to his mother. During the questioning the Japanese revealed that at one time he had been a Christian. Just as Bert was leaving to return to the compound, he mentioned that if the Japanese were really a Christian he would not keep the wings. The Japanese interrogator smiled and returned them to him.

On entering O'Donnell, another officer was found to have in his possession some Japanese coins. He was separated from our group of Americans and never seen again. Presumably he was shot.

Bill Miller and I, having served together in the Ammunition and Supply Train of the 88th Field Artillery Battalion, began to pool our meager resources. Bill's diarrhea was getting out of hand so I began scouring the compound early in the morning, trying to find bits of paper and old rags for him to wipe himself. At one point I thought I might have dysentery and so he was able to get a sulfanilamide tablet for me. He had some pesos, so he bought me an old raincoat since the rainy season was expected soon. Having a friend often made the difference between life and death. Young men, in particular, seemed to be dying more rapidly than the older men during those first weeks at O'Donnell.

Because there was so much time without anything to do

some men began to write poetry. A Major Small of the 31st Infantry wrote this poem which he titled "Eyes":

Your eyes still haunt me Ole Man
And I say "Ole man" with esteem.
I was a Major of thirty-three
And you a boy of nineteen.

I well knew, and you also knew
That today would see you leave
This role of tears that should hold years
For your pattern of life to weave.

As our eyes met over the bodies of men
Who were killed, not with guns but disease,
You were fighting a glorious battle,
Which at home you'd have won with ease.

But resting on ground of foreign soil
With the hope of medicine nil,
The only road that was open to you
Was the road that led over the hill.

After several weeks at Camp O'Donnell I felt stronger and could get my own chow and drinking water without nausea. Fortunately, I had found a deck of cards in a musette bag at the 200th Coast Artillery installation on the march out of Bataan. During the day we would play cards, talk about the war, express hopes that American forces would recapture us and always talk about food. Chaplain Howden conducted a communion service outside his barracks for those of us who were Episcopalians, at which time I used my little pocket prayer book. In the evening I would sit and look at the beautiful sunset and later simply lie on my back and look up at the twinkling stars. It was comforting to know they shown over much of the world that was still free.

One late afternoon after chow, I sat on a hillside and counted over 500 bodies being carried out of the Filipino compound to a burial ground. The bodies were in Army blankets tied at two corners. Then a bamboo pole was thrust through the ends making a kind of a hammock. It hurt to see our Filipino comrades in arms dying just as we were. God's world seemed terribly bleak and unfair. Why should innocent people like the Filipinos get caught up in Japan's will to expand and dominate the Far East? What right had the Japanese to invade China, Hong Kong, Singapore, the Philippines, Malaysia? And why hadn't we in America the political and military power to stop them? Yet what did I know about this part of the world? I felt caught up personally in tremendous forces which had trapped me and put my very life in danger.

In the middle of May our battalion commander, Lt. Col. William Ray, died. Three of us in his battalion went to the burial ground shortly after mid-day and dug his grave. The soil was hard clay so we had to chip away at it by pieces. We sweated well over an hour in the hot sun and still dug only a shallow grave. It was the first single grave in the hospital cemetery. All the others were group graves for fifteen to twenty men. When our grave digging was finished we returned to put a clean uniform on the body, which was something unusual. Most bodies in the hospital were stripped naked because we needed the clothing. When I put the clean khakis on Lt. Col. Ray his body was stiff, so I had difficulty pulling on his shirt sleeves. Looking down on the haggard face of this fine old man I saw a character I had come to love and admire. It was now so clear to me that the body is really only a shell that houses the spirit; there is so much more to a person than the physical frame. After we had him neatly dressed, we carried him to his single grave. Chaplain Curran was there and read a simple burial service, with our battalion officers standing in a circle.

He said some lovely things about our senior officer, who had led our part of the losing battle. Our ranks were now sadly depleted, some killed in combat, some died at O'Donnell. There was no distinction between Protestant, Catholic and Jew, which was as it should be under such tragic circumstances.

I returned to the barracks with my head spinning. Someone called Dr. Louis, our battalion doctor. I had a very high fever and a terrible headache. He diagnosed my illness as dingy fever, a common tropical fever in the Philippines.

On June 5th the Japanese began taking the Americans by truck to another prison camp called Cabanatuan. We had learned Correigador had surrendered and so it appeared we would join their forces and be fully separated from the Filipinos. I was too sick to be moved on the first day, but on June 6th Bill Miller and I joined a group from the hospital and went into a crowded truck to what was known as American Prisoner of War Camp No. 1. Our status was changed from captives to Prisoners of War.

One of our poets penned another poem, which I was so impressed with that I memorized it as a tribute to those who died at Camp O'Donnell. It was written by Fred Koenig.

THE VANQUISHED SPEAK

Here on this sun scorched hill we laid us down
In silence deep as is the silence of defeat.
Upon our wasted brow you placed no laurel crown,
But neither did you sound the trumpet for retreat.
Mourn not for us, for here defeat and victory are one;
We can no longer feel humanity's insidious harm,
The strife with famine, pain, and pestilence is done.
Our compromise with death, laid by that mortal storm.
Though chastened, well we know our mission is not dead.
Nor are the dreams of victory we dreamed in vain.
For lo, the dawn is in the east. The night is fled,
Before an August day which will be ours again.

So rest we here, dear comrades, on this foreign hill,
This alien clay made somehow richer by our dust
Provides us with a transitory couch, until
The loving hills of home enfold us in maternal trust.
We are assured brave hearts across the sea will not forget
The humble sacrifice we laid on Freedom's sacred shrine,
And hold that righteousness will be triumphant yet,
And o'er the earth again his star of Peace will shine.

That poem almost made me weep because it expressed so beautifully what we experienced at that burial ground. Oddly, there can be powerful meaning in tragedy, such as Jesus' death on the cross. The loss of a good life under these circumstances made poignant the meaning of life itself, whose preciousness we often take for granted. It is also true of our country in its defeat — a country we believed was so strong and yet had become so impotent that it could not rescue us from such terrible circumstances. But, like the poem, even in my numbness and sickness, I had some underlying hope I could survive — some way, some how.

7

CABANATUAN — A NEEDED CHANGE

Shortly after daylight on June 6th, the sick were crowded into trucks at the entrance to the prison camp and driven to Capas. There we were put again in box cars and shipped off like cattle to Cabanatuan. The train arrived around four o'clock in the afternoon, and from the train we were trucked to the new prison camp. It was a needed change from O'Donnell which had been a degrading experience. This prison camp was also surrounded by barbed-wire, with guard towers and lights around the perimeter. The barracks were better constructed than at O'Donnell, with corrugated iron roofs which did not leak; yet when it rained there was a terrible racket. The rainy season was beginning, so we were grateful for better cover. As our truck stopped for a head count a guard inside the gate looked at me and asked, "You like President Roosevelt?" I nodded. "He's no good, look at you!" the guard remarked with a sneer.

Then the truck moved into the compound; we were unloaded and taken to the hospital section of the prison camp. Inside these barracks were double-decker bays and a single long corridor running through the building. Bill Miller, who had become my close buddy, and I spotted some empty spaces in an upper bay, climbed up a support pole and lay down for another hot, tiring night. The temperature must have been between 95° and 100°. We had splurged before leaving O'Donnell using what little money we had left to buy a can of smuggled-in corned beef, which we devoured after dark. It was the first solid meat we had eaten for two months.

The following day we learned that another prison camp had been constructed not far away for additional forces from Correigador. Our large compound was divided into two sections, a hospital side and a side for supposedly well prisoners. My dingy fever was about gone and Bill's trots had subsided so the next day we decided to see what was going on around the camp. A few Correigador men were on the well side and appeared to be in good shape physically. In contrast, we were little more than skin and bones. Although they had not been starved as we were on Bataan and at Camp O'Donnell, they had been through nerve-wracking shelling and bombing and it showed. I asked several about their surrender and how the Japanese had landed on the small island fortress. They told of the Japanese landings and how they had been rounded up at the 42nd garage area below Melinta Tunnel. After sitting a long time in the hot sun, they were moved to Manila and paraded down Dewey Boulevard for the benefit of the Japanese command and the Filipino community. After that they were moved in boxcars to Cabanatuan.

When we returned to the barracks on the hospital side, several bodies were being carried out on rectangular window mats. We heard they had died during the night and it looked like quite a few more would follow the next day. Before much time had passed, my skin and eyeballs began to turn yellow. The ward doctor said I had yellow jaundice, which often follows dingy fever. I could hardly swallow the rice, even though I was hungry and needed the food. Because of nausea, I literally had to force myself to eat even though my body was starving. Both Bill and I knew that even though we were sick we had to get out of this terrible hospital if we were to survive. It was dirty, the smell was sickening, and there were many dysentery patients who simply could not control their bowels. A few corps men were amazingly dedicated to the sick, but it was obviously a "no-win" situation. Wet beriberi, resulting from dietary deficiency, showed up as swelling of the hands and feet and sometimes of the scrotum, which was horrible to see. There was also a lot of malarial fever and it was a common sight to see a man huddled up in a single Army blanket, shaking like a leaf from chills. It was a tragic scene.

In a few days I began to feel better, so Bill and I went to the ward doctor and asked him to let us go to the well side of the compound. He granted our request. We gathered our few belongings and went looking for a place to settle in, hopefully near friends. Circumstances looked a good deal better there. We saw men digging ditches beside the footpaths so that during the heavy rains there would be adequate drainage. Small clusters of men were huddled around fires preparing some "quan," which meant preparing some scavenged food to supplement the small daily ration. Others were just sitting around shooting the breeze. We passed friends who shouted greetings. We particularly noticed that some faces were animated, and at long last we began to hear some laughter. Checking several barracks, we finally found one with some empty space in an upper bay, the least desirable because you had to climb up a pole to get to the living space. But we did not care. It was such a relief to get away from the hospital and in a barracks with some friends.

After several days I went to find Chaplain Howden. When I located him he was with some 200 Coast Artillery men playing cribbage. The cards were dirty and worn around the edges but still usable. We greeted each other like long lost friends. He also had been through a bout of diarrhea and was given some drugs which caused a bad reaction. Now he had pellagra showing up on the backs of his hands in open sores. Nevertheless, he was cheerful and told me he was reading the

Book of the Prophet Isaiah which, under these circumstances, helped him understand the captivity of the Israelites.

Food at Cabanatuan was much improved over O'Donnell. What everyone looked forward to the most was a ration of mongo beans, a small native bean that was full of protein. Occasionally there was salty dried fish and carabao meat, so we did not feel we were purposely starved any longer. A commissary was available for those who had money. A prisoner could purchase cans of mackerel and sardines, small cans of corned beef, beans, luncheon sausages, rice candy, native cigarettes and, on rare occasions, scrawny chickens. The men from Correigador were able to bring with them books, magazines and Bibles, so a small lending library was set up in the headquarters building. Kindergarten books stood alongside philosophies and Ellery Queen's "who-dun-its." A few men tried to play baseball, but most were too weak to play anything rigorous. In time, everyone just sat around swapping stories, designing homes, discussing food, and talking about what to do once the war was over. I was personally interested in what actually happened during the fighting on Bataan and went about collecting information about various combat units and holding lines. Worship services were held daily by the Chaplains and there were large, well attended services on Sundays. Some men including one Baptist Chaplain, spent time in gambling. Although there were 45-50 men dying each day in a camp of 8,000, we could see that the death rate was on the decline. The Japanese began bringing in limited medical supplies, but the diet was so poor that the malnutrition diseases of beriberi, scurvy, pellagra, elephantiasis, along with malaria and dysentery, were on the rise. 2,500 Americans died within five months at Cabanatuan.

Each morning I began to visit Chaplain Howden. We would spend time reading the Bible together and talking about various religious subjects. Since his father had been a bishop, he knew a lot about the institutional church. Consequently, we would sit for hours and talk, forgetting about the horrors of war and difficulties we had to face in prison camp. I also knew the Chaplain worked hard visiting the many sick in the hospital and planning for worship services. He had an obvious affection for his men in the 200th C.A., made up of Indians, Mexicans and ranchers from New Mexico. He was a big man and the amount of food he received was not enough to supply his body's needs. His beriberi became progressively worse and I had a growing concern about his ability to survive.

Toward the end of June, six Americans were caught going under the fence to buy food and cigarettes from a barrio nearby. They would go out at night, make their purchases and then sneak back into the compound where they would sell their items at high prices. They had made a deal with a Japanese guard to do this, but apparently one night they were caught when a change had been made in the guard detail. Two Filipinos were also involved in the scheme. We were told the next day that the six Americans were to be shot outside the fence in view of prisoners in the camp. This was to teach us a lesson. I decided I did not want to witness the execution so stayed in the barracks. When I heard the shots ring out I was praying for the men being executed.

Other atrocities began to occur as some Americans became desperate to escape. Three men tried to get away in September and were beaten up by the guards. It was reported via the grapevine that one was buried alive, one had his head cut off and one was shot. I was shocked not long afterwards to see two Filipino heads dangling from bamboo poles brought down the road toward the Japanese headquarters. This let us know that the Japanese were fighting guerrillas in the mountains not far away.

To stop escapes, prisoners were divided up into groups of tens. If anyone escaped the nine left in a particular group would be shot. Such an incident occurred on a work detail at Calumpet bridge so we knew the Japanese meant business on this plan. Also, we were told to organize an interior perimeter guard of Americans who were to walk inside the fence and report to the Japanese guards outside if someone was seen trying to escape. One night in the middle of the rainy season I was assigned to this guard duty from 2:00 a.m. to 4:00 a.m. It was a dark night I will never forget, slopping back and forth in the mud in pouring rain. My only protection was my flimsy raincoat, which failed to keep out the water but did provide a little protection from the wind. Back and forth I marched under the bright lights, with a Japanese guard standing in a guard house watching me. When my time was over I was chilled to the bone.

After several months at Cabanatuan I became bored so volunteered as a message carrier at our headquarters. An American had left a Bible in the small room where the runners waited for messages to be carried to the various barracks leaders. Opening the Bible one day I turned to my favorite passage, I Corn. 13. I noticed someone had crossed out the last lines: "Faith, hope and love, these three, but the greatest of these is love." In pencil they had written, "We see very little of this in prison camp." It occurred to me that whoever had written this remark must not have had any friends. I crossed out this statement and wrote, "There is real love in prison camp because whatever we do for another is done with personal sacrifice."

One day I was placed in charge of the burial detail. At headquarters I was given a Japanese flag and put in charge of a detail of 76 men. We marched across an open area to the hospital where there were 38 dead lying on window slats. Quite a few were naked, and some had small bundles of grass on them to represent flowers. The men on the burial detail did not look far from death themselves. Two men carried a corpse on a slat. We began walking single file through the compound and as we did all prisoners near us stood at attention and saluted. A small number of guards walked with the column. We walked some distance and then stopped near an abandoned barracks during a light shower. The day was overcast and the soil was drenched with water from days of rain. When we reached the cemetery everyone was soaked to the skin. We came up to a big open pit which must have been dug that morning by another detail of prisoners. It was filling up with muddy water. I couldn't order the men into the pit, so they rolled the bodies in on top of each other. There was a horrified look on their faces. After a body splashed down in the mud the carriers went to one side to huddle together, ashamed of the whole procedure. A sergeant and I picked up two shovels and threw the mud as best we could on the emaciated bodies. Since there was no Chaplain I stood by myself near the open pit and said a prayer. Inside, I felt that no matter how awful the circumstances, there was a good God who was caring for the souls of these men. Jesus had promised us everlasting life so they were now released from the pain and struggle of war, prison camp and starvation, separation from loved ones, and disease. They were now safe in the love of God. No formal theology could convince me more about the relevance of life after death. There had to be something spiritual and eternal beyond the awful circumstances of this world.

In the latter part of September, 1942, the Japanese selected 700 electricians, plumbers, welders and men with other skills to go to Japan. They were given a medical inspection before setting out on the long trip. Early in October, a detail of 100 men were sent south to Mindinao to work on an airfield. There was a lot of talk about what the work would be like and to what extent was this a risk in leaving the main body of prisoners? Then it was announced that 1,000 men would be transferred to the Davao Penal Colony, also on Mindinao. This was the southernmost island of the Philippines and the largest of the island group, but also much of it undeveloped. Bill Miller's name came up on the long list, mine was not included. Chaplain Howden was in such bad shape that he volunteered as one of the chaplains in order to get out of Cabanatuan. Since I did not want to be separated from my good friends, I asked at Headquarters if I could substitute for someone else who didn't want to go. My request was granted without any difficulty.

Early in the morning on November 7th, our big detail lined up and marched out of the compound. There were many firm handshakes with those who weren't going, optimistic waves and shouts of encouragement. Our morale was high. Jimmie English, one of our battalion officers wanted to give me his last two pesos to seal our friendship, but I didn't take them.

We marched to the town of Cabanatuan, 13 kilometers away, in a light drizzle. During that march I kept thinking to myself, other American troops must be marching elsewhere in the world. Instead of being defeated, they were winning battles against the Japanese, Germans and Italians. How I wish I could see them fighting for freedom against the belligerent powers, because we were going to win — I never doubted that!

In our mess kits we had only cold rice and camotes for the day's ration, but who cared? We were going someplace else in the Philippines that had to be better than O'Donnell and Cabanatuan. There was another difference, we had new guards, mainly young men who were Japanese conscripts from Formosa. Over these were a number of battle hardened Japanese non-commissioned officers. We called the young guards "yard birds." They probably feared us more than we feared them, but it was obvious they tried to appear self-assured. We also learned that a Lieutenant Kempi Yuki, a Japanese lieutenant who spoke some English and had been a Christian, was to be in charge of the 1,000 man detail.

On arrival at Cabanatuan we marched straight to the railroad station where we were put in box-cars larger than before. Lt. Col. Mori, the Japanese Camp Commander stopped by each box-car and, in English, told us we were going to a place we would like. He said he was sorry that we could not be better fed, but not much food was available. He also asked if some of us wouldn't like to send notes to relatives at Santa Thomas, the civilian internment camp in Manila. Since Bill Miller's wife, Jerry, was there, he scribbled a short note and gave it to him. Apparently, this Japanese officer had owned and operated a bicycle shop in Manila before the invasion so was on friendly terms with Americans.

The train ride into Manila wasn't too bad. As we passed through towns and barrios, Filipino civilians tried to give us food. We could hear whispers, "God Bless America." Some gave us the "V" sign, or a wink of support. The train arrived in Manila shortly after dark. The streets were practically empty as we marched to Bilibid prison, a giant gray building surrounded by a high wall.

When we went inside there were joyful greetings between friends who hadn't seen each other since the fall of Bataan and Correigador. The old Spanish prison was now being used primarily for battle casualties, men with arms and legs off. The morale seemed excellent. Shortly, we were fed steamed rice and the best mutton stew I ever tasted. We slept on the hard stone floor, but it was clean and we felt good after an excellent meal.

At daylight we were fed again and then at 8:00 a.m. left the prison. We were marched through the central section of the city where there were many Filipinos standing on the sidewalk. The city now was fairly quiet, few vehicles were on the road and it looked badly scarred from the bombing. Some women were obviously crying; others kept their heads down so as not to look directly at us. Here and there I could see quick movements of the hands with thumbs up or a "V" Victory sign. We must have looked a pathetic sight in our ragged uniforms, worn out shoes and carrying a weird variety of bundles and knapsacks.

The Japanese marched us in front of the handsome, rich appearing Manila Hotel with its lush landscaping. We were abruptly stopped for a few minutes while Japanese officers in their polished black boots and samurai swords at their sides looked down at us from the porches and windows. They appeared as casual victors. There was an interminable silence for probably ten minutes, with the exception of some muttering among the Americans and whispering among the Japanese observers. I kept asking myself, "Now what could they be thinking?" "Have they brought us here in front of their high command to humiliate us?" "What kind of an ego trip was involved in this gesture?" The incident seemed small and insensitive, but there we were, Americans, defeated and broken by a much stronger military force. As a nation we had obviously been naive about the Far East and dismally unprepared to meet it's challenge.

After passing this review we were marched to Pier 7 where we embarked on a six to seven thousand ton cargo vessel. We were only one half of the 1,000 man detail; the remainder were to arrive for boarding the next day. We were directed into the hold of the vessel where we were fed a good meal of rice and corned beef, which we considered a real luxury. The next day the rest of the detail arrived, and after midday the small ship got underway. Once we were at sea Lt. Yuki allowed us to go on deck where we enjoyed the sea breeze. It was wonderful! There was movement again in our lives even though the future was full of uncertainty. The food was a high mark of the trip south. There was always plenty of rice along with salty dried fish, squash and, on several more occasions, corned beef with salted red cherries. I had scurvy so bad I could hardly eat the salty dried fish, but everything else went down all right.

Lt. Yuki was a stocky little man who smoked a lot of cigarettes. His English was understandable so he would come over to us at a roped off section of the deck several times a day and talk. He seemed pleasant and understanding of our difficult situation. What a contrast he was to all the other Japanese we had contact with so far. He didn't seem to mind our staying on deck at night instead of barely existing in the hot hold below. So he helped make it a wonderful experience, sailing through the tropics under a starlit sky with a round orange moon overhead.

In several days the ship docked at Iliolo on the Island of Panay where the ship disposed of some cargo. An American died during the night, so his body was taken ashore for burial by one of our chaplains and a few guards. On November 10th we sailed for Cebu City on the Island of Cebu which took us through narrow straits. The ship docked for several days, leaving on the 12th at 10:00 a.m. The next day another man died, so he was buried at sea. Lt. Yuki brought us some sail cloth to sew his body in. Then, just before dropping it over the side, Yuki appeared with a bugler. The Chaplain said some prayers and as the body was dropped over the side of the vessel we all stood at attention and saluted, including Yuki. His bugler played some kind of Japanese taps. Yuki had also brought along some flowers which he had presumably bought in Cebu for his cabin. They went into the ocean with the body. It was a moving experience for all of us, made so in large measure by one we knew as a Japanese friend.

As our ship sailed past white sandy beaches, groves of coconut trees, little nipa shacks tucked away in the thick foliage of bamboo and banana trees, hibiscus and bougainvillea vines, we began to appreciate what human freedom was all about. The natives we saw in these peaceful settings seemed to have everything in life worthwhile. The lovely blue sky banked by white clouds, the soft breeze, the vast blue ocean, made us feel that the storm we had been in for the past eleven months was over. I thanked God for the ship, Lt. Yuki, and the fact that I was still alive and going to a much better place than where I had been.

However, Chaplain Howden who had volunteered for the detail seemed to be getting weaker by the day. He found it difficult to eat, and climbing the ladder to get on deck to go to the latrine was exhausting. Finally, with Yuki's permission, we were able to get him moved to the aft deck for the rest of the journey. This area had to be clear of prisoners because it had a 75mm gun on it. Chaplain Albert Braun, a Roman Catholic priest was a close friend and helped as best he could by talking with Yuki about this special place on deck for the sick Chaplain.

On the afternoon of November 14th the ship arrived in the Gulf of Davao where it anchored all night. The following morning it went well into the Gulf and anchored near a small lumber mill called Lasang. Just before disembarking on lighters we were fed, and then we filled our mess kits with rice and salty red cherries in preparation for a long march. Once ashore, our individual baggage was loaded on trucks with the sick and transported to the Davao Penal Colony.

Yuki led the march with guards spread out along our flanks. We passed beautiful coconut groves, clusters of banana trees and many fruit orchards bearing oranges, lemons, avocados, breadfruit, guavanos and star apples. We came to the conclusion that this was the promised land of milk and honey which the Bible tells about. However, after several hours we began to walk through dense jungle where there were tremendous trees and vines reaching to the sky. I suspected these thick jungles were infested with snakes, wild buffalo, lizards, monkeys and exotic birds. As we trudged along, men would drop out of the column even though Yuki gave us a ten minute rest break at the end of each hour. An open-bed truck kept coming and going between the column and the Penal Colony, picking up those who couldn't walk any further. Even a few of the young guards began to groan after six or seven hours and were having trouble keeping up (which we found amusing).

Just at dusk we saw the lights of the Penal Colony up ahead so we began to sing. As soon as we walked inside the fence we were warmly greeted by our southern island forces, who had seen only a limited amount of combat. Men looked well fed, their uniforms were clean and none had the haggard, beaten look of a defeated army. Soon we were fed and assigned to permanent barracks where we fell exhausted into screened, double -decker bunks for the night.

8

FENCED AROUND THE GARDEN OF EDEN

The Davao Penal Colony was a large penal farm for hardened Filipino prisoners, isolated deep in the southern jungles of Mindinao. The farm was well developed with extensive rice fields located several kilometers from the main compound, vegetable gardens nearby the barbed wire enclosure and, a short distance away, a fruit orchard. It even had a herd of cattle and a sizable poultry industry. In short, it was a self-supporting penal institution for the Philippine government. The colony operated a small, narrow-gauge railroad between the rice fields and the main installation where the rice was milled. It also had a machine shop, sawmill and an abaca mill to cut up the abaca vines for rattan furniture, thus, making it possible to sell rice, produce, lumber and furniture on the common market. There were two large well-constructed bodagas (warehouses) where produce was kept. Among the variety of buildings, there was an open chapel for worship but used mostly for recreation. The Filipino prisoners were incarcerated for serious crimes committed before the war, and those trying to escape could be seen in leg irons. They were kept in a separate compound from Americans but had some contact with us through the work details.

The day following our arrival the Bataan/Correigador forces met for the first time with the Visayan/Mindinao forces. Those of us from Luzon could hardly believe our eyes. At the time of surrender the southern forces had been interned in a Philippine Army Camp in the central part of Mindinao called Malaybalay. These troops had been allowed to bring into the camp truckloads of food following their surrender. Consequently, they had lived on an adequate diet of food prior to our arrival. None had the dietary diseases we were faced with. The officers were not forced to work and the Japanese allowed plenty of recreation to go on inside their camp. In contrast, our men from Bataan and Correigador were dying off by the thousands. These men from the south looked physically fit and their morale was excellent. At the time of their internment they came under the command of another Japanese officer named Mori who apparently was a brother of Lt. Col. Mori in command of Cabauatuan on Luzon.

During the first two days we rested from our trip south and spent a lot of time exchanging experiences about what had happened in the war on its various fronts or in the prison camps. On the third day all able-bodied officers and enlisted men were put to work. We lined up in front of our barracks each morning at 7:00 a.m., counted off in Japanese and then were assigned to work details. One day I might be assigned to the vegetable garden harvesting camotes, another day planting corn or working in the rice mill. On one day I was assigned to work in the jungle cutting abaca. There the leeches stuck to my skin and sucked the blood until someone with a lighted cigarette burned them off. However, by this time my scurvy was so bad that, with some others, I was assigned to the fruit orchard detail under the leadership of Capt. Ed Dyess, an Air Force officer. In a very short time, by gently sucking lemons or eating oranges, the scurvy cleared up. The work schedule was from 7:00 a.m. in the morning until noon, when rations were brought out from the compound, and then 1:30 p.m. until 5:00 p.m. There were plenty of tools such as shovels, hoes, bolos (long knives), hammers, saws, etc. The colony also had three tractors and one bulldozer to do the heavy earth work when needed to clear more land, repair roads, or haul logs.

We considered the toilets wonderful after the slit trenches we had been used to. They were long open houses with box seats behind the barracks and soon became a place for conversation or jokes. The drainage of the camp was good but malaria was rampant, so everyone got a ration of quinine each week. A serious effort was made to clean out the ditches which were breeding areas for the malaria mosquito.

The fruit orchard work was easy and we were mostly in the shade while we harvested the fruit. There were plenty of ferns and I soon learned to pick off their curled heads to augment our limited rice and vegetables. However, one sad feature about the orchard detail was that the Japanese guards would never allow us to bring fruit back into the compound for other prisoners. Consequently, I would hide bananas and oranges in my clothing to bring to Bill Miller and Chaplain Howden. Both were put in the hospital upon their arrival at the Davao Penal Colony. The Chaplain's beriberi and pellagra continued to get worse and Bill was not able to get rid of his trots. He was also going blind as were a number of men who had faced the serious dietary deficiency at O'Donnell and Cabanatuan.

The Japanese commanding officer, Major Maeda, a man around sixty years old spent most of his time in Japanese Headquarters and seldom did any inspection of the P.O.W. camp. Of major importance among the Japanese staff was Lieutenant Nishimura, who had to be in on everything discussed around the facility. Captain Hoesuma commanded the guards and was senior officer next to Major Maeda. He was a tall, thin, haughty Japanese who obviously hated the Americans. Lieutenant Ora was a tall, gawky Japanese who always seemed to be in need of a shave, so we called him "five O'clock shadow." Some prisoners thought him to be a drug addict and for some time he supervised the vegetable garden detail. Lieutenant Sirayu was the quartermaster, an unattractive, heavyset Japanese who always seemed to block our getting more food. Lieutenant Shibota was a big fellow who laughed and seemed friendly, but there were some who felt he could not be trusted. He was in charge of the machine shop. Lieutenant Yasamura was the medical officer, who seemed to have more culture than the rest of the Japanese staff and who worked with our American doctors. Our original interpreter, Lt. Nishimura, was replaced by an excitable little civilian, Mr. Onada, whom we called "Running Wada" (water) because he always seemed to be on the run. Lt. Yuki, in charge of American prisoners, was always kind and considerate and made a point of seeing that our four Catholic and one Episcopal chaplains had communion wine and wafers for holy communion on Sundays. In summary, the Japanese staff were a very mixed bag of people from good to bad, and our welfare depended very much upon the nature and whims of these people.

We were paid a little money for our work at the Colony, maybe because it sold rice, fruit, lumber, abaca, coconuts, etc., as commercial products. The Japanese told us they were paying funds into personal bank accounts, so every two months we received a few pesos, the amount depending upon our rank. With this money we could make purchases of tobacco, candy, and fried bananas at a small commissary.

Bill Miller and I were separated when he had to go into the hospital and after that I developed a close friendship with Capt. Clyde Ely and Lt. Russel Hutchison whom everyone called "Hutch". Both men were in the 200th C.A., but by now organization identities had pretty well broken down. "Hutch" worked in the machine shop and eventually stole parts from old radio equipment so he could put together a radio which brought news into the camp. Clyde also had scurvy which originally brought us together on the fruit orchard detail, and later we worked together in the rice fields.

Chaplain Howden was getting weaker by the day. I would visit him in the hospital after finishing a work detail, but except for bringing him fruit there was little I could do for him. Shortly before Christmas when I returned from work I was told he had died that morning and was already buried. This made me sad because I would have wanted to be present for whatever kind of simple funeral was held for him. Then someone brought to me his personal Bible saying simply that he had left it for me. What a beautiful gift! Sixteen men died in our first six weeks at Dapecol (Davao Penal Colony), but after that there was not a single death for over a year.

One evening about 6:30 p.m. I walked out of the barracks and much to my surprise heard some beautiful music. Major Larry Pritchard, who had been a glee club director at West Point, had organized a fairly large group of P.O.W'.s into a Dapacol Glee Club. They sang the *Dartmouth Winter Song, Old Man Noah, Caroline* and other favorite tunes. What a lift this singing gave us!

In the week preceding Christmas everyone was getting into the spirit of the season in spite of the prison camp conditions. Lt. Yuki was instrumental in organizing a program in the chapel which included everyone: Americans, Filipinos and Japanese. We were allowed to decorate the building with rice stalks, palm fronds and flowers. A program was planned by the prisoners and Yuki from the different nationalities at the colony. The Filipino supervisors and their wives and children were allowed to attend and even a few guards came. Prior to the event, there was practicing in the chapel every night. We even had a band which included a tuba, violin, clarinet, a base vial, trumpet, drums and piano. The glee club had been practicing for weeks. I joined it even though I didn't have much to add in the way of a voice.

During these preparations, Lt. Howard Martin, knowing I had attended the Episcopal Theological School, asked me if I would hold a traditional midnight service Christmas Eve. I told him I could not celebrate the Holy Eucharist but I would be glad to conduct Evening Prayer in the place of Chaplain Howden. I talked the matter over with Father Albert Braun, who was the senior chaplain, and he couldn't have been more supportive and cooperative. He said he would announce the service and encourage attendance even though Father Carberry, one of his Catholic chaplains, was going to celebrate midnight mass. I arranged for our service in a small carpenter's shop in back of the barracks following the evening program.

On Christmas Eve we had a marvelous dinner of carabao meat (which was always a luxury), vegetables, rice and squash pudding. The program followed with the Japanese guards filing into the chapel first and sitting on the right side of the stage. The Filipino civilians sat across the aisle from the guards and we prisoners poured in from the rear and open sides of the building. Just before the curtains parted for the first program of the evening, Lt. Col. Nelson, the American Camp Commander, and Lt. Yuki made a few introductory remarks. Each expressed his feelings in a simple manner, saying how happy we all were to celebrate Christmas together. Then the program began with charming dances by young Filipino girls and some small children. Their costumes were lovely. There was a jitterbug dance by several sailors, one dressed as a girl in flat heeled shoes and a butterfly skirt. The Mexicans put on a dance by a male senorita and a dashing cavalier. A Japanese sergeant sang several songs and a Formosan guard performed magic tricks. The glee club sang Christmas carols and the band produced some happy American tunes under the direction of a Lt. Saunders. The program turned out to be a great success!

Before it was over I had an unhappy experience. Toward the end I dashed over to the carpenter's shop to be sure I had everything ready for the Episcopal Service. As I was walking across a small bridge over a stream between the chapel and the barracks, I was struck in the face and knocked to the ground. I looked up at a Japanese sergeant who apparently had struck me because I had failed to see him and salute. He pushed me toward the barracks and grunted. What a shock just before the service! Nevertheless, it was held with an estimated 25 men in attendance.

I felt that I had preached a terrible sermon, but the Holy Spirit seemed to be there and we celebrated the birth of our Lord in our Episcopal Prayer Book style at midnight.

This service began my ministry that lasted for the remaining 19 months I was at the Penal Colony. An Episcopal service was held on Wednesday nights and Sunday mornings through the cooperation of Father Braun, who in time became a very dear friend. It wasn't easy preparing sermons for Sunday, but out on the work details I would think about my subjects. I had no reference book but Chaplain Howden's Bible. Sometimes I would talk over my sermon topic with either Roman Catholic Chaplain Father Braun or Chaplain Brewster, who was a Presbyterian. Chaplain Brewster spent much of his time in the Dapecol Hospital. They were willing to share their knowledge both from seminary training and work in the ministry. I was always on the lookout for scraps of paper to use for preparing the sermons and in this "Hutch" was helpful. On occasion he kindly brought me scraps of paper from the machine shop, dusty and dirty, but usable.

After Christmas, morale got better. In January we received our first shipment of Red Cross supplies which included two food packages per man, medicines and a small supply of clothing. In the evenings men would build "quan-fires" where they would bring their ration and supplement it with Red Cross food. We began to gain weight and the dietary diseases started to disappear.

In February the Japanese held a special ceremony to celebrate the Emperor's birthday. All Americans were ordered out on the parade ground, and at a designated time we were to bow our heads and pray to the Emperor. The Japanese had us line up in parade ground fashion, facing the Japanese flag. We followed the designated procedure, but I'm sure there were no prayers offered the Emperor. Following the ceremony a Capt. Coleman returned to his barracks and penned the following poem:

A PRAYER FOR THE JAPANESE EMPEROR

O Lord of Hosts and Holy Ghosts
Hear us while we pray.
The Japanese nation, that land of starvation
Has had a birthday today.
A lineage unbroken and by that same token
One of virtue and grace,
Has ruled an empire, genealogically entire
And never lost a face.
Ten thousand years of blood and tears,
Yea, even six hundred and four
Have all passed by, how time does fly
They've all rotted to the core.
Now any nation in this creation
That piles up this addenda,
Begins to stink, and I really think
It's all just propaganda.
But if it's true, I'm asking you,
What it is that makes them strut,
It's plain to me and it's plain to see
By god they're in a rut!

This period of good living was not to last long. Soon after the first of the year the Americans asked Yuki if some prisoners working outside the fence near the vegetable gardens and at the fruit orchard could go to work without guards. A kind of trustee system was set up with Yuki and so morale was raised even further. But one night after work Capt. Hoesuma ordered a complete shakedown at the gate. Fruits and vegetables came from everywhere. Some men were carrying in a large squash and there were stalks of sugar cane and ripe pineapples. The assortment of food and its quantity was amazing! We had all become thieves. One nice Formosan guard who frisked me felt my pockets full of avocados but let me pass by as if I had nothing. I came through the gate grinning from ear to ear. The shakedown continued each night following work details for a week.

The following Sunday, early in the month of April, Ed Dyess and seven other officers from our orchard detail, two enlisted men, and several Filipinos escaped. All prisoners were promptly ordered to form up for "tinko" (roll call) in front of the barracks. The guards went through the barracks to locate anyone hiding and to try and figure out who had taken off. A detail of guards was immediately sent out to recapture the escapees, but apparently ran into some guerrillas and several Japanese were killed.

That Sunday morning before the escape I had gone to the barracks after breakfast to get my little Prayer Book and Bible for the Episcopal service. As I went down the bay I passed Ed Dyess, author of *The Dyess Story* who was sitting near his bunk greasing his shoes. I said, "Where do you think you're going Ed — to Davao?" And then I went on, anxious to get to the carpenter's shop. Little did I know what was on his mind at the time. He had once talked to me about the possibility of escaping, but I told him it seemed to me too big a risk because of the men in the hospital. Still, I knew it was a rule in our Armed Forces that if a man is ever captured, he should try to escape. Consequently, no one held it against Ed and his group for trying to get away from Dapecol.

For several days all work details were stopped and we were placed on a rice and salt diet. On Tuesday and Wednesday we were told by the Japanese that all men living in the same barracks as the men who had escaped were to be put into a disciplinary compound. An order was also put out from Japanese Headquarters that there were to be no meetings of any kind and church services were to be limited to prayer only. Four barracks of men out of the total eight were involved in the discipline. We were lined up, counted, and marched off to another somewhat isolated and less well built compound about a kilometer away. This compound had a triple barbed wire fence around it, eight guard towers and a strong iron gate at the entrance.

For several months those of us under discipline did nothing but talk, read the books from Malaybalay, play chess and bridge. At first this seemed like a nice vacation from work. Then one day Major Maeda and Lt. Yuki came into the compound. We were called out for an assembly. Major Maeda made certain threats and then told us the American Camp Commander, Lt. Col. Nelson, and all barrack leaders were relieved of their duties and a portion of their pay was deducted from their bank accounts. After he left the compound, Lt. Yuki addressed us in his broken English. He said he had trusted us to go out on details without guards but we had broken this trust. He was sorry the escape had happened, but he would forgive us. After a few other remarks he left. I was flabbergasted! There was no trace of bitterness in what he said and, in fact, he also remarked, "You have to live under difficult conditions and I understand." I could have wept for him, knowing he had lost his command.

The food during the disciplinary period of several months wasn't too bad and we received quite a lot of dried fish with our rice. When we returned to the main compound, we found a different atmosphere. The vegetable gardens had gone to seed since no weeding had been done. Everyone seemed to be complaining, especially the officers, about their rights. No one liked mass punishment and some felt this was the time to put pressure on the Japanese to follow the Rules of Land Warfare in regard to prisoners. All officers but two in the disciplinary compound signed a paper protesting being used for manual labor. This protest was given to the interpreter. The following day we learned from the new American Camp Commander, Lt. Col. John McGuire, that Major Maeda would send the protest to Manila where it would be submitted to higher authority. Several weeks later we received our answer. In general it was the following:

"If a man did not work, he would have to live on a much smaller quantity of food and his health would be seriously impaired. The Japanese policy was that all able-bodied men must work regardless of whether they were officers or not. This policy was being carried out by the Co-prosperity Sphere of the Japanese Government."

Since there was no contact with the International Red Cross, there was no one to complain to. At this point Capt. Hoesume took charge of all American prisoners and most of us were assigned to the Mactan detail, which involved working in the rice fields. All the Filipinos were sent away, and American details to such places as the fruit orchard, lumber mill and vegetable gardens ceased. Guarding of prisoners became strict and if anyone got out of line they were "straffed" or slapped. There were cuts in our rations of rice and vegetables. Even though assemblies had been ordered to be discontinued, including church services, I kept up my little Episcopal services in a place in the barracks where we could not be seen by the guards. We needed it for our morale.

The Japanese began flooding us with propaganda papers from Manila and Davao. In the main they had to do with the Japanese victory over Bataan and Correigador. But they also announced big successes in the southwest Pacific. However, it was impossible for them to keep out of their propaganda newspapers Allied victories in North Africa. When our mission in North Africa was completed the Japanese discontinued issuing any more papers. There was no information about landings in Sicily and Italy, but by the grapevine we were getting some good news about the war in the West. By September, 1943, we learned of the evacuation of Mussolini from Rome. What was happening in the Far East was a blank.

I began to develop a routine which was livable. I would get up at 4:30 or 5:00 a.m. depending upon the time our barracks of several hundred men would be called out for chow. After breakfast I would try and read a chapter in the Bible. At six o'clock we would be lined up for "tinko" and then form at the gate to be counted again for the Mactan detail. We would then march to the little train and at the "ok" of the guards, dash to the flat cars to get to sit down. I use to wait for a few seconds until the crowding was over, which gave me some time to see what was happening up and down the line of cars. It was always a friendly rat race to get to sit rather than stand. Most of the mornings going through the jungle were beautiful. The sun would come up just about the time the train pulled out of Dapecol so I could see the beautiful sunrise with all the colors in the sky. I loved to look at the mist in the tall trees, always appearing ghostly and forbidding. Often we would see monkeys swinging from vine to vine or among the branches making a lot of noise as we chugged past. There would be shrill calls of tropical birds and along the tracks the swishing sound of mud fish in the pools. It was common to see very large lizards in the murky ditches. During the forty-five minute ride I would say my prayers, often the ones from the family prayer section of the Prayer Book. As we reached the wide cultivated area of the rice fields we would always see the tall stately carabao birds, and as we approached they would flap their wings and fly into the air. Their legs straight behind them made them look like gliders. They would land on the backs of the big lumbering carabao, who seemed to be their friends. The rice fields themselves were beautiful. They seemed so organized; mainly in squares and rectangles delineated by dikes and canals. They were especially lovely just before harvest time when the tall yellow stalks would wave in the breeze. However, they became a mess during heavy rains when they would be blown down and we would have to pick up the heavy stalks from the sticky, stinking mud.

When we arrived at Mactan we would jump off the train and immediately line up to be counted, always in Japanese, of course. The guards would shout, "Tinko, tinko". This exercise of being counted seemed to go on about twenty times a day. When the counting was finished a small group, usually Mexicans and Indians, dashed off to catch the carabao for plowing and harrowing. Their speed was important because each man would fight to get a good work animal. The rest of us would be divided into different details to either plant seedlings, weed, or harvest the rice. In the wet paddies we would sink deep into the mud up to our knees, and following a long rope across the paddy, plant the seedlings in straight rows. As the sun rose to high noon it would blaze down on us glistening in the mud. All day long we would work through the muck, and if the paddy was drained and the shoots were secure, we would get down on our knees and pull out the weeds. A fun day would be to clear out the canals full of weeds and in doing so, often catch some mud fish. We were now completely converted to an Asian lifestyle. All we had to cover our bare bodies was a G-string and the needed broad-brimmed hat as a protection against the hot sun. Hours would pass quickly as we would converse along the planting line, talking about antique cars, college, Europe, history, the war, politics and religion. Sometimes there would be emotional debates about socialism, communism and capitalism. Since officers and enlisted men were on separate details, here we were, college educated and on an intellectual plane, doing the most humbling of work. But certainly, as a result of this experience, we would never be the same.

Mactan always had some unforeseen incident. A young guard secretly took off and returned with a jacket full of green and ripe papaya which he gave us. Once a cobra was underneath one of the big rice baskets and could have bitten someone. Another time a big python was curled up in the tall grass along a dike. There was great excitement as several men with long bamboo poles pushed him into the canal and then as it was crawling to the bank, I took my big cane knife and cut through it's body. We brought it into the compound that night to supplement our dinner. Because food by now was so short we were eating lizards, bird's eggs and even a stray dog that wandered into the compound.

September and October, 1943, were particularly bad

months for me. I had gotten malaria back in January, but even with quinine I was still having attacks of chills and fever. Also, we knew that those of us working in the rice fields had contracted some rare tropical disease. Red spots were showing up on our arms and legs and we had headaches and loss of appetite. The doctors in the hospital tried to figure out what the disease might be. Using an old microscope they discovered those of us working in the rice fields had a high white corpuscle count. At one point I felt so weak that a nice young doctor named Keeley gave me two weeks off to rest.

In November morale began to pick up again. A small group of officers and enlisted men started to put on a variety show every Sunday night. At first the Japanese said it should be stopped and then relented because our enthusiasm was so high. A Corporal Biggs had been a master of ceremonies at a night club in the States, so he organized the show. He was a big, rough, uncouth man but knew how to make everyone laugh. His show included a small band of a trumpet, clarinet, bass viola, and a five gallon can used as a drum. There were soloists, one act plays and comic artists. The opening bit tune was:

Hey, hey, the Yanks are comin'
That's the way the rumor's runnin.
Skies are starry, we're not sorry
The Yanks are comin' hurrah!
We'll see ole' Alabamie
As soon as Uncle Sammie
Will take this place
To save his face
The Yanks are comin' hurrah!
Think of the friends we've made here
Dur'in the time we've stayed here.
Think of the cash we've saved here
These are the treasures worth fight'in for.
The Yanks are comin' hurrah!
(So) Come now don't start a riot,

They'll be a change in diet
No more rice - o, it will be nice - o
The Yanks are comin' today, hurrah
The Yanks are comin' hurrah!

There was an added touch of patriotism cleverly injected into each program. One night was especially memorable. We had been at the Davao Penal Colony a full year. The situation had steadily gone downhill, especially after the big escape. We were in the rainy season and water poured from the sky in torrents. The night was dark and dismal. After the program was finished, Lt. Col. McGuire gave us a serious talk about having faith in America; he said we would win the war and some day be released. Then he asked everyone to come in close around him. Two men stood up and between them held a rolled up Army blanket. They let it roll open and before our eyes was an American flag sewed to the blanket. We then softly began to sing "God Bless America" and tears began to roll down our faces. Having been through so much intensified our love of America, our country of freedom and justice for all.

Two weeks before Christmas, 1943, we began to make preparations again to celebrate the time of our Lord's birth. The daily rations had been cut back considerably, our shoes had worn out, so most of us were going barefoot. Our clothes were in rags. We had little news of what was happening in the war; "Hutch" had not gotten his radio going again but he did talk of getting together the necessary parts. Christmas, of course, is far more than nice gifts, gay parties and Christmas decorations. More than ever we realized it was a spiritual matter, and so I was hard at work thinking out my sermon for Christmas Eve. There was an attempt to decorate the barracks using evergreen twigs, cotton and bits of colored paper, even small bits of tinfoil. I put in a requisition for candles to the two Japanese interpreters. To my great surprise they produced them.

At eight o'clock in the evening the camp program began in the chapel. It was decorated with tropical foliage, flowers and paper trimmings. Some of the Japanese officers and the two interpreters came to the event but there were no enlisted men present. Lt. Shibota sang a song to represent his group. The musical instruments were not in good shape but the band ripped off some swinging tunes and the Christmas caroling was lovely as usual. We had some fine soloists, which helped the program a lot, but it did not have the peaceful spirit of the previous Christmas.

At 11:30 I began our Episcopal Service in the hospital chapel. It was beautifully decorated and the candles added a lot to the atmosphere. The service was simple, fairly short and this year we had an excellent choir. My sermon seemed to go a bit better than the previous one. I guessed there were around 300 prisoners present in contrast to the 25 a year ago. When the service was over we joyfully shook hands and wished each other a Merry Christmas. The following morning fifty of us got up just before daylight and sang Christmas carols throughout the compound. The rest of the day was one of happy celebration despite the conditions we were under. Men put on their best khaki uniforms and insignia if they still had any. Lt. Clyde Fleming resurrected an old civilian suit and with a derby, cane, and reddened nose walked through the compound during the morning, pretending he was drunk. The noon chow was a disappointment with only rice and vines from the canals made into soup which we called "kang kong". But that night we had carabao meat, vegetables and rice. We ended the day feeling that it had indeed been a blessed Christmas with the spiritual side clearly in focus.

After Christmas there was a normal letdown, but it did not last long. We heard another shipment of Red Cross packages was due to come and at a time when we desperately needed it. Medical supplies from last year's shipment were exhausted and the hospital was full of sick men. In the middle of January, 100 enlisted men were sent to Davao to work on an airfield and a rumor circulated that 650 men would go to work on another airfield in February. Late in the month of February the Red Cross shipment did arrive. It contained four general weekly food packages per man, a quantity of medical supplies, 1,200 pairs of shoes, toothbrushes, toothpaste, razor blades and shaving cream, and a small quantity of clothing. I was overjoyed to see the razor blades since I had been using two gem blades since entering prison camp almost two years ago. There were some 10,000 letters which were parceled out to us from February into June. News from home was as good as food. In all I received fourteen letters from my parents and Pat Taylor, my fiancée.

About this time I was going to form a church vestry and an Episcopal congregation. One officer had made a small portable altar for me with the words "Holy, Holy, Holy" carved on the front of it. A nice sense of Christian community had developed among those who attended our prayer book services, some of whom were Episcopalians, some were not. One Sunday I simply read to the men aloud the Holy Communion Service, since they had not received communion after Chaplain Howden died. Even though there wasn't any consecrated bread and wine, we all felt we had received the elements spiritually.

The last week of February, 1944, the Japanese Camp Commander sent orders to our American Headquarters that 650 able-bodied men were to leave for the Lasang Airfield March 2nd. It appeared that even though there were 1,800 men interned, only about that number were strong enough to do heavy work and most of them were on the Mactan rice detail. Lieutenant Yasamura, the Japanese doctor, came into the compound to inspect the able-bodied. Our headquarters selected men by rank, and since there were not enough enlisted men to fill the quota, warrant officers and second and first lieutenants were included on the list to be shipped out. One of my Episcopalians, a Commander in the Navy, came to me and said, "Johnny, since this is going to be a tough detail we at Headquarters want you to go. There is no telling what will happen on this one. We want you in the group even though you cannot go as a chaplain."

Three days prior to our departure, Commander Portz, USN, a Senior officer of the American prisoners, presented a written protest to the Japanese. I did not see the document but was told it was based on The Rules of Land Warfare and had been prepared by Lt. Col. Marron who had a copy of them. There were references to the Hague Conference and the Geneva Conference and noted the Japanese had signed the Hague Conference, having to do with prisoners of war. In several days we received a negative answer to our protest.

On March 1st all of us on the detail were given new shoes which had come from the Red Cross shipment. Two days prior to that we had been given two Red Cross food packages. On March 2nd a large convoy of trucks came into the compound to take us to Lasang even though everyone was reluctant to leave. We were quite upset about being taken to a combat airfield to work and even personal protests were of no avail. My buddy, Capt. Clyde Ely, with whom I worked side-by-side in the rice fields, gave me his new Red Cross gloves which he had just received, believing I would have to work with my hands on the coral runway. Russel Hutchison gave me an old piece of canvas. As we left Dapecol we felt like a doomed work detail.

Just before leaving we were marched to the Japanese parade ground where Major Maeda gave us a speech through his interpreter Mr. "Running Wada". The Major told us he knew we had been hard workers because he had seen us at work in the rice fields. He promised that if we worked hard we would soon be returned to the Colony. So, following the speech, down the road we went in open trucks with a fairly large contingent of guards. In several hours we left the dense jungle and were back into civilization of sorts. It had been a long time since we had seen Filipino farms and their fruit orchards, the pigs and chickens underneath the buildings and the children playing in the dirt. For seventeen months we had been fenced in at Dapecol. All the way I kept wondering "What next, what next?"

9

DETESTABLE LASANG

"Guys this ain't no palace," said the prisoner next to me. "Yea, this looks worse than Alcatraz," said someone else. The trucks pulled into Lasang about 2:00 p.m. It was a bleak prison compound. There were no trees or bushes or room for any recreation. There were four rectangular barracks, a kitchen shack, two latrines and one well where we bathed behind the buildings. The barracks were crudely constructed with two-by-fours, plywood siding, and corrugated iron roofs. Not long after we arrived, the Japanese officers had our latrines moved between the barracks because they did not like the smell reaching their quarters. This not only created a sanitary problem for us, but proved to be a nuisance because of the flies. There was a guardhouse at the entrance of the compound, a double barbed wire fence, the usual lights shining in and around the compound at night and a single guard tower. There were no trees or shrubbery, only some grass and weeds in the compound. We were assigned to specific barracks: privates in numbers 1 and 2, officers in number 3, and non-commissioned officers in number 4. The American staff included Lt. Col. Rufus H. Rogers, C. O.; Capt. Griffeth M. Berg, Adjutant; Capt. Morrison C. Cleveland, Supply Officer; and Capt. Kenneth Wetzel, Mess Officer. Our three doctors were: Lt. Col. George T. Colvard, Major Luther C. Heidger and Major J.C. Trevaine.

Our dentist was Capt. Joe Allen. Two chaplains were: Capt. Joseph V. Lefluer, Roman Catholic and Capt. Morris Day, Lutheran. Knowing the difficult circumstances of the detail the staff was ready to do everything possible to assist in the morale and physical needs of the prisoners.

Among us we had agreed upon a plan that we would go out on the airfield, as directed, but do nothing in the way of work. The Japanese had made promises to feed us well, stating that we would be given 650 grams of rice, and 500 grams of vegetables per man a day, and weekly issues of fish and meat, sugar, salt and cooking oil. We had heard promises before that were not fulfilled so no one expected they would be met this time.

The following morning at 6:00 a.m. we were organized into working groups of 50 men each, and in columns of fours we were marched to the Lasang Airfield. The young Formosan guards were supplemented by Japanese soldiers. When we reached the airfield we found it to be a single coral runway estimated to be 1,600 feet long. There were six Japanese transport planes, ten fighter planes, and six bombers parked along the runway. No one liked the looks of the situation. Anger welled up inside me at this affront to our loyalty to the United States. Unquestionably this was a combat field and we were, once again, a part of the war zone but on the Japanese side.

The first day we did nothing but lean on our shovels in spite of the fact that all we had been instructed to do was to shave down the sides of the runway for drainage purposes. A Japanese civilian contractor outlined the work for each detail. Some men were directed to dig long drainage ditches down the length of the field. Large woven baskets, which we called "idiot baskets" were to be used by two men to haul the dirt. Long bamboo poles were to be shoved through the handles and then the baskets were to be hoisted to our shoulders for carrying purposes.

The Formosan guards seemed unusually quiet and we

guessed they were sympathetic toward us in this intolerable situation. About the middle of the morning our new Japanese Commanding Officer, Lt. Hoshida, arrived to inspect our work. He had a kind of round nose so very quickly we nicknamed him "Bubble Nose." He was accompanied by his second in command, Lt. Hashimoto, whom we nicknamed, "Little Caesar." Hashimoto was a fierce looking little Japanese officer with a fiery temper. Seeing that we weren't doing any work, Lt. Hoshida called for an assembly and he proceeded to give us a pep talk about working. When it was over we returned to our assigned areas and did nothing. We could see a serious discussion going on among the officers, and the interpreter, Mr. Nashamura, and the civilian supervisor. Detail leaders were called together to discuss the contract but still, no one did any work. The first day ended with absolutely nothing accomplished.

The second day we went out to the air strip and the same thing happened — no work. The civilian supervisor decreased the requirement, there were more assemblies and speeches by the Japanese officers, but no work on our part. Late in the afternoon it began to rain so we returned to the compound soaking wet. Camp morale was good because we had a strong determination to stick together. The third and fourth days were the same, so each evening after chow we were assembled in the compound for more speeches by the Japanese officers.

The situation became extremely tense because of an incident on the airstrip. During one of our assemblies, called by Lt. Hashimoto, one of our prisoners was standing on an ant hill. He moved, trying to brush off the ants which were biting his legs. Hashimoto called him to the front where he was standing on a hill and proceeded to lash him with his riding crop. We were furious. Our American prisoner didn't move, but just took it. "Little Caesar" earned his nickname and this incident only deepened our determination not to work. Our refusal to work continued for several more weeks, resulting in cutting back of our food. A pattern had developed — early breakfast before dawn, marching to the airstrip, review of the daily contract, no work. After several hours an assembly was called, then no work, lunch, no work, an assembly, no work, return to the compound. Most of the time we returned wet, tired and hungry, but would be assembled again after chow for a speech either by Lt. Hoshida or Lt. Hashimoto.

Then one afternoon a fighter plane got stuck on the coral strip with a wheel sunk in a pot hole. The guards near our detail ordered us to go to the plane and push it out of the hole. I refused to go. Here we were, men who had fought on Bataan and Correigador ordered to push a plane free so it could attack our forces! We had struggled so hard to defend ourselves, starved for weeks, made the death march, gone through O'Donnell, Cabanatuan and Dapecol, and now this deepest of all insults — ordered to work on a combat field. Tears came to my eyes. I didn't care if a guard shot me, I was not going to move toward that plane. A short distance away a young Formosan guard just stood quietly and watched. Wind blew the dust around me, some planes began landing on the field; I wished I were dead. God and country were so important in my life, and now intertwined with them was this terribly difficult situation.

Tony Montoya suddenly appeared beside me and said, "That's all-right Johnny, we all hate them, too. I'm not going over to the plane either." So the two of us stood there and watched our fellow prisoners grunting and groaning but the plane stayed stuck in the pothole. Shortly, the guards gave up. In about half-an-hour a group of Japanese and Filipino civilians were brought to the plane and without difficulty moved it from the pothole.

I was emotionally upset all that day. In the evening after chow, we were called to assemble behind the barracks — 650 men in long rows, 4 men deep. Ole "Bubble Nose" stood up on his box to harangue us about not working. What he said was translated in English through "Running Wada," the interpreter. We were told we were surrendered prisoners of war and therefore had no rights. We must always do what the Japanese told us to do. He went on to say that the Japanese never surrendered. He said that we were getting more rice and vegetables than the Japanese soldiers and civilians at the airfield (which we didn't believe). If we would do as we were told we would receive extra compensations such as tobacco rations and more meat. (At this point, from carabaos, we were getting the N.R.A. — nose, ribs and asshole). If we failed to work, our food rations would be cut even more.

When he completed his talk he began repeating the simple question, "Will you work? Will you work? Will you work? Will you work?", getting more emphatic with each repeat of the question. Something like an electric charge went through me. I said to myself, "Well, if you want to know, I'll tell you." Almost mechanically I found myself walking toward Lt. Hoshida. I saluted him and then said, "I am an officer and a soldier of the United States Army. I cannot work for you on this airfield." Running Wada said, "Go back, go back, you cannot speak for the group." Then I heard Lt. Col. Roger's voice from the back of the assembly. He was walking toward Lt. Hoshida saying, "What this officer has told you is the feeling of all of us. We do not want to work on this airfield and we want you to send us back to the Davao Penal Colony. You must know how we feel about this detail. We don't mind working for our food but we dislike this work very much." Running Wada mumbled something to Lt. Hoshida who immediately got off his box, the two walked away, and the assembly broke up.

Once inside our barracks, I discovered I was sort of a hero. An enthusiastic group of enlisted men came to me urging that we organize an escape.

The next day, as we were moving through the gate to go to the airstrip, Lt. Hoshida was standing near the guard house. As we were being counted I could see his eyes carefully look at me, so I knew I was a marked man. Lt. Col. Rogers suggested I go on sick leave for several days until the incident had passed over, which I did.

It now began raining heavily every day. Another week went by and we were coming down with chills and fever; we were putting on cold, wet clothing to go to work each morning. The food ration was cut to bare subsistence. One enlisted man detail had had enough so they finished their contract work on the airstrip in about an hour and then returned to their barracks. It wasn't long until another detail did the same. Now we were divided, with a few enlisted men details and all the officer details still holding out. Several days later Lt. Col. Rogers called us all together to tell us he had made a difficult decision. He said he now felt another approach was best for the whole camp and he did not feel our country would believe we had done wrong in following it. Beginning the next day he was ordering us to go to work on the airfield with the understanding that we would do a minimum amount of labor so we could return to the compound early and save our health. We would live as best we could under this difficult situation. He settled the matter for everyone and gave us a sense of unity again.

The following day we began this policy but always argued over each work contract to keep our labor at a minimum. This was irritating to the Japanese who, on occasion, would run at us with fixed bayonets to scare us as we sat in groups in the middle of the airstrip. But everyone held firm. There was a provocative incident when Lt. Hoshida had his guards bring up some small, narrow gauge rails. A detail was made to kneel down over the rails with their shin bones resting directly on the edge of the rail. Guards stood close by urging men to keep their backs straight and their heads up. Then we were told to finish our work, which we did as quickly as possible to relieve our comrades. The job was finished in about twenty minutes and the mistreated men were allowed to stand up and we had the usual "tinko" (counting). We were ordered to run back to the compound, some distance away. The gravel and coral under our feet was hard and sharp, but we ran like wild men and some of us outdistanced the guards. We laughed as we huffed and puffed our way through the gate with our heads high.

The Japanese had taken away our new Red Cross shoes just one month after we had arrived at the Lasang Air Field. One day, when some of us were working in the coral pit about six kilometers from the compound, we saw a Dapecol truck pass by which had three wounded Japanese guards in it. When we returned to the compound we learned that a Japanese sergeant had dropped the information that seven men had escaped from the Davao Penal Colony. We felt that if this was true we would never get our shoes back. Shoes were an important part of our lives, not only because of the kind of work we were doing but because walking through the jungles would be very difficult without shoes, and because of the morale factor. When a person has to walk over gravel or sharp coral the tendency is to keep the head down. This had a psychological effect on increasing our sense of being defeated. In fact, it created a slave mentality.

As time passed at Lasang we were developing a very deep anger toward the Japanese and some men began swearing at the guards. Of course, they disliked this profanity. One night during an assembly, the Japanese asked us to stop this swearing because their own guards were complaining and getting difficult to control.

By the middle of April all our Red Cross food had been eaten. The Japanese had stopped issuing cooking oil and fish and had cut back on our rice and vegetables. Instead of the 650 grams of rice per man per day, we were getting around 500. The vegetable issue was around 300 grams a day, so we were receiving about half the food promised us. Frequently, we went without salt which was so necessary when we were working in the heat of the tropical sun. (Lasang was located 7 degrees above the equator.) As time went on the food got more monotonous and tasteless. Sometimes we received nothing but boiled blue camotes in our mess kits. The Japanese knew we were irritable, angry and wanted to escape. They doubled the number of guards and revised the guard system in an effort to prevent any kind of mutiny.

In May, the Japanese officers and sergeants began talking to the detail leaders about an exchange of prisoners. Some men got so excited with the idea that they could hardly sleep at night. One man, Ezra McKinney, begged everyone to tell him about a rumor, regardless of how groundless it might be. Since we were so completely cut off from the outside world we were forced, more than ever, to depend on our own resources. We began to hold small group meetings. Ed Bewley was extremely knowledgeable about railroads and could talk intelligently about them. Chaplain Le Fleur held discussions on religion. Morris Shoss told us about a cadet's life at West Point. Jay Shands reviewed popular novels he had read. Stanley Maxwell, a Britisher, "took us on sightseeing trips" through the English countryside. Earl Spellman lectured on China. Bruno Ulak "took us sailing" on a pleasure cruise through South America.

Every day I read sections of the Bible until I had actually completed all the books. I did not hold any church services but enjoyed the Protestant services conducted by Chaplain Day on Sundays. I often talked about houses with Dick Cook who slept beside me. Since he was an architect he helped me design a house on some scraps of paper. He was an Episcopalian, and I told him about my two years at seminary. Milton Morgan who slept on the other side of me liked to discuss world politics, and under the circumstances it was a fascinating subject to consider.

At night we would have to be careful to keep our bare feet under the mosquito net because the rats would eat on our calluses while we slept. When you were wakened by a sudden sharp pain you knew a rat had started eating on the bottom of your foot.

In the latter part of May, commissioned officers were told they wouldn't have to work on the airstrip any longer. This seemed like a sure sign there was about to be a prisoner exchange. Consequently, we sat around the inside of the barracks waiting for something to happen. The only major event was that a large flight of locusts landed inside the compound. We quickly got our mosquito nets and caught skads of them. Someone said the tails were edible so we fried them in Barbasol shaving cream which had come with our Red Cross packages.

The rest period for the officers did not last long. Lt. Hoshida ordered all officers to wash the enlisted men's clothes, or what was left of them. He also had us line up in the morning to watch the enlisted men go to work. But Lt. Hashimoto somehow made it known that he felt Lt. Hoshida's command was unfair and that we should all bring out our clothing for display. The situation had now become quite strange. Trying to impress upon us his power, Lt. Hashimoto told us at assemblies that he would kill anyone who tried to escape. The job washing the enlisted men's clothing fizzled out and Hashimoto appeared more and more like a man with mental and emotional problems.

One day we were told that all officers including Lt. Col. Rogers, his staff and one half of the kitchen detail, were to work on the airfield. Once again we were back on the job, breaking the coral rock into small pieces and spreading it on the runway. The Japanese began to camouflage buildings and put planes into revetments or hide them under trees in case there was a bombing attack. Every day we would see fighter planes take off with extra gasoline tanks and bombs attached to their bellies. We felt increased tension among the Japanese officers and guards who appeared to have packed their equipment, ready to leave at anytime.

Dr. Allen, our dentist, made a trip to see the 100-man detail, located on an airstrip outside of Davao and brought back some interesting information. He reported that transport planes were arriving every day at that airfield, loaded with wounded Japanese soldiers. Also, heavy bombers were taking off from the field with their bays full of bombs.

In only a matter of days our airfield began to have air

raid alerts. At night we would see searchlights scan the sky looking for attack planes. During these alerts a Moro gong in the guard tower would be struck again and again and the guards would rush into the compound with bayonets on their rifles. They would stand around the barracks ready to stick anyone who came out. The guards counted off and at times Ed Lloyd would confuse them by adding a Japanese number (a trick which we found amusing). One night Private Tex Arnold, who had been sound asleep during an alert, woke up and dashed to the latrine. As he stepped out the door a guard stuck him with a bayonet between the ribs. By now the Japanese were frightened and they meant business if we got out of line in any way.

On August 4th all work was discontinued on the airfield. It appeared that final preparations were being made for our departure from Lasang. That night around 1:00 a.m. a low flying plane passed over the airfield and dropped three bombs. An alert was sounded and we all shouted with joy.

The very next day we received our last Red Cross box of food and our shoes were returned. For five months we had been waiting to receive this box, which we now really needed because the food at Lasang was terrible. Our morale immediately went sky high with the feel of good leather shoes on our feet again. Still, we were kept in the compound. The next day we were told to turn in our shoes again and our rations were cut to two meals a day. By now, a few men who had squandered their food or traded it for cigarettes hung around the garbage pit to find a few scraps or boiled up some weeds. Men addicted to cigarettes found themselves in a bad situation. I had no trouble trading off my several packages for canned meat or beans.

We waited day after day for the order to move out. This was an exciting time because we knew the Yanks were finally on the way. We had had four trying months of war and 2 1/2 years in prison camp so we had been through very difficult times. Now the big question was, "how do we gain our freedom?" The raids at night became more frequent so we even wondered if there could be a sudden invasion and we would be set free on Mindinao.

On August 19th we were told to get ready to depart Lasang the following day. Also, we were informed that our shoes would be returned to us once we had boarded a ship. Mosquito nets were turned in to the Japanese along with our kitchen equipment. That night Lt. Hoshida called an assembly and told us we were being taken to a safer place. He said that if we created any disturbance during the trip, we would be shot. It was obvious now that the Japanese were very much on the defensive.

Everyone was sick of Lasang — the work, the food, the confinement, the Japanese officers "Bubble Nose" and "Little Caesar," the drabness of the barracks. We knew, too, that if the American Air Force heavily bombed the airstrip, our compound nearby would probably be hit. Furthermore, the Japanese would not allow us to dig any foxholes to protect ourselves. For some months many men had been talking about an escape, in fact I dreamed about it. I'm sure most of us felt we needed to do something to break out of our situation, but the question was always, how?

One day I heard Dixie Dugan, an Air Force pilot whistling the *Dance Macabre*, Saint Saën's *"Dance of Death."* It gave me an indescribable feeling of doom.

At 3:30 a.m., August 20th, we were awake and our belongings were packed. Before dawn we had had breakfast. The orders were to be ready to leave at 6:00 a.m. When the time came, the Japanese lined us up in companies. They tied heavy hemp rope around the waist of each man and linked him to the man in front and the man in back. We were literally all tied together. There was a reinforcement of guards, two now for every four prisoners. Machine guns and automatic rifles were mounted on trucks in front and to the rear of the column. Escape was out of the question.

As we walked through the coconut groves I tried to

figure out what was happening and where we were going; to Manila, to Tokyo, to the Island of Formosa? A few Filipino bystanders watched our column without any expression on their faces. Barefooted, we walked to Tabunco, the pier for the lumber mill. There our shoes were given back to us, but we were told not to put them on until we were aboard the ship. As we were sitting on the pier waiting for lighters to take us to a freighter, out in the gulf, the Erie Maru, the 100 man detail from the Davao airfield arrived. These prisoners had their shoes on and were holding their final box of Red Cross food and cigarettes. We quickly learned that the airfield where they had been working had been bombed. It was good to be leaving Lasang, a place which was detested and which had compromised our loyalty to America.

10

HUMAN CARGO AT ITS WORST

Around noon on August 20th, seven hundred and fifty of us were taken by lighters to a freighter out in the Gulf of Davao. We climbed up the side of the ship on a wide lattice rope to the deck. Four hundred men were crowded into one hold, three hundred and fifty into another. At first there was hardly enough room to sit down, let alone stretch out on the floor. The Japanese had taken up space by placing a considerable amount of luggage in the crowded holds. Everyone tried to shift around to make room for seating space but, still, some had to stand. It was clear we would have to take turns standing as we settled in. Three five gallon cans and two latrine boxes were sent down through the hatch and were put in the middle of the hold for toilet purposes. Any eliminations had to be done in full view. The heat was terrible. In a very short time we were covered with sweat. I was glad Dick Cook and I had gone to the well before daylight and bathed. In this heat a dirty body would bring on skin rash which could open up into sores. Having traveled in the hold of a ship before, we knew what to expect. The Japanese had piled sacks of vegetables on the hatch covers above us limiting the amount of air coming down into the hold, making the situation even worse.

About 2:00 p.m. the Japanese called for our American

cooks to come up on deck to cook our food. That evening buckets of food were lowered down into the hold. Each man received a half mess kit of rice and an inch of watery soup in a canteen cup. We had been promised 300 grams of rice and 300 grams of vegetables per man each day but what we received couldn't even be considered a minimum ration. Our soup was made from the peelings of the camotes and squash, so it was hardly edible. Those of us who had carefully saved what we could of our Red Cross food were grateful for it.

That evening the ship moved in an unknown direction but we guessed not out of the Gulf. I had a pretty good place in the hold where I could see through the open hatch and look at the full moon. A mast of the ship slowly passed back and forth in front of this beautiful white light up in the sky. It gave me comfort even though we were literally human cargo at its worst, literally trapped in the hold of a dirty freighter. This was a time when prayer meant so much. I couldn't help but think of my days of freedom, especially when attending seminary. I wondered about my classmates and thought what a contrast between my situation and theirs. Probably, by now, they were ordained ministers. I re-lived moments with my fiancee, the happy life I had while growing up in Springfield, Ohio, the good fortune of having such fine parents. They were so precious to me now.

The next morning around ten o'clock, buckets of food consisting of rice and watery soup were sent down through the open hatch. Serving had just started when we heard the sound of an airplane. Through the open hatch I could see a four engine plane in the sky with American markings. Then we heard the swish of a bomb falling, followed by an explosion in the water. It had missed us but it was a close call. Immediately I heard the clatter of machine gun fire on deck and the banging of hatch covers over our hatch. The hobnailed shoes of the guards running on the steel deck made a terrible clatter. Some of us jumped from the center of the hold to get underneath the super structure of the ship. Gradually things began to settle down.

Because the hatch covers were still on the hatch, it was almost pitch black except for a little light that came through the slits between the hatch covers, enough to allow us to just barely see one another. Most of our ventilation was gone and we began to sweat. We felt absolutely trapped, but we were afraid to speak because even that would use energy and oxygen. Lt. Col. Rogers spoke up and said we should be very still. After a short while, some men began to get sick and others started to pass out due to lack of oxygen and the terrible heat. My whole body began to sting as the fluid inside had poured out in sweat. After (at least) two hours, Lt. Col. Rogers called up to the Japanese and asked that we be given some air. There was no response. Around the third hour he began to plead for the removal of the hatch covers. It was sad to hear our leader beg like a child for ventilation. We had become like fish that had been left out of water too long and were simply limp.

Finally the hatch covers were removed. In about twenty minutes we started to revive and some began talking. Then we saw Lt. Hashimoto look down into the hold. Possibly as many as 100 men had passed out in both holds, and two men simply went beserk and had to be tied down. Lt. Col. Rogers made a strong protest to Hashimoto, whose only response was that they had to do this because of what happened on a previous ship to Manila. In several hours we were fed again and now everyone in the hold was quiet and subdued. It had been an exhausting and frightening day.

That night the ship moved again. Information about what was happening on deck was brought to us by the men who went topside to empty the latrine cans. There was some firing the next morning and the hatch covers went over the opened hatch again. We were dehydrated for the second time and I experienced the stinging sensation for another two hours. It was a blessing to have a little Red Cross food still left. After this experience we opened a can at a time and shared with others around us. We could not live long on what we were getting from the Japanese so we scrupulously rationed what was left of our Red Cross food.

On the evening of August 22nd we were shut up in the hold for ten hours, with the result that the next morning everyone was in a terrible condition. Those with some strength left fanned the very weak. Hour after hour we bathed each other's heads with dirty damp rags and gave a sip of water to someone who hadn't the strength to lift a canteen to his mouth. Some men were now covered with open sores. The doctors worked like martyrs to help the sick.

On August 24th the ship arrived in Zamboanga in the late afternoon. For several days no one knew where we were because the ship had traveled slowly and would stop for a brief time and then start up again. Apparently, it was hugging the shoreline as it moved to its destination. Some men thought we were at Cebu, others Dumaguette. Finally, some old timers from the Philippines took the latrine cans up to the deck and took the opportunity to look carefully at our surroundings. When they returned they said it was their opinion that the ship was anchored at Zamboanga, even though there was some confusion in their minds because of the destruction of the port facilities. By this time we were very dirty and I was shocked at some of the skin rashes and running sores. Some men were also having blackouts. At this point, because of our condition, we were brought up on deck and hosed down with salt water and then immediately sent back down into the hold. It was hardly a bath, but it did help revive us.

Chaplain Le Fleur, I later learned, did a wonderful job holding daily prayer services and being a spiritual guide to those particularly in need of help. He also held a short general service each Sunday. Chaplain Day, in our hold, was too weak and sick to even get on his feet. He was unable to function in giving any spiritual help. Lt. Col. Rogers asked me if I would take his place in leading a Sunday service. I told him I would try to be of help. On the evening of the 26th, after we had settled down for the night, I said some prayers, read a chapter from the Bible and gave a short talk. To me, the most fitting subject at that time was suffering, so I told the prisoners about Job. I tried to present a dramatic picture of what he had to go through and yet he did not lose faith in God. Now that the bare essentials of life were denied us, the trials of Job seemed to have a realistic message for us. The men were all very attentive. The opportunity to speak to the prisoners was worth a whole life of ministry. Dripping in sweat, in bare feet, and with nothing but a pair of threadbare bluejeans on, I talked about faith in God.

The next Sunday, September 3rd, I had another opportunity to address the men. Because there were Jews as well as Christians and probably some non-believers in the hold, I picked a Bible lesson again from the Old Testament. I did not think there were any non-believers, but I realized that there must be at this point some who had difficulty in believing in a supreme being. In any case, trying to be sensitive to the situation and yet still preach as a Christian lay minister, I read Chapter 3 of Ecclesiastes:

> *"For everything there is an appointed time;*
> *And there is a time for every purpose under the heavens,*
> *A time to be born and a time to die—"*

There was now every indication that we were not to get out of the hold alive. I tried to be positive and said as Americans we had all enjoyed a wonderful past and now we shouldn't worry about the future. There was a set time for everything and there would be an end to this trip as there was a beginning. Regardless of what sort of men we had been, good or bad, still, we were all children of God and He still governs our lives, even in the hold of the prison ship. He is the one who ultimately is in control of our welfare. Regardless of whether a bomb would drop down into the hold and kill us, we are His creatures. If we are killed, we are still going to be all right. What we needed now was complete trust in a loving God, no matter what happened. In Him we will be returned to the goodness of his creation.

"Let us hear the conclusion of the whole matter: Fear God, and keep His commandments; for this is the whole duty of man.

For God shall bring every work into judgement, with every secret thing, whether it be good or whether it be evil."

I felt that with the great variety of religious backgrounds this was not a time to try and press for conversion to Christianity. But I did feel strongly that it was a time to affirm the certainty of God's love and that there was a condition in heaven where we would find release, freedom and the full awareness of His love. It was a moment of ministry I will never forget. God seemed to be speaking directly through me to men in suffering and great danger.

On September 4th, after being in the harbor ten days, we were ordered to move from the hold of the present ship to the hold of another ship docked beside us. Two hundred and fifty of us went into the forward hold of the second ship, five hundred into the aft hold. The move took place very rapidly, at night. The larger group was completely at the bottom of the second ship and apparently more crowded than ever. At night we could hear bombing raids on Zamboanga, so we knew we were in a target zone. The hatch covers were over the hatch again and I could feel the silent prayers of men in the darkness.

The following morning, on the 5th of September, the two hundred and fifty of us in the forward hold were transferred to a rear hold in order to make room for more Japanese baggage. When we made this transfer I could see we were in a sizable convoy of ships. By 11:00 a.m. we were underway.

About four o'clock in the afternoon we heard some loud commotion going on above us. Through the hatch opening I could see an elderly Japanese, with nothing around him but a towel, ordering the guards to take off the hatch covers, presumably so we could get more air. We were fairly certain he was the captain of the ship, who realized the deplorable condition we were in. That night the guards removed the hatch covers. What a relief!

The following morning there were more air raid alerts and the hatch covers were replaced. To make matters worse, a tarpaulin was pulled over them, shutting off all air. We were shocked at this. There was absolutely nothing to do but to pray. Fortunately, the alert did not last long and the tarpaulin was removed. However, the whole day seemed full of one short alert after another. The ship moved and then it would stop, then move again. It was obvious we were in submarine waters.

On the 7th day of September, Lt. Hashimoto rearranged the hatch covers to allow about four inches of air space between them. The covers looked like wide bars across the opening of the hold. We could see that the covers were lashed down with ropes so they could not be lifted from the inside. Ever since the ship had left Zamboanga we had not been allowed on deck to empty the latrine cans. Instead, we had to pass them up to the guards by the use of ropes. The guard's indifference about emptying the cans created added difficulties. In time the ship started speeding ahead. We talked a lot about the movement of the ship. For a very short time we felt the worst part of the journey was over. Still, I was apprehensive and looked carefully around me to see how I could possibly get out of the hold if the ship were attacked. A wooden partition separated our hold from one next to us. I was determined somehow to get through the partition in case of a crisis. All around me were men so weak and sick they could not even stand to receive their meager chow.

Suddenly, in the late afternoon there was one terrific explosion followed by a second. The hold immediately filled with dust and vapor. Men were lying all around me in mangled positions. There was a lot of moaning from those in shock and bewilderment. The face of the man in front of me was covered with blood. I put my hands to my face to see if I was bleeding, too, but I was not. Some large, heavy object had hit me on the forehead, but I was all right. My mind was still clear and so I started looking for a way out of the hold. Before the explosion I was stretched out like everyone else, packed like sardines in a can. Beside me was Lt. Massey who had become so weak during the 19 days in the hold that he could not stand to get his chow, so some of us nearby would get it for him. He was moaning and calling for help. I tried to release him from the debris, but had to leave him because it was impossible to get him loose and I certainly couldn't carry him. The ship began to lurch, so I knew I could not stay in the hold any longer. My mind was clear and racing madly to find a way out. Turning around to look at the partition, I realized it was blown away and a few men were passing through it into the next hold. I quickly followed, climbed over some luggage, and then went through an open hatch and got up on deck. Strewn around were a number of mangled Japanese bodies, probably ripped to pieces by flying hatch covers or other heavy objects on deck. Even so there were numerous guards shooting at Americans in the holds and in the water. Some were throwing hand grenades into the hold. There were guards so close to me I could have touched them but they, too, were in a state of shock and confusion. Far off in the distance I could see land. Several Americans, their faces full of fear, shouted, "We can't swim, we can't swim!"

By this time I could see the front end of the vessel listing down into the water where 500 men had been trapped. Debris began floating alongside the ship so I quickly stripped off my blue denims and jumped over the side of the ship into the water. I scraped my side on the way down because the ship was no longer upright. As soon as I hit the water I felt exhilarated. Above me there were guards along the rail shooting at prisoners in the water, so I swam toward some Japanese who had life preservers on, trying to create some protection by being near them. Then I grabbed several floating timbers. An American flailing in the water shouted to me, "I can't swim!" I yelled, "Grab onto the boards with me!" Then he was shot and his head fell forward on the boards so I had to push him away with my foot. I felt terrible about this. Up on the bridge I could see Lt. Hashimoto directing the rifle fire of the guards. Around me must have been ten or more Japanese with life preservers on. Overhead were three Japanese planes dropping depth charges trying to hit the submarine that had torpedoed us. The ship's whistle was screeching like a wounded child.

I decided that with the timber helping to keep me afloat I would scissor kick my way toward land, getting away from the ship as fast as I could. Some distance away I saw the bald head of Major Harry Fischer and called to him. He was swimming alone so I urged him to wait and hold on to the boards with me. (The boards were two-by-fours about six feet long.) Soon we were together, swimming toward the coastline. Hearing a loud crackling sound we turned our heads back toward the torpedoed ship. Like the crumpling of heavy tinfoil, the ship went up on its stern and down into the deep water. Japanese, now in life boats or in the water with life preservers on, began singing. The other Japanese ships in the convoy were circling the area picking up survivors, including twenty-nine Americans who were later shot off the end of one of the vessels with their hands tied behind their backs. One of them escaped to tell the story.

As Major Fischer and I approached the shoreline we saw a large vessel which had been run up on the beach. We knew we should stay clear of it. Some distance from us we could see a few heads in the water; they had to be prisoners like ourselves escaping from the Japanese. Sporadic bursts of gun fire came toward us from the ship on the beach. About 200 yards away we saw Master Sergeant Robinett. We called to him and said we would meet him underneath the foliage that ringed the beachfront. When we reached shore we found it was mainly coral rock which cut into our feet, but at long last we were free! Running into the underbrush we heard a hissing sound ... then looked into the grinning faces of three Filipinos who said full of excitement, "Guerrillas, guerrillas!" I hugged one of them.

11

THE ESCAPE

"Would we be able to really escape?" My mind was racing with excitement. Major Fischer and I followed the Filipinos up a dirt path, hitting the ground when a burst of machine gun fire went over our heads. But we were free and that was an exhilarating feeling. My feet hurt from the coral cuts and I was really stiff from the long swim and having no exercise on the ship, but I didn't care. Soon we were walking in the dark along the path where Filipinos holding candles gave us raw eggs, bananas, and boiled camotes. They were as thrilled as we were since in their little pocket of resistance they had been fighting off the Japanese close to three years.

Soon we came to a bamboo shack where a French priest lived. He gave us a little more food and then we were taken to a sergeant's house to rest and make plans to go inland. By now other Americans were arriving, some with bullet wounds, some with broken bones and deep lacerations and one man, Hayes Bolitho, had a broken jaw along with broken ribs. Like myself , they had held onto debris floating about the sinking ship and eventually made it to shore with the help of the tide. When the moon came up the Filipinos started us on a trek inland; around twenty-five of us either walking or riding carabao, and in the case of Bolitho, being carried on a bed. As the sun rose we could see Filipino farmers going to work in what I believed to be the most peaceful scene in my life. There was no hurry, nò shouting, no guns firing, no clatter of tanks or explosion of bombs. It seemed to me at the moment this was the way God wanted his world to be, but in so many ways we human beings had turned it into chaos.

Sometime in the morning we arrived at a vacant bamboo shack situated on a hill. By this time we were exhausted and simply needed rest. Filipinos began bringing us food, and a nice, intelligent looking nurse arrived with clean rags and a bottle of methyolate. With the help of several corpsmen we began to clean and bandage wounds as best we could. For the rest of the day we watched survivors come down the road to our collecting point until we numbered about fifty. A few men had a dazed look in their eyes, obviously still in emotional shock.

The next day, September 9th, Major Fischer, the guerrillas and I got together to discuss what we should do. The Filipinos suggested a plan of dispersing the able bodied men with farmers in the area and moving the wounded to the guerrilla hospital, across Sindangan Bay to the town of Sindangan. Since Major Fischer was the senior officer of our survivor group, he was in command and asked me to be his Adjutant. Seven of us felt we could travel right away, but it was obvious most of the survivors needed time to rest and be looked at by a doctor and a dentist who had arrived on the second day of the escape to help us. They had brought with them a limited amount of first aid equipment.

On the third day of freedom the seven of us, along with our Filipino guerrilla guides, went down to a little barrio called Liloy. There we waited until nightfall for two outrigger canoes to take us to a Moro village not far away. Someone mentioned it was Sunday, so I held a simple prayer service as a kind of memorial to the many Americans who had lost their lives.

Fortunately, I had memorized St. Paul's great hymn of love, I Corinthians: 13, and so repeated the chapter and used it as the theme for my talk. God seemed more real to us now than ever before in our lives. However, the tragic death of our many close comrades was something we could hardly accept at the time. Their deaths will always linger as a kind of silent hurt inside us.

That night we were loaded into the outrigger canoes and in several hours reached the Moro village, where houses were constructed out on the water. The Moros that we met were big fishermen, quite different in looks and stature from the Filipinos, and had a reputation for being fierce warriors. They provided us with a cumpet with a broad sail to take us across the bay. We hadn't gone very far from the village when we heard the sound of an airplane, so the Moros covered us over with a straw mat so the Japanese observation plane would not see us. A while later the wind picked up and it started to rain. The old sail tore and we had to put in to shore. While waiting for the sail to be mended, we stayed with a Moro chief who seemed very anxious to show his loyalty to the United States. Consequently, Major Fischer asked me to write a flowery statement of friendship and appreciation for all the Datto (chief) was doing for us. The Major and the Datto then pierced their arms to draw blood and together signed the statement which I had quickly prepared. The chief and his wives and children all stood proudly together while the ceremony took place in the dim light of coconut oil lamps. It was a very interesting cross-cultural experience.

On reaching the town of Sindangan, Capt. Salvador Fangon helped us organize the caretaking arrangements with the Filipino farmers in the area. The next day the rest of the survivors arrived in a fairly large boat from Liloy with additional men who had landed on the beaches at various places along the coast. Altogether, we now numbered eighty-three. However, one man named Pritchard was so weak from the long 19 day trip in the hold of the prison ship and exposure in the water that he died, undoubtedly of pneumonia. With several of his friends and some Filipinos we selected a lovely little clearing where we dug his grave. Since I knew the 23rd Psalm, I used this Scripture for the basis of what I had to say. It was sad because this young American had come so far in the war, survived prison camps and the horrible prison ship and now, at this moment of freedom, his body had reached the final breaking point.

Several days later, Lt. Col. John McGee appeared and told us about his escape from a prison ship in June off the Port of Zamboanga. He said he had been designated at guerrilla headquarters to take charge of the survivors and to begin developing a security camp where we would be supplied with food, clothing, arms and ammunition. All the able bodied were to be divided into three platoons and trained in the use of the new American carbine. His orders came from Lt. Col. Bowler, commander of all the guerrilla units in western Mindinao. He then appointed Major Fischer as his Executive Officer and I was given the job of Adjutant responsible for administration matters and records. Lt. Jim Gardner was given the duty of Supply Officer and Master Sergeant George Robinett was placed in charge of the mess once it was established.

With the help of a primitive tribe of river people called the Subanos, who were still in loin cloths and using bows, arrows and spears, the security camp was established. Its location was fairly deep in the mountains, requiring seventeen crossings of a fast mountain stream to reach it. Two radio experts, Lt. Richard Cook, and Sergeant Joseph Coe, helped repair the guerrilla radio, which had ceased to function. I was asked to prepare a statement of what had happened and the condition of the survivors, which would be radioed to General MacArthur's Headquarters in Hollandia, New Guinea. Major injuries included two compound fractures of the legs; eight other fractures including a broken jaw, arms and ribs; eight bullet wounds; shrapnel wounds; twenty-eight cases of broken ear drums; as well as numerous other lacerations and bruises. By now gangrene had set in some of the wounds so we were in need of immediate help or there could be more deaths.

Soon after Lt. Col. McGee arrived, a boat came into Sindangan with khaki clothing, shoes, rifles and ammunition; so, we were definitely back in the war on the American side. For roughly a week life was quiet since the city had been pretty well abandoned. Two platoons went up to the security camp while I stayed on in Sindangan in Capt. Fangan's house, which we used as a kind of headquarters. He had an old typewriter which I began using to make reports. Finally, the remainder of the survivors were instructed to go up to the security camp so all the able-bodied men would be together. Not long after we started out of the town we heard planes. Several Japanese planes came out of the clouds and one landed in the bay in front of us. Apparently it had engine trouble, so landed to make repairs. The Filipino guerrillas got excited and as the plane taxied to shore, they opened fire.

The plane's guns began strafing the beach, so I went running back to the Fangan house. Salvador's wife had just had a baby and she hadn't left the house yet. I asked what I could do. I took his wife, the baby, a rifle, and two house boys who carried luggage on their heads and we started inland. We crossed over several streams and I heard more strafing as we came to a stream too deep and swift to cross. I told her I would go back and tell Salvador where she was, but to wait there with the house boys. When I returned to the bay, I could see two planes out on the water. Then the Captain dashed up, all smiles; he had been waiting to get into a fight and was pleased to have a crack at the Japs. The pilots of the downed plane swam out to sea where the second plane had landed and picked them up. Then the second plane took to the air and began dropping bombs to try and destroy the abandoned plane which gradually floated to the shore and was captured.

As I was going to the security camp alone, I met Lt. Col. McGee on the way down and gave him a radio message from Col. Bowler which stated there was a possibility some survivors might be evacuated by submarine. That was exciting news! When I arrived at the base camp the situation did not look good. It was very damp in the mountains. Some men had to sleep without blankets, and under these conditions, colds, chills, and fevers started up. The Subanos had finished building the needed barracks for roughly fifty men, but to my eyes they were little more than bamboo lean-tos. It was obvious this situation could not be maintained for very long.

There was now a big question about the size of the submarine and what would happen if the Japanese attacked Sindangan, which we felt was a good possibility. After all, the Japanese had lost to the guerrillas a good sea plane, completely in fact except for some engine trouble which could be fixed.

At the security camp, each man had a rifle and there were sixty rounds of ammunition apiece, so we were all set to continue to fight. However, things were now changing fast. Lt. Col. McGee was keen to get us out before an attack might take place, so on the following morning I received a message from him stating I was to take a priority group straight to the town of Siari as quickly as possible.

In spite of overcast skies the Japanese sent in two seaplanes which bombed the city. One plane crashed into the bay, probably because of the terrible weather conditions. Two crew members swam to shore where the guerrillas captured them; when one of the airmen tried to escape, he was shot.

We, of course, heard the bombing on the way from base camp. 1st Lt. Paul Snowden carried a heavy automatic rifle, but the rest of us had nothing to carry except our carbines and ammunition. Hooked to our belts were coconut shells which would serve as a cup for food or drink. On leaving, I told the men that this was a forced march because we had an important place to go and when we got there we would have something good waiting for us. I wanted to say a submarine but I could not be sure that the plan would work out.

Going through Sindangan I could see the plane, which had been beached in front of the house where I had been staying. We went across the open beach on the run because there was always the possibility that the Japanese would return for still another bombing. After walking roughly 20 kilometers we met our sick and wounded men who had been in the guerrilla hospital. The two with compound fractures, Pultice and Mapes, were being pulled on carabao sleds. Others rode carabao or walked in agony, like my friend Jack Playter who had a hole in his thigh so large and deep one could see the bone. Each step was sheer agony for the wounded, who in many cases pulled themselves along with poles. Somehow we crossed mountains and streams, determined to reach our destination. Lt. Col. Chenoweth who was in charge of the sick and wounded had, as I recall, a broken eardrum and a seriously injured back which later would have him in a cast for weeks.

When we arrived at Siari, another small barrio on the edge of the bay, it was about dark. We waited one and a half hours on the beach and then went into the large plantation home of Jacquin Macias who owned and operated the copra plantation. We were fed a wonderful meal of rice and meat, eating as much as we wanted. Ricardo was a big, smiling Filipino who was prepared to do anything he could for us.

The next day Major Fischer arrived with the rest of our men from the base camp. We were given numbers with the low numbers going to the sick and wounded and the high numbers to the most able-bodied. We were all told to stay inside Jacquin's house so we couldn't be seen from the bay or from the air. That night we went to the beach again and gathered around a large fire of dry coconut fronds. Some men were anxious to stay on with the guerrillas and be on the beaches when the Americans arrived, which showed the courage and loyalty of our group of survivors. But we were skin and bones, fighting malaria and dysentery and living in a body which had reached its outer limits of endurance. Consequently, in all our minds was the question, will I be included? At this point we numbered eighty, plus Lt. Col. McGee and Captain Lim, a medical doctor from guerrilla headquarters who would accompany us. (Cook and Coe stayed behind to operate the guerrilla radio).

Suddenly, we heard the submarine had arrived, (although we could not see it in the darkness) and learned that all eighty two would go! What a thrill! Outrigger canoes and two rubber boats went back and forth from shore to the submarine, taking men by their assigned numbers. Those of us with arms stacked them and put our ammunition in a small pile nearby. This was another date we would never forget — September 29, 1944, just twenty-two days after the sinking of the prison ship!

When my number came up I climbed into an outrigger canoe and, with two Filipino paddlers, we went into the darkness. Then I heard a muffled sound of an engine turning over and a strong American voice called, "Here, catch a line." Ahead of us loomed a half submerged submarine, the USS Narwhal*, one of the two largest in the U.S. Navy and under the command of Captain J.C. Titus. The steel deck felt good to my feet as I reached a narrow deck, and then I was directed down through the coning tower into the submarine.

Crowded into the forward torpedo room were roughly half of the survivors, including a lot of the wounded. One of the guerrillas was standing among them with the most patched shorts and shirt I had ever seen. So, I was able to pull him aside and we traded clothes. Shortly, we were underway and without delay were fed sandwiches and Campbell's vegetable soup. What a wonderful American meal! We were told we ate forty-eight loaves of bread and sixteen pounds of butter. Major Fischer said the bread tasted like cake. That night I heard poor Mapes groaning; everyone else was sound asleep. I said, "Victor, what's wrong? Can I do anything for you?" He replied, "Johnny, I'm so dirty, I haven't bathed for weeks!" So I bathed him as best I could, working around his compound fractured leg.

On the second day out from Siari a Japanese plane spotted us and began circling overhead. The Narwhal dived, but instead of making a 6-8 degree dive, it was making a 20' dive. I was standing by a torpedo man who began shaking like a leaf. "This is it," he said. Then we heard Capt. Titus over the

P.A. system order, "All hands back aft." As best we could we scrambled toward the rear of the submarine; we could hear the engines go into reverse and learned later that seamen manually operated the aft diving planes. The solenoid mechanism controlling the diving fins had stuck. The airplane above us did not drop any bombs so we moved on, traveling on the surface through heavy seas. The only other interesting event was the passing of a Japanese hospital ship. We trim dived and some men saw the ship through the periscope. Most people aboard got sea sick, including some of the crew.

The Executive Officer, Lt. Comdr. C.R. Gebhart and I became friends since he allowed me to use his tiny office to work on compiling a list of all who were killed on the prison ship. Amazingly, I was able to pull together from our survivors the names, rank and towns or cities of the six hundred sixty-seven men who presumably died. This seemed to be my job as Adjutant of our group of survivors. The list, of course, was later turned over to the War Department. Apparently after our arrival at Mios Woendi, a submarine base off the tip of northern New Guinea, Cmdr. Gebhart wrote a letter to his wife. In one paragraph of the letter, which was undated, he wrote,

"While I have been out here, I've met a 1st Lt. in the Army that I think is a darned nice boy. He's had some tough experiences and he's on his way back to the States now for rehabilitation. He was a student for the ministry before the war. In fact he had one year to go before being an Episcopal minister. His name is John J. Morrett or "Johnny" as everyone calls him. He's going to be in New York soon and he said he would drop by and see you and tell you all about me, that I'm well, happy and everything."

(Apparently, somewhere in the letter my home town must have been mentioned to Mrs. Gebhart. She first telephoned my father in Springfield, Ohio, and later sent the above part of the correspondence having to do with me. My parents were overjoyed to know I was free.) Oct. 5th we arrived at our destination — we had embarked the night of September 29th —

roughly six days at sea.

At Mois Woendi we were fed royally and those who could still travel went by P.T. boat to Aowi Island, a large combat airbase where we stayed all night. On the way over we traveled with Commander "Chick" Parsons, liaison officer for the guerrilla forces in the Philippines. To greet us at the beach were a few Red Cross women, the first white women we had seen in over two and one-half years. And what a thrill that was!

The airfield at Aowi Island was busy, planes arriving and taking off continuously. We stayed there all night and in the morning boarded four planes which flew down the coast of New Guinea stopping off at Hollandia, General MacArthur's Headquarters. It was there that we saw the largest flotilla of combat ships in the world preparing to make an attack on Leyete. We also met General Carlos Romulo who was very interested in our situation. We traveled on to Nanzab where we remained one night and then on to Townsville and finally Brisbane, Australia.

From the 42nd General Hospital at Brisbane I wrote the following letter dated Oct. 9, 1944:

Dear Mother and Dad,

Am well, happy and back with our own forces again.

Will have to save the story until later. Am wondering about Pat. Worried considerably about Pix (my older brother) but am confident in his ability to take care of himself. Hope you are both well. News of me, I know, will be of considerable relief. My hopes are to be home by Christmas, but I have no information on furloughs yet. It still is a great big beautiful world and God has been with us all the way.

My love to Sis, Janie and Johnny and the children. Words cannot express how wonderful it all is. Keep up the old spirit, it won't be long.

Love,
Jack

On October 22, 1944, orders were issued for all but eight of our survivor group to board the S.S. Monterey, a troop ship bound for San Francisco. The seriously wounded needed a longer period of hospitalization.

---

* Saturday Evening Post, June 16 and 23, 1945 — "Twenty Thousand Headaches Under The Sea".

12

HOME AGAIN!

"Pat, darling. I'm Home! I've missed you so much!" My emotions were running so deep that I could hardly talk.

Our ship, the Monterey, had been a large passenger liner for Matson Navigation Company. During the war it turned into a massive troop ship and took us from Brisbane, Australia to San Francisco. On November 7, 1944, just two months after our escape, it passed under the Golden Gate Bridge. Our P. O. W. group, upon disembarking, went to Fort Mason where we were greeted by some family members and friends. It was a thrilling experience. I ran to a telephone to call my parents and find the location of my fiancee, Pat Taylor. Mother said I would have to call my sister, Janie, about her number, which I did immediately. Janie said Pat was on duty as a WAVE in the Navy, stationed in Washington, D. C. and gave me her number. I was so excited I could hardly dial. When I reached Pat she sounded very surprised. "Jack, I can hardly believe it! Where are you?" She seemed responsive and pleased to hear my voice, but I sensed an undercurrent of restraint in our conversation. Still I was so excited that nothing really mattered except to hear her voice. I was so overjoyed at being able to contact her that I wanted to buy her a lovely present. As soon as possible

I went into downtown San Francisco and bought her a string of pearls.

On the second evening at Ft. Mason, the wife of a P.O.W. Major came to see me. I had heard her husband had been killed on the march out of Bataan. She was a lovely middle aged woman, sitting quietly in my room asking for news of her husband. Instead of her breaking down over the bad news, I suddenly found myself weeping as I gave her the information I had. It must have been a combination of empathy over her hurt, which I felt so deeply, and my own hurt. She was understanding about my poor witness of strength and we began to commiserate together. I realized there was a deep agony inside me about those who wouldn't return, and I was going to have to deal with this in the weeks ahead.

In a few days a small number of us were flown to Washington and were met by a Major Ellis Gay who took us to the Chief, Captured Personnel and Material Branch in the Pentagon. It was very nice to find that reservations for us had been made at the Statler Hotel instead of at a military facility. While in Brisbane I had started doing a lot of social things with Bert Schwarz and Gene Dale, both Captains in the Air Force, so we were together in the Statler. We had a list of people to see and, particularly in my case, the Casualty Branch since I had compiled the list of men killed when the prison ship was torpedoed. Bert and Gene were well informed about the installation at the Lasang Airfield so they were asked to draw maps, location of facilities, etc. There was keen interest in the treatment of POW's by the Japanese, so the Judge Advocate General's Office and the State Department queried us for a long time about this.

During the first day I contacted Pat Taylor on the telephone and she said she would meet me at the Statler Hotel after work. When she came to my room I was impressed with her trim, athletic figure and how stunning she looked in the blue Wave uniform. I was in seventh heaven. After some talking we went to the main dining room for dinner, and since it was a little on the early side of the dinner time we were seated without delay. The dining room looked like a palace after the wretchedness of prison camp for two and one-half years. Toward the end of the dinner I excused myself to go to the men's room. When I returned, there was a crowd of people around the entrance waiting for tables. I tapped a woman on the shoulder to get through the crowd. She turned her head and, in a rude tone as I passed her, she said, "Don't you know there's a war on! " I had no ribbons to show I had been overseas. It struck me how some people were totally unaware of the tragedy of this war and who they might be talking to in uniform.

I made a date to take Pat to dinner the following night. In the course of this dinner Pat said that my return had come as a big surprise, and, in fact, since I had been missing in action so long, she had started dating someone in the Navy. This comment didn't seem alarming at first but then I recalled the little element of restraint in her voice at the time I had phoned her from San Francisco.

On the following night we had dinner in her apartment with her father present, since he was visiting from Columbus, Ohio. He excused himself when the dinner was over so we could talk privately. Pat, in her forthright but gentle manner, acknowledged that she had been seriously dating a Lt. Comdr. in the Navy and now she was not sure where she stood regarding our engagement. The conversation became quite involved and I am sure I reacted badly to this information. I later learned from my sister that Pat and her mother had gone to Springfield at one point and made an effort to return the engagement ring. My sister was indignant and refused to take it. In any case, I was not about to try and move back into the dating game with Pat, although she seemed open to it but with both suitors. I was sorry for her, sorry for myself and, quite honestly, not sorry for the Lt. Comdr. Certainly, a lot of the difficulty was my fault and the predicament I got myself into, but I was devastated.

It was about this time that Dad and Mother arrived at the

railroad station in Washington, arrangements having been made by the War Department. It was quite evident that the War Department was doing everything possible to make our return a positive one. To see my dear parents was a thrill and helped to counter-balance my broken engagement.

Another thrill came when our small group was invited to meet General George Marshall and Secretary of War Henry L. Stimson in the General's office. Naturally, both were interested in learning about our treatment as POW's. At the end of our discussion the General, in his quiet, dignified manner, said he was very sorry help could not reach us when we needed it so badly on Bataan and Corregidor. However, in the overall picture American forces were not in a position at the time to rescue us. Also, in terms of strategy, the main forces had to be in England and North Africa rather than the Far East in the initial stages of the war. We appreciated his frankness — he offered no excuses nor did he sidetrack the critical issue in regard to the need for help which never came. At the time I realized we were talking with two historic figures in this great war.

There was a scheduled awards ceremony when most of our group arrived by train from San Francisco. Consequently, we were busy writing up commendations for awards to be presented in the office of the Army Chief of Staff. The event took place November 18th at which time some men received the Legion of Merit, some the Bronze Star, and all the survivors received the Purple Heart.

The Rt. Rev. Angus Dun, Bishop of Washington, and the former Dean of the Episcopal Theological School, telephoned me and suggested I come and stay with him and his wife Kitty in the Bishopric at the Washington Cathedral. I had always like the Duns, so I checked out of the hotel and stayed with them in the warm atmosphere of their home.

One other incident occurred in Washington which turned out to have a lot of significance later on. Bert Schwarz and Gene Dale suggested I go with them to meet the head of the Air Force,

General Henry H. (Hap) Arnold. When we arrived at his office we were introduced to Major Corey Ford and Captain Alastair MacBain, former writers for Colliers magazine but now writers for the Air Force. General Arnold suggested that we write about our experiences for publication and these two men would help us as ghost writers. Since we were to be given three months leave time, we could compile our material at home and it would be worked up later into an interesting narrative. The proceeds from the article, hopefully published by Colliers, would be divided, one-half to the Air Force Aid Society and one-half for us. Corey Ford asked about some sketches of prison camp scenes so we suggested Lt. Murray Sneddon, a POW artist who would probably produce something for the story. He would be included in the proceeds for his work. Before leaving the General's office we worked out a plan. We were to begin separate narratives during our leave time and then meet in New York in January with the ghost writers to put the material together. (The article sold for $10,000, half of which went to the Air Force Aid Society.)

Before leaving to go home, I was eager to know how our U.S. military treated Japanese prisoners of war. As a result of this request orders were issued on December 4, 1944, arranging for travel to Camp McCoy, Wisconson. There I saw our facilities which I felt certain met the Rules of Land Warfare in regard to prisoners of war. I was impressed, but dejected thinking about Americans and Filipinos still in prison camps.

Happily, I was back in Springfield, Ohio, two weeks before Christmas. POW's were returning heroes at this point so I was approached to give speeches, and in the mail were letters from relatives requesting information about loved ones. My father made available his secretary, Miss Bertha Unkle, who began typing out my part of the story for publication, and I would answer the many letters in long hand. Consequently going home did not turn out to be any kind of a rest but, nevertheless, it was exhilarating. My brother, Pixley was with

General Patton's Army in Europe so Mother and Dad still worried about him. Subsequently, we learned that he had been wounded and missing for a short period of time. Because of nerves, Mother's hands had broken out in open sores and were bandaged for a while. At this point I realized what a heavy toll had been paid by family and friends whose loved ones had been lost, killed or wounded during the past three years.

In January I went to New York to discuss the Collier's article with the ghost writers and Bert and Gene. Bert Schwarz was married on January 11, 1945, in Mayor Laguardia's office, with Gene as his best man and me as a witness. Bert's wife, Gaham was a beautiful woman, a John Powers model, originally from Georgia. I could understand why Bert fell in love with her — she was so lovely. Her good friend, Fay Hancock Miller, was also a beautiful model; people would stare at her when she walked down the street. Gene began dating her, so she was also a witness at the wedding. However, there was just one problem, she was married to an Army officer who was fighting in Europe.

Bert had loads of friends in New York since it was his home, so the partying began. I was introduced to Elaine Reuben who was a dear person and someone I could have easily fallen in love with. We hit the nightclub circuit; Club 21, the Cotton Club, Sardies, etc. — all the popular spots of New York. However, I was still weak and got a terrible cold so Elaine arranged for a doctor to see me. It wasn't long before we finished our work with Corey Ford and Alastair MacBain, so I went to Washington to settle some matters with the Casualty Branch of the War Department and stayed with the Duns again.

The Rev. Frank Sayre, now Lt. Comdr. Sayre, was in Washington following a tour of duty on the cruiser, San Francisco. I was invited to have dinner with his father, High Commissioner Francis Sayre and his wife Betty, step-mother to Frank. It was a real reunion since we had last seen each other on Corregidor. All three of the Sayres had contacted my family at various times, and through Betty my parents had received my last letter from Bataan dated February 24, 1942. The Sayres had also gotten out of the Philippines by submarine. Betty wrote a splendid two installment article for the Atlantic Monthly entitled, "Submarine From Corregidor."

The Collier's articles entitled, "We Lived to Tell," were published March 3rd, 10th, and 17th of 1945, and brought me many more letters of inquiry and some personal publicity. The letters I tried to answer as best I could but it was difficult.

Through the suggestion of Col. John McGee, Major General S.G. Henry, Asst. Chief of Staff G-1, sent me a cable asking if I would be interested in an assignment with the Bureau of Public Relations, War Department for temporary duty of three to four months. The job was to interview next of kin of personnel missing in action in the Philippines, speak to civic groups promoting relief for American Prisoners of War, and appear at War Bond rallies. This would involve traveling throughout the country. Since this was not an order, I politely declined because I did not feel I had either the physical or emotional strength to do the job, particularly after the incident at Ft. Mason, San Francisco. Facing that widow with bad news, and my subsequent breakdown, made me realize how raw my nerves were.

On the 26th of April, accompanied by my parents, I went to the Army Ground and Services Forces Redistribution Station at Santa Monica, California. My parents stayed with me one week at the government's expense. This was for rest at the Edgewater Beach Club, a rather large hotel-type beach facility. By now I was beginning to see blood in my stools and after a physical examination was diagnosed as having amoebic dysentery. I was told I could be treated as an outpatient if I was careful to take my medicine. Normally this diagnosis would have required hospitalization, but since I had been confined so long in prison camps the examining doctor agreed to give me as much freedom as possible.

The Edgewater Beach Club was just what I needed to have some quiet time with my parents away from the telephone. They needed the rest as badly as I did, having worked as volunteers in the war effort at home and worried over two sons involved in combat overseas. Captain Richard Cook, a person who slept beside me at the Lasang Air Field, had returned to the States following a short period of time with the guerrillas, repairing their radio equipment. Dick was living in Westwood with his family. He introduced me to Elnora Day, a beautiful girl who lived in Beverly Hills on Roxbury Drive. I am sure I fell in love with her on our first date. We went to the Coconut Grove and danced to Freddie Martin's band and then returned to her house where we talked. I told her about the Philippine experience, especially the time when I spoke to the men shortly before the prison ship was torpedoed. She liked to tell people I preached a sermon to her on our first night out together.

Elnora was not only beautiful and enthusiastic, but she also had a marvelous sense of humor. She loved a joke, especially if it was a little off color. There was, at times, a block stammer in her speech, especially when she got excited or felt insecure with someone. Once when we were going up on an elevator she blocked and then giggled and said, "I sound like a PT boat." The night of our first date she was dressed beautifully. I admired the lovely beige coat she was wearing, with its fur around the collar and down the front. When I remarked about it she smiled, opened up to the inside lining, and there I saw a patch which read "Day Original." I learned that she designed and made most of her clothes. We saw a great deal of each other for about a month, generally at the beach during the day and going out to night spots in the evening with her many friends. The most favorite was the "Tail of the Cock" on La Cieneqa Blvd. She seemed to be known and loved by everyone, especially her Pi Phi Society sisters from U.S.C. and the many graduates of Beverly Hills High School.

While in Santa Monica, a businessman linked to the movie industry telephoned me about the Collier's magazine articles. He said he would like to take me around to Fox, MGM, and Paramount to see if anyone of them would be interested in the story. I agreed to go. In a few days a luncheon was planned with Daryl Zanuck, famous movie director at Fox Studios. He walked into the private dining room dressed in riding britches and with a scarf around his neck. He sat at the head of the long table with a number of producers and looked every bit the part of a famous director. Following dessert I told about some of the POW experiences. As we were leaving one of the producers followed us out and said, "Captain Morrett, I would like to arrange for a screen test for you." "Thank you," I replied, "That kind of thing is not for me, I am going to be a missionary to China." But that did not discourage him. Within three or four days I received a call from Fox saying the screen test had been arranged on such and such a day and time, would I please come to the studio for it? I politely refused again, but was a little flattered.

One other incident occurred in the studios. It was with Lucille Ball and Buster Keaton. (In Buster's rather strange office were two large erector-set contraptions which took up a lot of space.) Despite the crowded quarters we talked for at least two hours. Both were keenly interested in hearing about the prison camp experience, so much so that I did not get a chance to ask about their lives. I felt a little strange being questioned by two such gifted comics and movie stars. Nevertheless, it was fun being with them.

A letter dated March 30th from Colonel Jason S. Joy to Julian Johnson regarding the "We Lived to Tell" story, had in the second paragraph: "As picture material, it is not for us, because as any subject undertaken now is probably a year distant from the public, at least, we have begun to edge away from out-and-out war pictures of the brutal kind, and the Philippine scene, during Jap occupation, will be well covered in our forthcoming picture, "American Guerrilla in the Philippines."

Within three weeks Elnora and I were talking seriously about our lives and our future. When she learned I had been a divinity student for two years and planned to go to China as a missionary some red flags went up. She was frank to say religion wasn't her bag although she always remembered her grandmother saying, "God so loved the world that he gave his only begotten son to the end that all that believeth in him should not perish but have everlasting life." (John 3:16) It was obvious she had absolutely no interest in the church institution, let alone becoming a missionary wife in China, of all places. But by now she had become my "Sparkle Plenty" with her warm, charismatic personality and complete charm when it came to people. Everyone loved Elnora!

I faced a dilemma which I talked over with Dick Cook who agreed Elnora was definitely not the missionary type. So I decided to break things off and explained why to her. But we both fumed and fussed for a week by ourselves — no telephone calls, no dates. After a week's time I couldn't stand not seeing her so telephoned and asked her to the beach. Sometime later we talked alone in my room, especially about my finishing seminary and going to China; life up the Yantze River without much contact with the Western world. She admitted her love for me and I for her. Finally she said if I really felt a calling to go, she would go with me. But she went on to say she was not going to be a drab, serious missionary type. Yet she would do the best she could to support me.

I knew that with the war still on, if I were to be transferred to the East Coast or elsewhere I could easily lose her. Consequently, in the next several days we went to a jeweler and selected an engagement ring. I talked with her father and in the old fashioned way asked for her hand in marriage. He agreed although he did not care for the missionary part. However, in some sense I appeared as a war hero which the Collier's articles helped to establish, and we could go ahead with a marriage as far as he was concerned. Elnora had two older sisters who were twins, Catherine and Lorraine, and both were married, so he knew the routine of giving away a daughter and Elnora's mother seemed thrilled.

In discussing a new assignment with a military counselor I was told about an Army Ground Force Liaison School being held at Lexington, Virginia. Men who had received the purple heart were taught to help amputees coming from overseas with their pay and allowances, insurance, and getting proper awards following a serious wound in combat. The amputee was often quickly evacuated from the combat zone, in emotional shock over the loss of arms or legs, frustrated over insurance or about not receiving a purple heart. Since this was in line with the pastoral ministry, I agreed to take this training in the month of May. Elnora and I set the date for our marriage June 12th at All Saints Episcopal Church, Beverly Hills. Only my mother came for the wedding since it was difficult to get rail transportation and Dad was tied up in business. During May, I attended the course of instruction at the School for Personnel Services, Lexington, Virginia.

On June 1, 1945, I was issued orders to depart from Lexington June 6th, with ten days leave. I went to Springfield to pick up my mother and by rail we traveled together to Los Angeles. The wedding at All Saints Church, Beverly Hills, on June 12th was lovely. We spent our honeymoon night in the bridal suite of the Bel Air Hotel and then by rail went to Washington. My close cousin, John Southmayd, arranged for us to occupy a furnished apartment at the Broadmore Hotel for several months and then to the Falkland Apartments at Silver Springs, Maryland. John and I had a wonderful, close relationship for many years. He was married to Jean Duke, and because of poor eyesight, never saw military service. John, Jean, Elnora and I became very close. Soon after our arrival we were visiting John and Jean in their apartment and he turned to me and said, "Couz, I have only one word of advice, stay out of the kitchen!" He was standing in the kitchen with an apron on, washing dishes.

The work at Walter Reed was challenging and interesting. Ward after ward were filled with amputees, arms and legs off, and in several cases men had lost all four limbs — they were called "basket cases." There was anger, hurt, frustration, pain, resentment among them. "I've lost my leg and didn't even get a purple heart," some man might say to me in resentment. Or, "I was on the (firing) line for four months and now can't even get a Combat Infantryman's Badge." There were times when I would get almost as angry as the men and once laid it on some bureaucratic person in New York over a combat infantry man's badge because of a snarl-up in his records. I said over the telephone, "The man is in a wheel chair with two legs off, cut out the shit and cut the order." Within a week he had his badge and so he made it a point to come to the office and thank me.

Elnora and Jean Southmayd got along famously. They both loved parties, clothes and entertaining. Soon we were living across the street from the Southmayd's and Walter Reed was only several miles away. We couldn't have been happier in Washington.

While there, Gene Dale and Fay Hancock Miller came to visit us on a weekend. Before their departure, as Gene walked out of the door, he said to me, "Johnny, I really love Fay and intend to marry her." My response was, "Yes, I know, but Gene, she's married. You had better leave her alone until her husband comes back from overseas and they resolve things."

Some time later John Southmayd telephoned and said, "Couz, have you seen the papers today?" I said, "No." "Well, there is an article about Capt. Gene Dale, former POW in the Philippines, who was shot and killed in a woman's bedroom in New York." I was shocked!

Washington Post, December 29, 1945, headlines read:

CAPT. DALE, HERO OF PHILIPPINES,
SHOT BY JEALOUS AAF OFFICER

Another article read at the time of the trial:

New York Herald Tribune, Thursday, May 30, 1946:

ARMY CAPTAIN ADMITS HE SLEW WIFE'S VISITOR

Poor Gene, poor Fay, and poor Captain Miller were all involved in a love tragedy that should never have happened. I felt sorry for all three of them.

I soon discovered Elnora was marvelous when it came to decorating, along with getting the most out of every dollar. We bought second-hand furniture so she made chair and sofa covers using attractive fabric; she made curtains and a bedspread to match and utilized every wedding present, so it wasn't long until we had a beautiful apartment. The Falkland complex was filled with young military families, which created a nice, friendly atmosphere. The war was going our way so enthusiasm was high. The Germans had surrendered in Italy on April 29, 1945, so the pressure was off in the western theater and amputees stopped coming in to Walter Reed. On August 6th the first atomic bomb was dropped on Hiroshima and another on Nagasaki August 9th, so the surrender followed August 10th. Washington was ecstatic! The streets filled with people and literally everyone celebrated. We stayed up all night, going from one party to another whether we knew the people or not, and alcohol flowed like water. Elnora and I came home early in the morning exhausted.

One day at Walter Reed I ran into a Col. Stubbs whom I had known at the Davao Penal Colony. He said, "Johnny, have you had a stool specimen checked for schistosomaisis?" I said I didn't know what he was talking about. Then he told me that all POW's who worked in the rice fields undoubtedly had picked up this disease and should be checked. I turned in a stool specimen without delay and was loaded with the "schisto," a small organism that comes from a snail and which lodges itself in the intestines. The disease can be fatal. Treatment was started at the out-patient department immediately and I was released from my assignment in the A.G.L. office December 21, 1945. Elnora and I spent Christmas at home and then we went to Cambridge, Mass. where I began seminary classes, even though I was still in the Army and checking regularly with Cushing General Hospital, Cushingham, Massachusetts. The lab there required stool specimens every two weeks. On May 1, 1946, following three months of checkups, I reverted to inactive status. I was given four months leave and left the Army officially September 1, 1946 — over five years in the service — half of which was served in prison camps.

Despite the trauma of the war years in the military, I felt privileged to have served my country in its long travail in WWII. I was fortunate to survive despite numerous challenges in combat, disease, starvation, the loss of a fiancée and the emotional wear and tear of the times. But I had no regrets and was determined to lay aside the war years and get on with the completion of seminary and be ordained an Episcopal priest. Having been away from school for five years, I was glad to take a year and a half to finish training for a degree. I use to say, "It took me eight and one-half years to complete seminary, an unusual kind of record."

Elnora and I were given a delightful, tiny third floor apartment above the dining hall at the Episcopal Theological School. Just as back in Washington, she fixed up the attic space attractively and became the perfect hostess for students and their wives who frequently came for after dinner coffee. We had a little bell attached outside one window with a long string attached so friends could ring it to let us know they were coming up the winding flight of stairs. Most of the students had military service so the atmosphere of the school was completely different than pre-war days. There was a lightheartedness about the school which everyone, including the faculty liked. Many men and their wives were in their late twenties or early thirties.

I was thrilled to be back getting into the meat of theology, Christian ethics, Biblical interpretation, homoletics and pastoral theology. My assigned tutors were both favorites: Dr. Massey Shepherd, eminent historian and liturgist, and Dr. Sherman Johnson, a fine New Testament scholar. Since we were an affiliated school with Harvard, I was also fortunate to take at Harvard Chinese history from Professor John Fairbanks, eminent Chinese scholar, and Japanese history from Professor Edwin Reishauer, who later became our Ambassador to Japan. Since this was right after the war, these men had a good grasp of both oriental history, and the problems and politics of the Far East.

Two of our closest friends on campus were Dr. and Mrs. Charles Buck. "Charlie," as he was affectionately called by both faculty and students, had been a senior during my middle year before the war. He was a brilliant young man who, as I recall, received a Ph.D. at age 21. He had graduated from the seminary in 1942, went into the Navy as a chaplain, and subsequently married Betty, who was a Wave. He was now on campus as a lecturer in New Testament and Greek. Betty and Elnora hit it off right away and became dear friends. There were other husbands and wives we came to know and love, too. Off campus in the historic Longfellow House, located next to Lawrence Hall, lived Tom and Romey Edwards who served as paid custodians. It was loads of fun to go over there for our exclusive parties in these charming old surroundings.

By the spring Elnora needed a break from staid old Cambridge so she went home for a month to visit her family. Soon after her return we began to think about summer work. Mrs. Drown, who knew everything about the Episcopal Church and especially the Diocese of Massachusetts, told me about a Dr. Howard Chandler Robbins who had formerly been Dean of the Cathedral of St. John the Divine in New York City. Dr. Robbins had become a famous writer and preacher but in his later years had spells of depression. His wife mentioned to Mrs. Drown that she would like a companion for her husband during their summer months in Heath, Massachusetts. Some bishops, clergy, and such eminent theologians as Rheinhold Niebuhr spent their vacations at Heath. Elnora and I went to see the Robbins in their nearby apartment overlooking the Charles River. They seemed quite pleasant, although Mrs.

Robbins did all the talking while Dr. Robbins listened quietly to the conversation.

Several days later Elnora had Betty Buck, Romey Edwards and Kay Tierny for lunch and bridge in our apartment. Shortly after they had left Mrs. Robbins appeared at the door to see Elnora. In the course of their conversation she made direct statements which Elnora recorded in her diary, "We could not work for them if she wore cosmetics, polished fingernails and high heels." She concluded that if Elnora was not to hurt me in my ministry she would have to change the way she presented herself to the public.

When I returned to our apartment after a tutorial, Elnora fell into my arms sobbing. She said she felt she was going to hurt me in my ministry and that she had made a terrible mistake in marrying me. At that moment she needed a lot of comforting and affirmation because she was deeply hurt.

After this incident Elnora began to change a little and adapt to a more somber way of dressing. She made for herself a heavy black coat and the materials she would buy for dresses were subdued. She was always helping her girlfriends with their sewing and even made curtains for a Dr. Batten, a bachelor on the faculty. I declined to take the summer job with the Robbins and instead accepted an invitation to help the Rev. Almus Thorp, who was Rector of St. Stephen's Church, Columbus, Ohio. This parish was located next to the campus of Ohio State University.

On returning to Cambridge in the fall I knew my study habits had to settle down to a solid routine of hard work, getting ready for oral examinations the first of the year and written final examinations in June. Elnora became pregnant and the projected date of our first baby was July 8th.

On May 15th Elnora flew home to be with her family prior to her delivery and to give me plenty of time alone for study in preparation for the final exams. A week before graduation Mrs. Drown asked me to come and stay at her house. Graduation took place June 5th and I was ordained to the deaconate at Christ Church, Springfield, Ohio by Bishop Henry W. Hobson on June 19, 1947. Because of my good contacts in Springfield, I was able to purchase for Elnora's mother a new Mercury, since new civilian cars were hard to come by, and drove to Los Angeles. I arrived July 1st and Scott Day Morrett was born at St. Vincent's Hospital July 3rd.

The days that followed were busy preparing for China. They involved thorough physical examinations, purchasing a kerosene stove and refrigerator, buying cartons of baby food, two bicycles, medicines, etc. There were many farewell parties, especially for Elnora. We knew so little of what we were getting into, but the die was cast and my mind had one goal about to be reached after so many years of anticipation — China.

13

CHINA BOUND

On October 18, 1947, we sailed on the S.S. General Meigs for China. I had told Elnora about the lovely accommodations we had on the President Coolidge going out to the Philippines, but soon we discovered the Meigs was something else. It was a passenger liner turned into a troop ship during the war. I was directed to take Elnora and Scotty to a stateroom where there were three-decker bunks locked to the bulkhead. Inside were five or six oriental women with their many bags and bundles. The stateroom was sweltering and Scotty immediately threw up. Elnora began to cry, when suddenly a Salvation Army lady appeared and immediately said, "You don't belong here! All mothers and babies are assigned to the hospital ward at the top of the ship." She took us up several ladders to an airy cabin for twenty-six persons, a large room with plenty of portholes and only thirteen women, four babies and three small children in it. Scotty was given a crib which was strapped alongside Elnora's bunk. Once they were settled to my great relief, I made my way three decks down to a cabin with the three-decker bunks which ten men had already occupied. On this deck the ship was full of old Chinese returning to their homeland to die. There were also a few missionary men, State Department personnel, and a few men going to Manila, Hong Kong, and Shanghai on business.

We were fortunate to be assigned to the purser's table in the dining room, with Virginia Wright whose husband was with American Electric Co., and Margaret Copeland and her two children returning to a missionary husband in Shanghai. Soon we also teamed up with Tom and Margaret Gilliand who were with the Museum of Natural History in New York City. Mr. Kantzar, the Purser, would invite us to his cabin for after-dinner drinks and coffee on frequent occasions. At midnight we sailed for Manila, arriving November 4th. The first leg of the trip turned out to be a lot of fun, especially since it involved a layover in Honolulu. Canon Anson Stokes at St. Andrew's Cathedral showed us around and we went to tea at the home of Mr. and Mrs. Carter Galt. Elnora fell in love with the city.

We reached Manila on November 4th. I was surprised to see so many sunken ships in the harbor and also a lot of visible destruction in the city from WWII. Since the Meigs was to be docked in the harbor several days for unloading cargo, we went to our missionary compound where I again met Dr. Spackman, who was going to help me with my theological studies before the war broke out. His dear wife suggested she take care of Scotty while we toured around the city. Elnora and I had a delightful time together sightseeing, going to the Army Navy Club to see the sunset, dinner at a French restaurant and dancing at the Riveria Club. The next day Dr. Spackman and I visited St. Andrews Episcopal Seminary. The ship sailed for Hong Kong at ten o'clock p.m. Elnora wrote in her diary on November 5th: "Loved Manila but wish I could have seen it before the war."

In Hong Kong we had a marvelous time with Lew Nordeen, a Beverly Hills High School friend of Elnora's who was employed by Caltex. So despite the twenty-five day trip to the Orient aboard a troop ship, the voyage worked out well.

We landed in Shanghai November 11th at six-thirty p.m. and were met by Bishop and Mrs. William Roberts and Mr. Carl Gilson, a layman in charge of the mission office. The scene at the wharf and through the streets of Shanghai was like a nightmare. It was unbelievably crowded with people, squalor, awful colored neon signs in Chinese characters, and traffic was amazingly congested. It was dark by the time we retrieved our baggage and were ready to go to the mission compound in a jeep. I had the impression of a grim city filled with confusion. We could not have entered into a worse scene to begin our tour as missionaries to China. The Roberts were pleasant and friendly but the house was cold and drab and without central heating. I gave it three "D's": damp, dark and dreary. In several days Scotty and I had colds.

On November 17th Elnora wrote in her diary:

"Just another depressive day. Don't see how John and I can be happy here in China."

Sunday November 23rd she wrote:

"John preached at the evening service at St. John's Chapel. No one said he was good. Can't figure out why. (She was always my biggest supporter) . Only the Gilson's said it was good and John was just what they needed out here. If we stay more than five years I'll die."

Elnora was going through a real culture shock made far worse by the terrible conditions of the city, just recovering from WWII, and living in a bleak missionary compound at the beginning of winter. I soon went up the Yantze River to Wuhu to meet Bishop Lloyd Craighill to get some orientation regarding where we were to be stationed and to learn about the Anwhei Diocese of Central China. Soon after my return on December 11th, we boarded the Kaing An, a Chinese river steamer, to go to Anking , about four hundred miles up river. We had a nice cabin to ourselves but all over the decks were Chinese with their bundles, bags, chickens and ducks, so we had to walk over and around people just to get to the dining room. We learned that the ship dare not stop at Nanking where it could be easily conscripted and taken over by the military. I soon learned that China was still very much at war. We passed Nanking the first day, China's capital, and arrived at Wuhu the second. Bishop and Mrs. Craighill and some of the Sisters of the Transfiguration were there to meet us with their wonderful smiles and joyful greetings. The Bishop went to China in 1915 under the Episcopal Mission Board and on the same boat was Marion Gardner, who had gone out under the Presbyterian mission. They met on the ship and were subsequently married. Pearl S. Buck, famous author about China, who was present at the marriage, wrote up the event for the Shanghai newspaper. Both spoke fluent Chinese and had spent most of their time as missionaries at Nanchang where we were to be posted, and in fact we were to live in their former residence. Out of a total of thirty-three years in and out of China they spent twenty of them in Nanchang, which is located south of the Yantze River.

The following day, the 14th of November, we arrived in Anking. There to meet us were the Rev. Henri Pickens, missionary in charge of the mission station and Dr. and Mrs. Harry Taylor. Dr. Taylor was an outstanding surgeon who came to China in 1905, so his career extended over forty years. His wife, Alma, at this point had served over thirty years. We couldn't have been in more seasoned hands. Harry Taylor had a delightful sense of humor, constantly making funny remarks with a twinkle in his eye so (privately) I nicknamed him "Harry the Limb." Alma was quite serious about almost everything, and especially about matters of which she had personal concern so I nicknamed her "Alma Dalma".

"Alma Dalma" and "Harry the Limb" made a good team helping us get adjusted to a strange new world. The house was cold, heated by wood stoves, and since there was no running water the toilets had buckets inside of them which were emptied daily by an amah. With my prison camp experience behind me, I could swing with anything, but for someone brought up in Beverly Hills, California, this was a drastic change in environment and lifestyle. Elnora had done a lot of camping with her parents growing up, but she had absolutely no preparation for this missionary way of life in China.

Anking was an old city with an estimated population of

50,000. It was surrounded by a twenty to forty foot high wall backed by mounds of dirt to protect the city from bandits, revolutionary armies, and marauding soldiers. The distinctive feature about the city was its tall pagoda, seven stories high and well proportioned. The views from it were magnificent: the wide Yantze River to the south and, off in the distance, a range of mountains. To the north we could see lakes and fields, and not far away the "great dragon mountain." The pagoda is a place where the spirits of the air and those of the earth meet and harmonize to bring peace and good crops. Embedded on each side of the entrance to the pagoda, facing the river, were large iron anchors with long sharp flukes or barbs that went into the ground. These were intended to keep the city from slipping off down the river.

The city was obviously very old with many narrow streets and alleyways where people lived, usually behind walls and in tiny houses surrounding a central courtyard. The Kuomintang military were very much in evidence and it appeared to me there must have been one battalion of field artillery. As time went on, generally at night, we could hear small arms firing from the walls. This was a bit disconcerting. Because there were Communists moving about in the countryside, none of the foreigners were allowed to leave the city.

We lived in the large mission compound which was surrounded by its own wall. It had a main gate with guest rooms on either side, a separate house for women workers, St. James hospital (a large plain gray brick building), St. Paul's Boys School, a building for women's industrial work, the church, and missionary homes. The church was typically Chinese in style and would seat two hundred people.

The Taylor house was three storied, constructed of solid gray brick with the basement for the kitchen and servant's quarters; the second floor for an entrance hall, living room, dining room, and study; and the third floor for a chapel, bedrooms, baths, and another nice study. The house was barely heated by wood stoves, so we had to wear a lot of clothing to keep warm until our padded Chinese gowns were made. I immediately showed my ignorance by ordering a short gown which is generally only worn by laborers, instead of the long gown always worn by scholars. I really didn't mind, but I am sure the servants were amused.

We soon met Miss Margaret Monteiro, who had three little adopted Chinese girls in tow. She was called "Maggie" by everyone. She was born in Richmond, Virginia of Portuguese parents and I was told she spoke Chinese with a southern accent. Under the Episcopal Mission Board she went to Anking in 1920 and worked there mainly as a woman evangelist until 1940. During the Japanese occupation of the city she crossed over into free China where she worked with Miss Emeline Bowne, the former head nurse of St. James Hospital. There they collected many orphans and had officially adopted three of them. At the time of our arrival in Anking Miss Bowne was in the U.S. on furlough and Maggie was due one since she had not been out of the country for seven years. The three little orphans followed her everywhere so Maggie use to say, "Where the old hen goes the chicks will follow." Toward the end of WWII Maggie had made a 1,400 mile trek to Kunming, where she continued her work at St. John's Mission. She was a gay spirit, not unlike St. Francis of Assisi, smiling and laughing, emanating good will. She was a born evangelist and worked mainly in the women's industrial building.

The Treasurer was Miss Blanch Meyers, a very nice person, small and pleasant, who kept the books of the mission station.

The Rev. Henri Pickens and his sweet wife, Berkley, had two children, Robert and Janet, ages six and ten years. They had been interned at Santa Tomas in Manila during WWII. They were in their middle thirties and were very much on edge about the ability of the Kuomintang to hold off the Communists from taking over the country. However, they were very pleasant to us and provided lunch and dinner for our little family each day because we were of a similar age and they had an exceptionally good cook. Henri, with an excellent Chinese priest, Graham Gwei, were in charge of the Chinese congregation who attended the church.

I immediately started a course in Chinese at the "CIM," China Inland Mission Language School, which was not far from our compound. Because of the need to look after Scotty, Elnora began her language study with a tutor, a Miss Ching, who was originally from north China and spoke excellent Mandarin. She had a much better ear for the four tones in Mandarin than I did, and worked closely with our baby's amah, Hu Soadza. Consequently, she started picking up the language right away. My progress was slower in that I began the fall term late and, also, the school placed considerable emphasis on reading and writing rather than speaking. I was always working with flash cards, trying to memorize characters.

The students at the school lived a spartan life with only an open well for bathing. In the winter, with snow on the ground, the well was freezing cold. The CIM was a fundamentalist group of Christians who had been in China since 1853, mainly as evangelists in contrast to our kind of mission that built churches, schools, and hospitals and did other kinds of institutional work. It was a good experience being with them, even though we might disagree on their fundamentalist approach to the Bible. I soon discovered that missionaries in China made a great point of getting along with each other even though their approach to Christianity might be quite different, plus the fact that they often needed each other in times of crisis — there were many!

While living with Dr. Taylor, I became interested in the hospital. He did everything from performing examinations and prescribing medicines for two hundred patients a day, to operating and even pulling teeth. He was the only surgeon in a two hundred mile radius, so he and Dr. Sun, his co-worker, were often busy at the operating table. I asked if I could watch some operations and I thought he was pleased at my interest.

So, Saturday mornings when there were no classes I would go to surgery, get scrubbed up and watch Dr. Taylor operate. At the time of the first incision he would have everyone come close around him, raise both hands with a scalpel in one, and then pray for God's guidance. I thought that was wonderful. He invited me to stand right at the table along with him and the nurses to see what he was doing. Elnora would hear us talk about the operations afterwards, so she asked if she could watch, too. She made one attempt. Just at the beginning of a cut on a woman who had been terribly damaged by a mid-wife, I looked up at her eyes behind the mask. They got very large and then she dashed out of surgery. She told me later that she spilled all her cookies outside, but she was a "trooper" and complained very little about the circumstances, saving her complaints for her diary:

On January 23, 1948, she wrote:

"Same old routine. I could endure if I thought we were going home soon. From the looks of things we may go sooner than later, we think. All missionaries are leaving areas northwest of Hankow. I guess we will be next. I don't like this at all."

Nevertheless, she got into the swing of things and enjoyed the Chinese feasts, bridge with the Pickens, and interesting walks with me along the top of the wall and to the great Anking pagoda. It was also fun to go down to the river and see the activity, ships unloading cargo, rickshaws lined up for passengers and the many small food stalls selling all kinds of interesting things to eat.

On December 28, 1947, I wrote to my parents:

Dear Mother and Dad,

The three of us are still in central China and not doing too badly at this point. Christmas wasn't as joyful a day as it might have been because we missed our families and our childhood environments. However, the Taylor household is very pleasant and, with decorations, put us in the spirit of things. We all had stockings which were hung up over the fireplace and little Scottie's looked so cute. His was placed in the middle of the four of ours. There was a wonderful Chinese lantern procession Christmas Eve and a lot of caroling. Elnora and I found it difficult to appreciate the firecrackers which gave the whole festival a tinge of Independence Day. There were many church services and we attended most of them. I appreciated more than anything else the holiday from school; Wed. through Fri. This Chinese is every bit as difficult as one might imagine because there is practically nothing to it that compares to English. Woe is me — but others learn so I guess I can, too.

To date I have no exciting news about the political situation. We seldom see newspapers here which, when they arrive in a bundle, are usually two weeks outdated. Our radio only works at night when the electric power is on and even then the reception I get is poor. I have no decent antenna up as yet, which is probably the reason. The Russians dropping out of the London Conference appears to be a terrible blow to an assurance for world peace in the future. Our whole globe is in another great state of unrest and I feel we have cause to fear a threat to world peace. I wish our Christian Gospel were more of a potent factor to stabilize things. Our present crisis just points up the fact of how pagan this world still is and what a tremendous job we have to convert it. I feel like a bit of lint on a massive blanket and here, completely useless and helpless. It is hopeful to see each Sunday a filled church with a congregation apparently faithful and devoted to Christ. But the tremendous problem of pulling China out of her cultural lag and chaotic economic situation is breathtaking. The poverty, filth and ignorance of the general populace is appalling. I never cease to wonder how this civilization has kept intact for some 4,000 years. China's deep rut is just one of many; Palestine, India, the Philippines, and all of Europe. It almost appears that the more aged we become, the more ruthlessly we destroy that which we build. My old friend in Compton, N.H. (Robert Miller) suggests that in blue moods and those of despair, I should always turn to the New Testament. That is just what the world should be doing. So many of our necessary answers to great problems can be found in Christ's words and actions.

Time is passing on and I must stop. But a last word about little Scotty, who continues to be a charmer. He brings immeasurable joy each day as he chirps, laughs, and blows bubbles to amuse his proud parents. How you would love him as everyone does. My best to all the rest of the family and I hope your Christmas Season was a joyful one.

Love,
Jack

On March 16th the 6,000 troops in Anking pulled out which left the city unprotected except for its high walls. On March 20th Henri Pickens decided to get his family out and I was to take them, accompanied by Elnora and Scotty, to Wuhu where there were both Kuomintang Army and Navy forces stationed. On the night of the 22nd we boarded a dirty launch and, into a tiny stateroom, we packed Berkley, her two children, Elnora, Scotty, and our amah. Because of the crowded conditions I stayed out on deck with the Chinese.

At Wuhu, the Pickens' and our family were to live in the home of Mr. B.W. Lamphear, who was away on furlough, but shortly the Pickens decided to take their children and go to Shanghai. They continued to be extremely concerned about the way things were going in China. I was concerned, too, but not to the same extent. In any case, we moved in with Bishop and Mrs. Craighill which was delightful. They lived in a new, modern house with running water and central heating, which was now a luxury for us.

The compound was situated on Lion Hill with a marvelous view of the city below and not far away was the Yantze River with its constant traffic of junks and sanpans. Elnora had felt buried in Anking, which could only be reached by boat — there were no main roads to it. Here there was more of a sense of security with the army and two Chinese gunboats nearby on the river, and besides, the weather was turning warm. Both of us soon had a tutor and Elnora seemed to be doing well with her Chinese while my progress was slow. A lot of it had to do, I'm sure, with the fact that I am not a linguist.

The Sisters of the Transfiguration were located in a lovely compound just across from ours and were doing a marvelous work with orphans and sewing ecclesiastical vestments. There were dear little Chinese nuns wearing thick eye glasses who did embroidery work. Three nice, friendly American Sisters from Cincinnati, Ohio, were stationed with them. They, too were gay spirits and Sister Louise had experienced WWII in free China and so didn't seem to be concerned about the political situation.

On April 10th I wrote:

Dear Mother and Dad,

It is a beautiful day here in Wuhu, following an evening of rain. There is a stout breeze and so the boats on the river are sailing along at a fast clip. Mountains in the distance are visible through a slight mist. Shrubs and trees are all out in bloom and the brilliant green of the rape fields makes a breathtaking sight from the top of Lion Hill. I am typing out on a light, airy sunporch with all this before me. Days are pleasant here. We rise at 7:00 a.m. and have breakfast at 7:30. Following breakfast there are morning prayers of an informal sort and Elnora feeds the little man. I then study until 10:30 a.m. and my teacher, Mr. Chao arrives for the morning lesson. We read together, make sentences from a new vocabulary or discuss problems of Chinese grammar. On Friday mornings both Elnora and I have a writing lesson with Mr. Chao. When I get a little better, I will write you a letter using only the characters. Elnora has sent one to her parents already. It is a lot of fun writing but a real art and not picked up quickly. Mr. Chao leaves at twelve and lunch is at 12:30. After lunch I study a while or succumb to a magazine to get a breathing spell from my Chinese. A Mrs. Chao arrives at 1:30 and gives Elnora a lesson for an hour and then I read with her from 2:30 to 4:00. It is difficult for Elnora to work with a teacher for more than an hour because of the block stammer. Reading is a nervous strain, even on me. Not only do you have to be familiar with the odd looking characters, but also know the tones, which is an element foreign to our speech. While studying with Mrs. Chao the day before yesterday, a man from the office came in with a letter for her. The letter was written in English by Miss Mollie Townsend who is a missionary living in KuiKang. Miss Townsend is taking care of Mrs. Chao's son, Peter, who is a boy about ten years old. Naturally, the mother was anxious to hear about her son and so asked me to translate the letter in Chinese. This I did without much difficulty so I am getting the blasted stuff, difficult as it may be. Following the lesson, all the household go into the dining room to have tea, which is usually around 4:00 p.m. After tea I study and Elnora prepares the baby's supper. We have dinner at 7:00 p.m. and with Mrs. Craighill presiding at the table, there is always a lot of happy chatter. Dinner over, we retire to the living room to read, talk, write letters and listen to the short wave broadcasts of the news. Generally we go to bed between 9:30 and 10:00 p.m. By next week I will be playing tennis on a nearby court which will add some sport to this routine existence. On Saturday mornings I go to the Methodist Hospital and watch Dr. Waters operate. Surgery is a marvelous profession and had I not gone into the ministry this would be my chosen field. Well, there you have my life outlined. Elnora follows this general schedule. Almost everyday she runs over to the Sister's compound situated right back of ours. The Sisters run a handicraft or needlework shop and this, as you would guess, keeps her fascinated. The Wuhu situation is much more congenial for Elnora and I am sure we will be very happy here.

All best wishes and we think of you often.

Love,
Jack

In May we received a letter from Jim Pott, acting President of St. John's University, Shanghai, suggesting we might like to stay in his house during July and August when he and his wife Agnes and son Bobby would be at a summer home in Tsingtao. Most missionaries left the Yantze Valley during the hot summer and went to Kuling in the mountains. However, this invitation sounded fine to us.

On June 11th, after passing canonical examinations I was ordained to the priesthood at St. Liobas Chapel in the Sister's Compound. Poor Kimber Den from Nanchang, the man who was to be my co-worker there, had bad travel connections so arrived three hours late and could not preach the sermon. Consequently, Bishop Robin Chen, the assistant bishop of the Anwhei Diocese, preached and the Rev. Hunter Yen presented me to Bishop Craghill. Most of the foreign community in Wuhu attended, along with many Chinese Christians. The day was perfectly beautiful.

On June 20th I wrote the following long narrative letter to my parents:

Dear Mother and Dad,

Before departing from Wuhu I want to describe for you some of the world around me. To make it personal I will first describe myself at the moment. I am dressed in an old brown shirt with the neck open, a pair of shorts, tan socks and white tennis shoes. My feet are propped up on a brick and cement railing on the south porch and I am comfortably seated in an old canvas camp chair. A school bell in the distance clangs, a vegetable seller calls out his produce from the street below, a woman in the distance slaps her washing with a stick, and I can barely hear the jingle of the blind man's little clapper gong. Birds sing and twitter all around the house and in the garden, trees and shrubbery. In the sky, there are swallows diving here and there and white cranes whiz by in front of me like white comets. And now I can hear the singing of coolies and am looking toward the road beneath me and to the right. Four men come into view all jogging along, bent under carrying poles with a heavy wooden casket swinging between them. The road has other figures on it. Two men with loads on the ends of their "pien tans," single carrying poles, have stopped to chat. A rickshaw coolie with his odd little two wheeled vehicle trots past them. There is the leisurely movement of other people up and down the highway like miniature puppets, each with some insignificant part to play on our particular stage. And now looking in the same direction a coolie has come out of one of the mud huts with two buckets on the ends of his "pien tan" and fills them from the brown water in the canal running along the road. His straw hat shines in the bright sun.

But, let's turn (now) to the bigger picture. There are two predominate colors everywhere, a vivid green and a chalky brown. The trees on Lion Hill are in lovely foliage and their lush, full branches surround the house. Besides the green of the trees there are the rice fields, like giant green blankets covering every inch of space away from the houses, roads and river. In the middle of this green I see little specks moving around, no doubt men and women weeding their rice crop with long bamboo rakes.

Then there is the brown coloring of the dry straw roofs of the mud village, the dusty straight road past Lion Hill, the brown brick buildings of a Catholic Convent to the southwest, the main canal that winds through the countryside feeding the thirsty rice fields and most prominent of all, the vast ageless and untiring Yantze. I can hardly find words to describe this great artery through the heart of China. It speaks of years, peoples and civilizations that are beyond my scope of understanding. It seems to carry on its back thousands of little white sails and low varnished teakwood boats of the same style, and carrying the same kind of people as it carried two to three thousand years ago. Steamers of ocean going size also ply up and down its great length and broad expanse, but they seem only to do so by special privilege. When they overstep their bounds they get stuck on reefs, or are robbed by pip-squeak pirates, or face engine trouble and must linger in port for repairs. But the little boats with squarish looking sails and a family of five or six human beings belong to this old gnarled and twisting mother of waters. The Yantze is a law unto itself so to speak and yet still only a part of the vast panorama before me.

Across the river is a low plain dotted by small green trees which stipple the green of the rice fields. Miles off in the distance there is a faint blue mist backed by high mountains. This northern side of the river has a foreboding aspect about it akin to the way the Japanese front lines looked after four months on Bataan. As my mind turns to the Communists, a column of young Nationalist soldiers can be seen walking down the road singing some kind of war song. Only yesterday, a Philip Rao, a Chinese man on our staff told me about a pitched battle that took place a short distance away from Wuhu. I see gun boats patrolling the river and suspect trouble even here. Constant complaints reach our ears that the poor farmers north of the river are having a hard time of it since both Nationalist and Communist soldiers loot their houses and steal their crops. If they don't get their rice crop in they will starve and so in the fields a farmer's life is in constant danger. China is a romantic, shining, fascinating country and yet also revolting, nauseating and disgusting. We have a silly house amah who sometimes refuses to dust and sweep because she says it is the houseboy's work. We have young men in the compound, some sons of coolies, who having been educated without cost by the mission schools, and are now able to read and write, wear the long gowns and absolutely refuse to do manual labor. We have servants who refuse to see a doctor when ill, but prefer to take quack medicine bought on the dirty street. We have before our eyes a fight for survival that has turned a vast proportion of the population into beasts and haggling madmen over a worthless piece of paper called CNC (Chinese Nationalist Currency). If it weren't for these immense problems I wouldn't be here and yet when I consider the magnitude of the job, I feel like I am slapping myself in the face. Me, one man with an unobtainable ideal to begin trying to help a nation and a people that sometimes prefer to wallow in their own filth. The Cross, fortunately, is the Christian pattern, anything less would be insignificant. Christianity is no longer a sunshine religion, Christ's words have a cutting edge that could only come from God above. He did speak with authority and God helps us as we attempt to put His word into action.

Just a final note old dears. Will you buy us a box of Christmas trimmings, bells, tinsel, etc. and send them c/o The Rev. Kimber Den, St. Matthews Church, Nanchang, China? Also, some cheap 10cts store presents to give to Chinese friends. I suggest about five yards of plastic curtain material. The Chinese use these for table cloths. My best to all. Scotty & Elnora are grand.

Love,
Jack

The financial situation in China was now critical, with inflation beyond anyone's imagination. I was receiving a salary of $144.66 a month and after a few deductions in Shanghai received $136.19. At the exchange rate of 144,000 yuan to a dollar, my salary going into the Hong Kong-Shanghai Bank netted $19,611,360.00. The most popular note was a 10,000 yuan bill, but there were also 20,000 yuan bills in circulation.

14

HANDWRITING ON THE WALL

Just prior to departing Wuhu for Shanghai I went to see Bishop Robin Chen, assistant bishop to Bishop Craighill. Both bishops had been consecrated on St. Andrew's Day, 1940. It was a wise move in that Bishop Craighill and his family had to leave China when our country entered the war. It was now clear that more and more of the foreign leadership had to be turned over to the Chinese.

I frankly asked Bishop Chen what he thought about the stability of the situation. He answered somewhat like this: "John, China is in a terrible mess now, and I believe very near collapse. My guess is the Communists will win, so I will probably become a barber to survive. However, as much as I disagree with Communism, it may be a good thing for the time being. We cannot continue as we have in the past; China must come into the twentieth century and this will be difficult and take time. But the church will carry on as it has done in the past."

On June 21st we left Wuhu in the Methodist Hospital truck for Nanking; Elnora, Scotty and the driver in the cab, and I was in the back with Hu Saotzu, Scotty's amah, and several hospital personnel. It was a four hour bumpy ride, but under the circumstances, not bad. That night we took the train to

Shanghai.

We were warmly greeted by the Potts who lived in a lovely house on the campus of St. John's University. Jim was a tall half-Chinese, half-American whose father, a priest of our church, had founded St. John's University many years ago. He was very much the gentleman, quiet spoken but perceptive and wise. He once said to me, "John, how on earth could you have ever brought Elnora to China?" Agnus, whom he met in a POW Camp in Shanghai during WWII, was full of life, like Elnora. She had been a nurse at St. John's Hospital in Shanghai. The two women were a lot alike. She also loved parties, clothes, shopping, and interior decorating. A day of fun for them was to go out shopping, with bargaining a major challenge in every shop they entered. There were some interesting techniques to bargaining in Shanghai which Agnus passed on to Elnora with great delight. There was nothing superficial about Agnus and I'm sure she was an excellent nurse, but she did love to bargain, especially for beautiful things.

Elnora wrote in her diary June 23rd:

"Agnus took me shopping and I purchased some silks. Really wonderful. The silks are out of this world and so cheap. I'm just going wild over them. Tonight Agnus is having a dinner party for us and we'll go out for cocktails at the Maury Votaws. Her house is like a dream. White Peking rugs, lovely lamps and curtains. She has done it all herself.'

It was evident the hard days for Elnora were over. Throughout the rest of the summer we were alone, since the Potts left a week after our arrival to Tsingtao. I had a tutor for Chinese language lessons and we were busy entertaining and being entertained. Elnora's diary filled up with happy comments and references to the social world she knew and loved. I preached, spoke over the radio and did some counseling, especially with a nice white Russian woman who was desperate to get out of the country. Shanghai was now full of beggers and refugees.

I made a special trip to Nanchang where I was to be

eventually posted in the Kiangsi Province south of the Yantze River. I was to work with the Rev. Kimber Den, one of our mission school graduates and an able and committed Christian. He was the most enthusiastic man I had ever met, full of the Gospel and devoted to the church. He would bring children to the mission compound by playing an accordion through the streets and out into the countryside near Nanchang. On arrival by train, he took me to the Craighill house which was to be the place where we were to live. It was now covered over with vines, and inside were cubicles constructed around a living room. It had been used during the Japanese occupation as a brothel. Elnora and I would face a real challenge to repair and decorate it, but there were possibilities if we worked hard.

Kimber took me to the lovely St. Matthews Church, completely oriental in style except for the altar, pulpit and lectern. Bishop Craighill had built it during his years as a missionary there. On the first floor there was a fine parish hall and on the second the church. Around the main building were classrooms for a primary school. At the entrance to the compound was a dispensary for sick people coming off the streets. Not far away we went to a large blind children's school also operated by the mission. Kimber then suggested we go by jeep to three places outside the city which would be interesting to see. The first was a leper colony operated by the church, and where I was shocked to see for the first time people with ears, noses, fingers and toes eaten away by the disease. A number of lepers were making bricks for sale to provide some self-support.

We then went to a large war memorial which commemorated soldiers lost in a great battle and leading to the ascendancy of General Chang Kai-shek and the Nationalist government. He had spent a good deal of time in the city with his wife, who became a close friend of the Craighills. It was here that the New Life Movement got started in China. In any case, as Kimber and I walked up on the wide square platform surrounding the tower, I noticed a dirty, disheveled young woman playing with loose tiles on the deck. We walked to the top of the tower where Kimber pointed out the battlefield and told me something about the struggle between the Communists and Nationalists. As I looked down on the young woman, she seemed to represent to me the confusion China was in at this time.

From there we went to a lovely Taoist monastery with two delightful courtyards, in the center of which were some very ancient gnarled trees. We sat with the monks and drank some tea.

As we were about to return to Nanchang, and just before I got into the jeep, Kimber put his hand on my knee and said, "Wait a minute, John. We can see from here the War Memorial and the Christian leper colony. These three places represent three philosophies of life today in China. This monastery represents some men's retreat from the chaos of the world. The war memorial represents some men's drive for power and military control. The leper colony represents our faith in Jesus, which results in Christian service and sacrifice." Kimber said so much about the goals of life, using as examples these three different places we had been. He was later imprisoned by the Communists.

I returned to the St. John's campus with a vision of what our missionary work would be like. The university had closed down for the summer, due in large measure to unrest during the spring term because of Communist activity among the students. The president had resigned and Jim Pott was serving as "Acting President" and now the key man in holding things together. We, too, felt an anti-foreign, anti-American attitude stemming from a resentment over America's support of the Nationalist Chinese. I couldn't help but support General George Marshall, who was there to assist the Kuomintang, but not until it showed actual proof of helping itself through stopping the corruption in the government. On one Tuesday the US dollar went from 2,500,000 yuan to Friday when it soared to 4,200,000. Inflation had gone out of sight and reason.

In this situation the merchants were keen to get US dollars and so would sell beautiful things such as linens, silks, furniture, and rugs at ridiculous prices.

Bishop Craighill wrote to me with news that I had been accepted at the College of Chinese Studies, better known as the Peking Language School, for the fall term. I made plans to go to Peking (Beijing) by myself on a coastal steamer to Tientsen with our heavy baggage while Elnora and Scotty would follow by plane. I arrived in Peking on September 16th after a very interesting trip north. The railroad from Tientsen to Peking had tracks blown out in various places, so at this point I felt I had jumped from the frying pan into the fire. However, Peking was the old imperial capital of China and no one believed it would be seriously damaged in the fighting for control of the country.

Elnora and Scotty arrived several days later. I knew she would love the city because it was so beautiful.

We were assigned to two small rooms in a modern steam-heated hostel for eight families. We ate in a large dining hall which was fine except the food was bland and there was little variety. Elnora had become pregnant while we were in Shanghai. It was a relief to be living in Peking where pure Mandarin was spoken instead of the Yantze dialect, so now we would hear on the streets the same language we were learning in the classroom. The school arranged for an excellent baby amah who was used to foreigners and Scotty liked her immediately.

I fell in love with the city, as everyone does who ever lives there. At the time it was pure Chinese with lovely tree lined boulevards, handsome large buildings with yellow tile roofs and their upturned corners. Long camel trains carrying coal could be seen coming into the city and the pedicabs (three wheeled taxis) were quiet with only sweet sounding tinkling bells to break the silence. Peking was a city within cities because there was first a large four square Manchu city with high brick walls surrounded by an outside moat. It was entered into on four sides by large handsome gates. In the center of the city was the Imperial City and in the center of the Imperial City was the Forbidden City. This was where the imperial family lived for centuries and held audiences with diplomats from around the world. We loved it, and at that time there were very few tourists so sightseeing was a pure pleasure. It wasn't long until we were visiting the Forbidden City, Tien An Min Square, the gate of Heavenly Peace, the Temple of Heaven, the beautiful Beihai Park and Coal Hill. On one weekend we went out to the Summer Palace which was perfectly beautiful on a lovely fall day. Visiting the Great Wall was restricted except for one weekend, due to Communist activity in the area, so we didn't see it. At this point I was not about to take any chances. The Communists seemed to have control of all North China except for the large cities and, in fact, had control of an area only five miles from the west gate to Peking.

General Chiang Kai-Shek arrived, so there were rumors of his giving North China to General Fu-Tsa-yi, a strong general in control of a number of armies in our region. Our American Consulate committed itself to moving us out in one to six months, depending upon how critical the situation was.

Three couples of us at the school found a marvelous traditional Chinese house to move into rent free and all furnished, but we would have to do some repair work and provide the heating. This was exciting.

On October 30th I wrote:

Dear Mother and Dad,

I expect by the time this letter reaches you a good deal of important information will be known about Manchuria and North China. The Communists have broadcast that five Nationalist Armies have gone over to them. The United States Information Service in Nanking also reports that the Nationalists are pulling out of Manchuria and consolidating south of the Great Wall. All sorts of rumors are floating around and no real facts to speak of. British subjects yesterday received letters from their consulate advising evacuation, but as yet the Americans are only told to move their heavy goods south. Elnora and I have a big trunk already packed and will have it crated tomorrow for shipment. It seems almost certain we will have to leave Peking in a matter of a few months, but nothing is definite. Life is peaceful as usual, but now is the time to take precautions. I don't believe the situation merits our immediate withdrawal, but it seems certain we cannot stay the winter out. We will probably have to leave by plane when we go. Again, let me repeat, as I have done in the past, there isn't anything to get upset about. I write this information so as to keep you informed about our situation here. I expect I made a mistake in requesting that you send our Christmas boxes here. If they are not already on the way, have them sent to our Shanghai office, 152 Minghong Road."

Two days later all Americans received a circular letter from the American Consulate advising evacuation. The Consul indicated a ship would be available for American citizens at Tientsin between the 15th of November and the 1st of December. At the same time Dr. Fenn, director of the language school, announced it was closing immediately since Mukden had fallen, so we were now vulnerable to attack. I did not feel I wanted to take any chances, so I rushed to the China Air Lines office to make reservations to leave with Elnora and Scotty on the first available plane — I lucked out, two seats were available on the 6th of November for Shanghai. I also made reservations for Elnora and Scotty to leave for Los Angeles November 19th. It was fortunate I moved so fast because some of our students got caught and were in Peking when the Communists occupied the city. At the airport, upon our departure, people wildly rushed to the plane, afraid they would be left behind.

On November 10, 1948, I wrote:

Dear Mother and Dad,

I am sure you have been reading a good deal about China in the newspapers and are probably quite concerned over our welfare. The situation is as chaotic as the news describes it and I am afraid the Nationalists are about finished. As soon as I received my warning letter from the Consulate in Peking I made arrangements for our departure. Very good luck got us out of Peking at such an early date as the 6th. The only reservations I could get through normal channels were for February 6th.

At present I have plane reservations for Elnora and Scotty to leave for Los Angeles November 19th. We are in the midst of selling many things, heaters, stove, refrigerator, etc., and buying rugs and furniture. The mission has ordered out all women and children and so my family will have to be broken up for a while. I can leave, but feel I should stay until things become more crystallized. It is a tough decision and I haven't completely made up my mind on the matter. But I refuse to conclude my term in China and the missionary career at this date and stage of the game.

However, I don't intend being caught again either, and so will have to be very cautious in my actions. You will understand my point of view better than most people and realize I have you in mind when taking the next step. I have put the matter up to Bishop Craighill this way: Either go now and attend language school in the U.S. with the intention of coming back to China, or staying for the time being and make a tour through the Diocese with Bishop Chen. It is our last chance to drive home the point of Christianity, and even though what I have to say will be translated, it may do a little good. We can't drop the Chinese Christians now in a time when they need us most. There is nothing heroic about this point of view. It is simply a job which I feel I should do. The whole business probably looks pretty terrible from a distance but it isn't so bad. The thing that really counts now is to get Elnora and Scotty out and, if it weren't for all the buying, Elnora would be leaving tomorrow. Now she hates to leave China and talks of coming back.

We are once again living with the Potts who will stick it out at St. John's until the end. Most of our mission people are staying and will put up with the Communists until asked to leave. We are at war with Communism everywhere and might as well deal with it on the battle front as at the rear echelon. Christianity will win out but it will be a long hard struggle. Communism is another vicious ideology and yet in China you can hardly blame a man for not being one. The government made a perfect mess of the currency reform and now the economics here are worse than ever. People are going hungry and in one rice riot this morning there were over 2,000 people involved. Conditions in the interior are somewhat better.

I will keep you informed and please try not to worry. We are all well and have plenty of food. I am happy Scotty is going back at this cute age and I hope you can see him in the very near future. Sorry about the Christmas parcels, will probably get them eventually.

All our love,
Jack

The Potts had welcomed us with open arms when we reached Shanghai. We were relieved to be together again. In a day or so Elnora said, "Oh, John, couldn't we take some Peking rugs back with us to the States?" I had no need of a kerosene stove and refrigerator or our two bicycles, which we had never ridden and were simply at our mission warehouse at some point to be shipped to Nanchang, so I agreed. As I sold, Elnora and Agnus went to the stores and bought things at ridiculous prices. In the morning they would put on old clothes and with a fierce determination in their eyes go out to bargain. In the afternoon they would return excited about some lovely purchases. I was told later by our mission businessman, Carl Gilson, that our purchased items were shipped on the last boat out of Shanghai to the United States.

On November 19th Elnora and Scotty boarded a plane for Los Angeles, with a layover of one day in Honolulu. As I was about to say goodbye I said to Elnora, "Anson Stokes has written to me several times saying if we had to leave China, he could use me at the Cathedral. See if he has a job and let me know. I have already wired asking him to meet you at the airport."

At this point I hardly knew what to do. Should I return to Wuhu, go to Nanchang to be with Kimber Den, or return to the States? Shanghai was now crowded with refugees coming down from the north as was Nanking and Wuhu. Beggars were everywhere. It was obvious the collapse was underway.

My dilemma was short lived. In a few days a wire came from Anson Stokes urging me to come to Honolulu. Bishop Craighill had experience with the Communists over many years and he knew of their bitter anti-foreign attitude. Therefore, he felt that the Chinese Christians had much more hope of existing as an entity without Americans among them. Consequently, he began sending word to the foreign missionaries in his diocese to leave without delay.

At the same time our State Department arranged for the SS General Anderson, a large passenger vessel, to go to Shanghai and take as many Americans as possible back to the U.S. Shortly, I joined up with our three American Sisters from our convent in Wuhu and we left with hundreds of other Americans who poured down the Yantze River to leave on the ship. A few Americans stayed behind, but not many.

The SS General Anderson arrived in San Francisco December 24th, so I caught a train and made it to Beverly Hills late Christmas Eve.

Elnora wrote in her diary December 24th:

"John arrived from China. Thank heavens he is out of that mess. We are going to Honolulu next. Whee-e."

15

THE CHURCH OF THE "HOLY ACTIVITY"

By 1949 the occupation of thousands of military forces in Hawaii was over and the civilian population was on the rise. The city of Honolulu was vibrant with new life, of business opportunity and the need for housing of young families. A new housing development was started in a valley three miles east of the city called "Aina Haina", meaning "the land of the Hinds." Mr. Robert Hind had operated a dairy farm in the valley for many years, but a strike in 1947 caused the dairy to be sold and the office, milking rooms, bottling and shipping plant were abandoned. A small group of Episcopalians, mainly belonging to St. Andrew's Cathedral, began holding informal Sunday services in their homes instead of driving into town. They were encouraged to consider starting a mission by the Rev. Canon Anson P. Stokes, Rector of the Cathedral congregation. When I became available, the Rt. Rev. Harry S. Kennedy, Bishop of the Missionary District of Hawaii, and Canon Stokes arranged for the use of the rapidly deteriorating facilities of the dairy to start a congregation with me as the Vicar. Prior to my arrival, several dozen kindergarten chairs were loaned from the Cathedral for church school purposes and Bishop Kennedy obtained an old altar and one hundred chairs from a war surplus store.

A number of laity began to enthusiastically clean up the office to turn it into a chapel.

On January 23, 1949, Bishop Kennedy held the first service, since Scotty was sick and our travel had been delayed. On that first Sunday there were twenty-eight adults and thirty children in attendance. I arrived with Elnora and Scotty the first of February and held my first service February 4th. Bishop Kennedy had appointed a Bishop's Committee to help me formulate plans for the mission, meeting with me for the first time at the home of Mr. and Mrs. Richard Kimbal. Half of my salary was to come from the Overseas Department of the Episcopal Church and the other half plus housing were to be provided by the mission; the Missionary District provided an old second hand car for travel. In a few months the infant church began to explode with people.

Emphasis had to be placed on children and youth, simply because there were so many of them. Aina Haina was called "Mortgage Meadows" since there were many young families buying houses in the area with mortgages, most of them with military backgrounds because of the recent war. They were full of enthusiasm to get started in civilian life, and the birth rate was high.

Although the office had been cleaned up for the Sunday services the rest of the facility was a mess, with graffiti on the walls, broken window panes, doors barely hanging on rusty hinges, trash everywhere. But the congregation was young and strong and above all, visionary. At the outset this young mission had to be far more than a Sunday affair. In weeks we turned into a hard working mission requiring involvement in plain hard labor, to getting a variety of organizations started, along with raising of funds. Since many people who started attending services were not Episcopalians they had to be introduced to the mysteries of the *Prayer Book and Hymnal* with music supplied by a WWII foot pedal organ. Also, in the summer of 1949, I was asked to start a day school since public and private schools were in Honolulu.

By September we had over two hundred children in our Sunday School, using every available space in the dairy for classrooms, and forty children enrolled in the day school's kindergarten and first grade. By 1950 there were three hundred children in the Sunday School and ninety children in the day school. Activities by this time included children and adult choirs, a Women's Guild and Men's Organization, Brownies, Cub and Boy Scout troops, Hui Lina Kokua (Club of the Helping Hands), and a vacation Bible school which we called "Summer Fun." The adult membership by the fall of 1950 had increased to over four hundred members, which meant there were many baptism and confirmation classes.

Early on in the establishment of the mission we had to have a name and three were proposed by members of the congregation: Holy Nativity, St. Matthews and St. Bartholomew's. On a Sunday morning following the second service (services were now held at 7:30 a.m. and 9:30 a.m.), a vote was taken. Holy Nativity won out by a wide margin since it was felt by many that the church had been started in a dairy barn. The nickname "The Church of the Holy Activity" was quickly picked up when a youngster from Sunday School on the day of the vote came home and announced to his mother the permanent name was now "The Church of the Holy Activity." Everyone felt this was an appropriate take-off on what we were about.

Two blessings were soon evident, as far as I was concerned. The first was outstanding lay leadership, since many men and women in the congregation had fine organizational skills and were sincerely committed to getting the mission started. They had no time to waste on confusion and lack of direction. Without the many capable laity, I never could have functioned as well as I did. The second blessing was the appearance of Aunt Maggie Monteiro, my friend from Anking, China, who came to teach at St. Andrew's Priory. She enlisted a Mrs. Bloomfield, who was also a Priory teacher, to help out in the Sunday School, but Maggie gave her whole weekends to help me in whatever way she could. That sometimes included listening to my sermons before they were presented Sunday morning. Maggie had a masters degree in education, but most of all she brought her marvelous Christian spirit, which everyone came to love and admire. She was a real seasoning to an already delicious menu of people from many walks of life.

When we occupied the dairy we were made aware of the fact that our time was limited. Fortunately, in memory of the late Senator and Mrs. Robert Hind, his children donated 48,000 square feet of land on the Kalanianaole Highway to the church. Mrs. Mona Hind Holmes, their daughter, was an active member of the mission. One morning in early 1950 as I was walking to the church, Mr. Willis Jennings, Business Manager for Robert Hind, Ltd. approached me. He said, "John, the Hind Estate has sold the Dairy to the Department of Public Instruction. I cannot tell you when a new elementary school will be built, but maybe you have a year to find another place."

This meant that the church had to move into top speed to build a church building of its own on the Hind land next to the highway. It also meant we had to raise a lot of money rather quickly. The good women didn't bat an eye when they heard the news and immediately organized themselves with an enthusiastic member of the congregation, Mrs. Stanley Kennedy, at the helm to sponsor a church fair. This was a mystery to me, but I was impressed with the first fair on the grounds of the dairy and it brought in the whole community to buy things. The proceeds amounted to around $7,000. I chose Mr. Herbert Keppeler, an engineer heading up the Land Department of American Factors, to be chairman of a building committee whose first charge was to select an architect to design a church. Herbert talked of a long range master plan, which sounded right to me. The plan was to include a church, children's chapel, offices, classrooms, youth center, and a columbarium for the urns of the dead. I felt that some day many of those who helped organize and build the church would want to be buried there. Back of this idea was the communion of the saints and the burial place as a link between the living and the dead. We chose a Biblical text to give us our direction: I Chronicles 28:10, "The Lord hath chosen thee to build a house — be strong and do it." We hired Robert Law as our architect. A building fund drive got underway and cash or pledges were added to the support of the church budget. A loan from the National Council's Emergency Loan Fund, a fund created solely for assisting work in new, rapidly expanding areas, helped us through this critical time.

The development of the mission had come so fast that I was unsure how large the church should be, considering the rapid growth of the community. Therefore, the building committee agreed we should put off the design and construction of the main church for the time being. There was some disagreement over this since some parishioners believed we should build the main church first. But we held to our position and constructed a lovely chapel with one set of sliding doors opening onto a classroom and another opening onto a large lanai in the back. This arrangement made it possible to seat six hundred people. In addition, we planned for school rooms, offices, kitchen and toilet facilities. We chose "puka puka" rock (volcanic rock with holes) to be taken from the upper valley, redwood sheathing, shake shingles and poured concrete flooring. Ground was broken on August 30, 1950, a year-and-a-half after starting the mission. On March 4, 1951, the chapel and church school were dedicated. Forty-one persons were confirmed, four hundred forty adults were present and two hundred fifty children.

I had raised some funds from the families of deceased prisoners of war to buy pews, so on Memorial Day, May 30, 1951, these were dedicated. Each pew had two name plates of men who had died, a total of thirty-eight in number. This was a moving experience for me, particularly since the men were close friends and some belonged to my little Episcopal congregation at Dapecol.

On January 18, 1952, I was awarded the Honolulu Junior

Chamber of Commerce Award for distinguished work in the community involving expansion of the church into a community center, encouragement of Scouting activity, establishment of a day school, increasing church membership in three years from thirty-two to eight hundred members, and membership in various community organizations. This was a lovely award, but none of the accomplishments would have been possible without the many laity of Holy Nativity and a patient, supportive wife.

Elnora by now was really in the swing of things as a clergyman's wife. She loved all the activity of the church and the young, vibrant congregation responded to her beauty and personal charm. She gave birth to Danny our second son in the spring of 1949 and to our daughter Lisa in the spring of 1953. The Women's Guild was a power house of young women (we had only three grandmothers) who were sincere in wanting to be good wives, mothers and devoted Christians. Elnora fitted in with them perfectly. She made cute costumes for her volunteers to wear in her ice cream booth at the fair, modeled for the Women's Guild fashion shows and did a lot of entertaining.

The Sunday School continued to bulge, even with the new facilities, so we had to use fair booths for Sunday School classes. In desperation we hired a contractor who agreed to build two more classrooms at cost or below. His work appeared to be good, and the guild had raised some $13,000 which could be made available. The contractor, Hong Lee, quickly built the classrooms at this figure and I profusely thanked him at a dedication service. Not much later I picked up the paper to read on the front page that $200,000 of narcotics had been found on a Hong Lee, alias "Little Snake" at the Honolulu Airport. It was both amusing and embarrassing, but we did get the needed classrooms. About this time we were registering six to seven hundred children in Sunday School and the day school was pushing two hundred. Our children's choirs numbered over sixty, and I personally focused attention on a group of thirty young boys who sang in the choir and were called "God's Gang." Mrs. A.E. Minville, the choir director worked well with children and at one point she had four separate choirs: God's Gang, Cherub Choristers, Keiki Choir and the Adult Choir. Because of the size of the church school I prevailed on one of our volunteer teachers, Barbara Goss, to work as a full time Christian Education Director. She had no formal training in Christian Education but she brought to the job intelligence, a lot of integrity and a beautiful Christian spirit.

Finally, on September 12, 1954, at 3:00 p.m. the main church was completed and dedicated by Bishop Kennedy. It was a joyous occasion, completing five years of hard work. In 1955 the church received a National Architectural Award from the Church Architectural Guild of America. It was described: "Built of lava stone gathered from the surrounding hills, the church has a quality of openness and spaciousness which is emphasized by the clear span of glulam arches by Timber Structures, Inc. Floors are concrete slab on coral fill with carpeted aisles and sanctuary. Roof surface is cedar shakes over two inch redwood sheathing. Lighting features simple reflector fixtures concealed behind the arches. Seating capacity is three hundred eighty, which can be increased to five hundred by using lanais on either side of the church."

I personally emphasized two features of the building which I felt important. At the entrance there was carved in the large travatine flooring blocks an Alpha and Omega, the first and last letters of the Greek alphabet. They symbolized in their placement the beginning and ending of a life in the church. Hanging from the ceiling over a marble, free-standing altar in the sanctuary was a large marble cross. It created a powerful focus for the whole church — Christ crucified, yet Savior of the world. Mrs. Edward G. Harrison, one of our pioneers and generous donors, gave a beautiful stained glass window of the Nativity scene, which was located over the entrance. The church building, with its native volcanic rock walls, simple

Hawaiian lines and appropriate appointments, possessed a spiritual quality which one always seeks in a church. We endeavored to create the feeling that the presence of Jesus was in this place and was in the process of changing lives.

Bishop Kennedy, realizing I was under a lot of pressure, brought to my attention a young Maori priest from New Zealand who was anxious to come to Hawaii for a year to broaden his experience with the Episcopal Church in America. The Rev. Manu Bennett and his wife, Kaa, did come at our invitation and were of tremendous help at a crucial time of growth. It was Manu who suggested on the first anniversary of the new church to "clip" it. This, apparently, is an old Anglican custom to surround the church building on its birthday by holding hands in a lovely symbol of embrace at the time of the benediction. Manu was a brilliant preacher who spoke from a few notes in his hand while I laboriously wrote out all my sermons as I was taught in seminary. His explanation for this was that the Maoris for many years did not have a written language, so naturally developed their gifts of oratory. In twelve months the Bennetts became a rich and beloved part of the vigorous young congregation.

The concept of a youth congregation became strong as our many children of elementary age were going on to Junior High and High School. I again asked Bishop Kennedy for help and he agreed to allow us to call a priest specifically for a ministry to youth. An empty lot across the street from the church was purchased through the financial help of Mr. George Gannon, Mr. Gayer Domminick, and Mrs. Edward Harrison, who appreciated the vision I had for young people. We financed first the building of a residence on this property, with help from the Women's Guild. The Rev. Richard Aiken and his attractive wife Carol came to us in 1956 to develop a youth congregation. Once again we went into a building fund drive, our third since 1949. The Aikens were just what we needed at the time. Dick was a tall, good looking young man, a graduate of Trinity College where he was a varsity football player and a recent graduate of Virginia Seminary. I assigned him the job of working solely with the youth while I handled the adult congregation. With Dick and the building committee, plus a representative from the youth congregation interested in architecture and Mr. Cyril Lemmon, architect, we designed an outstanding youth center. It combined a gymnasium and auditorium of 6,000 square feet with a stage, recessed sanctuary, kitchen, craft room, meeting lanai, lavatory, dressing rooms and office. The altar within the sanctuary was backed by a colorful Italian mosaic which had on it the symbols of the tree of life. On a Sunday morning the stage was turned into a choir and sanctuary area. Organizations besides the youth congregation included Explorers, Boy and Girl Scouts, the Kalanianaole Athletic League, Junior Achievement and other community groups. The name given to the youth congregation was "Halepule Opio" (Hawaiian for "House of prayer for youth"). In two years Dick Aiken took the number of young people from thirty-five to a congregation of three hundred and fifty, and a pledging budget from the youth of $4,000 a year. They paid for their own expenses, including rent for their buildings, and bought their own organ for $2,000 as well as buying a fishing boat for missionary work in Formosa. Dick once said, "If we work an effective ministry to youth, we will not have the tremendous pastoral load of adults." The youth center was written up in the religious section of Time magazine December 6, 1963.

Due to all the construction for the church plant and clergy housing, we had difficulty in relieving the Missionary District of financial assistance, but on February 2, 1959, at our tenth year anniversary, the mission became a fully self-supporting parish. I was grateful to Bishop Kennedy for his patience allowing the congregation time to maximize its potential in this rapidly growing area. He was always keenly interested in what we were about and supported our vision, which naturally had many financial ramifications.

Uppermost in my mind was the spiritual life of the

congregation, because if we did not have Christ at our very center of parish life, whatever we did could not possibly sustain. Jesus was very real in my life and so I tried to help individuals and groups tap into His power as I had. Therefore, we programmed schools of prayer and retreats for men, women and youth. There were quiet days, Aunt Maggie's Bible Class, Lenten study programs, Wednesday morning healing services, etc. as a rich part of our continuous spiritual growth. We benefited from Lenten missions with such fine spiritual leaders as Dr. Shelton Hale Bishop and the Very Rev. Paul Roberts, retired priests. I worked hard developing spiritual growth in baptism, confirmation and marriage classes. Our teachers, both in Sunday School and the day school, were chosen for not only teaching skills but Christian character. To my mind, a prayer base was essential to all that we did whether it be before a committee meeting or at the outset of an annual fair. I felt we had some marvelous prayer warriors in the congregation, both men and women, who knew in their hearts a personal God and were constantly inspired by the Person of Jesus Christ. They were the rocks of the congregation. Some parishioners were only on the surface of "Holy Activity," but there was always the potential to grow and we had to start where they were in the spirit and take them up higher.

After the main church was completed in 1954, Bishop Kennedy came to visit me in my office. He said he had been talking with the Presiding Bishop, the Rt. Rev. Henry Knox Sherrill, the night before. Apparently, the Presiding Bishop had made a unilateral decision to change the general convention meeting place in 1955 from Houston, Texas to Honolulu over the strong objection of Bishop Quinn, who was to be the host bishop. The problem was over racial segregation which then existed in Houston. The long distance and additional expense were problems to face for the Presiding Bishop, along with the fact that we now had limited time to prepare for the event. Bishop Kennedy asked me to be hospitality chairman, which at the time would involve at least 3,000 delegates and visitors to be met, housed and entertained. This was a sizable challenge but I agreed to do it. Without delay I began to organize a committee, mainly of Holy Nativity people, but others as well. We met with Mr. Bill Cogswell, Director of the infant Hawaiian Visitors Bureau which had never dealt with such a large convention before. Nevertheless, we placed ourselves in high gear, met every ship and plane with leis and aloha, organized entertainment troops, made reservations in our limited number of hotels and did a job of hospitality. The Presiding Bishop was most appreciative and we had a marvelous convention held for the most part at Iolani Boy's School.

For missionaries overseas, and since Hawaii was still a Missionary District, a furlough arrangement was granted every three years whereby a family could return home and speak on behalf of missions. On our first furlough, Elnora and I returned to our respective homes with Scotty and Danny and I did a lot of speaking, along with attending the College of Preachers for one week in Washington, D.C. While at the College I met Dr. Reuel Howe who presented lectures on "Man's Need and God's Action," which later were printed in book form. The lectures made a powerful impression on me because they dealt with our real life situation. From that point on I became a devotee of Dr. Howe, reading his books, attending his seminars at Bloomfield, Michigan and, after his retirement, was privileged to have him in my home as a guest. Of all the leaders and professors I have known in the Episcopal Church, Dr. Howe made the greatest and most lasting impression theologically and from the pastoral training standpoint.

In 1956, a time for our second furlough, Elnora and I needed a good break and I was keen on attending St. Augustine's College, Canterbury England, the Central College of the Anglican Communion. In exchange with my sister, Mrs. John McGregor, for taking care of our three children, Scott, Daniel and Lisa, we would take her daughter Susan to Europe with us. This was a marvelous broadening experience beginning in Rome and then Florence, Geneva, Paris, London and

Canterbury. While I was in school, Elnora and Susan went on to Scotland, Holland and Belgium. The world of western Christian art and architecture opened up to me in a powerful way. The Vatican in Rome, the Coliseum, the Chapel of Domine Quo Vadis and the Catacombs brought early Christianity before my very eyes. But there were fun things to do also. We had lunch at the American Embassy with John and Mary Jernigan, number two man after Clare Luce Booth, and at restaurants we ran into the movie star Rock Hudson three times. Susie couldn't resist at one time dashing over and asking him for his autograph. Of all of Italy, we fell in love with Florence and its great art galleries and medieval atmosphere. But when we went to Assisi I felt I was on a spiritual pilgrimage to the grave of the great Saint, Francis. I knelt beside it with an American Franciscan monk in his brown Friars habit, knowing he was a spiritual brother of Father Albert Brawn, my dear friend of POW days. We said a prayer for peace together and he gave me a little copy of St. Francis' famous prayer on peace which I cherished. Geneva, Paris and London were fun and Elnora and Susan loved their shopping tours, while I never tired of cathedrals, especially Notre Dame and Chartres.

At St. Augustine's College, Canterbury, I joined with over thirty priests from around the world to consider problems of Christian ethics and work of the Holy Spirit in and through the church. It was the first time I was made aware of the terrible problems in South Africa and the involvement of the church in this severe political, social and religious issue.

We went to a garden party at Lambeth Palace, at which time I met the Most Rev. Geoffrey Fischer, whom I would later meet in Honolulu. I was literally filled with a new dimension of the church which up to this point was totally American. One of the clergy, a black priest from Kenya was asked rather bluntly what his theology was. I will never forget his simple answer: "I believe in Christ crucified as my Lord and Savior".

Because of the growing pastoral ministry with alcoholics in the congregation, while on my third furlough in 1959, I attended a month long course at the Yale School for Alcoholism. This experience, coupled with my involvement in the Hawaii Council for Alcoholism and a large AA group at Holy Nativity, extended my knowledge of this healing ministry. As time went on I began to do more and more counseling in areas on alcoholism, marriage and divorce, teen-age difficulties and with men who had problems on their jobs. I felt an affinity with men who lived under the stress of business pursuits. Many of them simply wanted a confidant to talk with other than their wives.

By 1959 the *Honolulu Advertiser* began to take a poll of the best dressed women in the city. In the Advertiser, February 9, 1959, there was an article with a full length picture of Elnora in a royal blue dress of linen weave silk which she had designed and made herself. The caption above the article read: "Mrs. Morrett Is Named In Style Poll".

But Elnora was not all surface in terms of clothes and appearance. In a long article about her in the January, 1956 issue of *Forth* magazine she says:

"One of my own best ways of getting to know the women in the church has been to visit new mothers, to give them small booklets about baptism. I find that chatting with a proud mother over the crib of a tiny new baby brings about an unforgettable meeting of the minds. I made one unhappy discovery however: All mothers do not instinctively love their new babies. John had a call from a downtown area, where neighbors had been shocked over the neglect of a teen-aged military wife who left her baby to go off with a man other than her husband. It was a weekend and welfare agencies were closed."

Elnora and I brought the baby home, dirty, hungry, and neglected. She fed her, soaked the encrusted filth from the abandoned child and then both of us worked toward the reconciliation of the husband and wife. When the chips were down Elnora could be magnificent, and I think she was the most non-judgmental person in the world. She did something special for that young, confused military wife.

Statehood was a big event in 1959. On March 12th, I wrote to my parents:

Dear Mother and Dad,

We have just been celebrating the passage of the Statehood Bill. Alma (Hutchinson, my secretary) had her radio going so we heard immediately when sufficient votes had passed to carry the Bill in our favor. I went and got the chimes going, which could be heard all over the valley. We beat the air raid sirens by about ten minutes. Then the day school children and their teachers filed into the church some two hundred strong for a short service. I gave them a short talk and then Dick (Aiken, my assistant) rang a chime and we counted to fifty. After that we said a prayer and concluded with "My Country Tis' of Thee". It was very touching. The faces of the little children were so serious and interested. What it will bring in the future is hard to say. Our mixed races, of course, feel the impact of this probably more so than many of us who have experienced voting powers on the mainland. Everyone is celebrating in one way or another and in Aina Haina a huge bonfire is now burning on the park strip. There will be entertaining and dancing at the Palace, City Hall, and at various large shopping centers. No doubt a big crowd will gather at the airport when Governor Bill Quinn, Delegate John Burns, and others return from Washington for some formal ceremonies here. Tomorrow as well as the rest of today have been declared a legal holiday but I expect the main celebrations will be when they return. The military will get in the act sometime soon with the firing of many guns and the display of aerial strength.

There are conservatives who feel we probably are not ready yet, but most of the people from the big industrialist down to the laborers are for it.

Our love,
Jack

March 13, 1959

Dear Mother and Dad,

I have just returned from old Kawaiahao Church founded by the first missionaries. All the Protestant clergy and the legislature along with many of the old Hawaiian Societies and, of course, hundreds of people gathered for the service. We formed a procession at the Palace and walked up King Street. It seemed to me the most impressive church service I have ever attended. The Rev. Abraham Akaka, the pure Hawaiian clergyman of the church, preached a wonderful sermon. When we marched by the Palace there were thousands of people assembled for the festivities of the day. Many military personnel were present and batteries of guns in place for salutes which will probably come later.

Tonight our choir has been selected to sing the Hawaiian anthem, "Hawaii Ponoi," and will be right up on the porch of the Palace overlooking the crowd. There is to be held a tremendous pageant and then we anticipate the governor and other dignitaries from the mainland to make speeches. This is really quite an historic occasion and, of course, the Hawaiian people are so proud and dignified about it. The orientals, too are inwardly as well as outwardly pleased. Now that we have arrived, and I see the reaction of these people, I can appreciate the value of this status. Fifty percent citizenship is never quite enough and especially for people who need a sense of status. Mr. Akaka spoke so well on the subject of "Aloha," which in Hawaiian also means "God," and which will overcome fear in the face of responsibility.

If the pageant is shown on television on the mainland, I hope you will look for some white choir gowns and red hats You just might spot us.

Love,
Jack

There was a lightness and humor about the Holy Nativity congregation, a lot of it centered around the annual fair when people simply had fun together. The auction of a calf or an old automobile or knitted carnations from someone's attic brought both money and laughs. Skits were often performed at the after-fair dinners or the annual meetings with the Bishop and his lovely wife Catherine, always there to enjoy the good jokes. (He would always tell a few himself).

The Very Rev. James S. Cox, Dean of St. Andrew's Cathedral, resigned in January, 1962, to become rector of the Church of the Incarnation, Dallas, Texas. A search process was started and in February the Very Rev. Paul Roberts (retired) came to the Cathedral as interim dean. We played a good deal of golf together and so he confided that I was being considered among others to be dean of the Cathedral. Eventually, I met with the search committee and then Bishop Kennedy informed me that I was chosen and should meet with him and the Cathedral Chapter. This was a big move for me and a call which I felt honored to accept. A contract was made in regard to salary, housing, automobile, pension, health plan, and moving expenses. In my letter of acceptance, March 20, 1962, I wrote:

"The Deanship of the Cathedral, I am sure, is a real challenge and a heavy responsibility. I know that I am not capable of meeting the full challenge without the help of the Holy Spirit, and so my constant prayer these days is that He will strengthen and guide me in the vital task ahead."

My election became official April 29, 1962, so I preached my last sermon at Holy Nativity on Easter Day, April 22nd. It was in many ways a wrench to leave Holy Nativity with its vision, many friends, pastoral relationships and beautiful Christian atmosphere, but I also knew it was time for me to move on into another dimension of the church, the city and the state. A lovely farewell was planned in the Youth Center, with kindly remarks and gifts. Holy Nativity, once again, combined seriousness with lightheartedness. In one of the skits there were three women on the stage seated before a table top on saw horses. They were Aunt Maggie (Parish Worker) , Alma Hutchinson (Secretary), and Barbara Goss (Christian Education Director). A man representing me said, "There are several people I cannot overlook or say enough about. Aunt Maggie has been with me for many years. I call her my 'Saturday Girl'. And, of course, the one who has been my right arm for so many years is Alma Hutchinson, my 'Morning Girl.' Another member on our staff whom we couldn't do without is Barbara Goss, our Christian Education Director, my 'Afternoon Girl'.

That about takes care of everyone at the Head Table, except my dear wife Elnora — my 'Night Girl'." Elnora enters the stage in negligee and peignoir — gives an enticing stretch and yawns.

Although we always had fun at Holy Nativity, beneath it all was a seriousness in our relationships which was made possible by our relationship with the Lord. It was said by the theologian Reinhold Niebuhr that, "Humor is the vestibule of faith". People gravitate to joy and happiness and that is one reason why many people came to Holy Nativity in its early days. It was fun to be there. It is true that conditions were right for churches to be built in new communities in 1949 where there was a lot of expansion, happy family life and the energy of youth. But there was something more — a Christian faith which brought people together into a new and vibrant congregation. Sometimes, it may have seemed like Holy Nativity was too social and too materialistic because we were so involved in raising funds to build the church. But in large measure we had our eyes on that big marble cross and all it symbolized to us in the post war era. As a congregation, we did not try to be righteous or perfect, we wanted to be ourselves, authentic human beings with weaknesses and strengths. With our humanity we had a vision of the church, both spiritual and material, the temple of God on earth if you will, sometimes misty and unclear but still there it was: "The Church of the Holy Activity".

Before I left the church to go to St. Andrew's Cathedral

two good things happened. Mr. Harold Hughes came to see me and said he wanted to give the vacant lot back of the Youth Center to expand our property. This extremely generous gift came quietly and without any desire for recognition. It amounted to quite a few thousands of dollars and more precious land. Secondly, I appointed George (Pete) Goss, husband of Barbara Goss, to head up a committee to build the columbarium. I knew I could trust "Pete" to get the job done. Churches for centuries have been the burial ground for Christians who were laid to rest near the sacred place that had been the center of their spiritual life on earth. I had hoped many of those who worked so hard to build and sustain the church could someday have their final resting place there. It wasn't many years until the columbarium was completed, fulfilling another dream.

16

AROUND THE WORLD IN EIGHTY DAYS

At the time I was called to be Dean of St. Andrew's Cathedral, Honolulu, in April, 1962, a three month furlough was due. An agreement was made about this with the Bishop and the Cathedral Chapter. It was arranged that the retired Dean of Grace Cathedral, San Francisco, would supply for me until I made a trip around the world. Elnora and I needed a break after a busy thirteen years establishing Holy Nativity and we had been blessed by some inheritance, so we decided to splurge and do some extensive traveling. We arranged for Scott to go to a boys ranch in Arizona, Dan to camp in the Redwoods of California and Lisa was to stay with her Aunt Catherine Older in Los Angeles, where she would attend a summer art school. We felt good about these arrangements and the children were thrilled to have some adventures on their own. Once they were taken care of, we went to Springfield, Ohio, where I performed the marriage ceremony for my niece, Susan McGregor. It was then off to "Around the World in Eighty Days," which was to be a trip of a lifetime.

I saw two primary purposes in the travel: 1) To visit the Holy Land, and 2) To witness the other great religions of the world as they were lived out in their particular cultures. On June 22nd we sailed from New York on the S.S. France for Le Havre. The ship was new, having made it's maiden voyage in January. In contrast to the troop ship, the General Meigs, on which we sailed to China, Elnora now had the best when it came to transoceanic travel — and she loved it. We met charming people, enjoyed the French cuisine and the beautiful appointments of a luxury liner. Instead of being in the hold of a prison ship with hardly anything to eat, I was enjoying the finest food. I thought, what strange, unpredictable things can happen in people's lives!

At Le Havre, France, we took a train to Paris where I picked up a little Simca for driving to Rome via Germany, Luxemburg, Austria and Switzerland.

In Rome, the Rev. Bill Woodhams, whom I had known in seminary and was our American Episcopal Church liaison to the Vatican, arranged for us to see Pope John XXIII at his summer palace. This was a thrill. There must have been three hundred people in the audience hall, yet we had excellent seats. The Pope emanated that warm, loving personality which literally opened up the Catholic Church to the rest of the Christian world.

From Rome we flew to Athens and had our first experience with authentic, Greek culture which has so profoundly influenced the Western World. We loved the Parthenon, the marvelous temple to Athena, the museums, the Greek food and the pleasant attitude of the people.

As we were flying into Beirut, Lebanon, the thought came to me that since we would end our trip in Japan, why not try to see Lt. Yuki, the Japanese officer who helped the American POW's at the Davao Penal Colony. Upon our arrival at the hotel I sent a letter off to the Rev. Kenneth Helm, our Episcopal liaison officer to the Japanese church. I gave him Lt. Yuki's name and the place where I had last seen him in 1943. Hopefully, he could arrange a meeting for us and I could thank him for all he tried to do for us under extremely difficult circumstances at Dapecol.

Beirut at the time was a handsome city on the coast of the beautiful Mediterranean, and we thoroughly enjoyed our short stay there at the King George Hotel. We never could have dreamed it would end up in shambles as it is today.

We then flew to Jerusalem, going first to the Jordanian side of the city. The American Colony Hotel where we stayed was moderately priced and situated next to a small mosque, which had a single minaret. We had no more than gotten into our hotel room when the muezzin, the man who calls Moslems to prayer five times a day, stepped out onto the balcony of the little tower and began calling out. We could easily see him from our window. I learned later what he was saying:

God is greatest! God is greatest!
I testify there is no god but God.
I testify that Mohammed is God's messenger.
Come to prayer! Come to salvation!
God is greatest! There is no god but God!

Should we as Christians be so eloquently reminded of our faith in God five times a day? Now I was really in touch with another of the world's great religions and it was a thrill.

Jerusalem, I knew, was a city fought over by an amazing number of tribes and nations: Hebrews, Assyrians, Babylonians, Persians, Greeks, Romans, Arabs, Turks and Crusaders. Even the British couldn't hold it with a mandate from the League of Nations. "Whose Land is Palestine?," was a good question. Now the poor country was divided between Arabs and Jews under very unfriendly circumstances. To enter the country we had to fly into Jordan, which controlled most of the old city and was divided by a no-man's land from Israel. We think of it as a "holy city" because of the three monotheistic religions which exist there and its long religious past, but in some respects it seemed to me lacking spiritually in many ways.

On our first day I began talking to a nice looking, elderly Arab in the lobby of the hotel. He told me he had formerly built a home and owned property on the Israeli side, but with the 1948-49 Arab-Israeli war he lost all his possessions and was forced to live in Jordan. I suddenly realized the deep bitterness that had resulted from the Israeli occupation of Palestine.

But when we visited the Church of the Holy Sepulcher I could see Christian Palestine also had its intense differences and drive to control space. There in this venerable old building, supposedly the scene of the crucifixion and burial of our Lord, were six rival denominations all determined to keep tight control over their own chapels: Eastern Orthodox, Armenian, Roman Catholic, Coptic, Syrian and Ethiopian. The Ethiopians had to hold services on the roof in order to have some space to themselves.

After completing our scheduled tours we packed our bags and went through the no-man's land and the Matalbaum Gate over to the Israeli side of the city. Soldiers had their rifles and machine guns pointed at us while a young Arab boy pulled the heavy luggage on a cart. The atmosphere of Jerusalem suddenly changed from the relaxed, poor Arab environment to the aggressive, rich Jewish environment. As we entered the lobby of the King David Hotel we could see it was filled with wealthy Jews, mostly women wearing heavy jewelry and, we guessed, from New York. In my private thoughts I felt sorry for the poor Arabs.

For a day we visited other Christian sites and then drove to Tel Aviv, Caesaria and Haifa. Our trip to Nazareth was lovely, followed by a nice drive down to the Sea of Galilee which I looked forward to with real anticipation. When we arrived at Tiberias our driver took us to a seaside restaurant where young Israelis were drinking beer and dancing the twist to rock music. This took the edge off of things, but when we went up to the Mt. of Beatitudes where Jesus taught the Sermon on the Mount, the atmosphere was much different — peaceful and quiet, and I could feel the presence of Jesus in this place. We went on to historic Capernaum, which was lovely and then back to Haifa to catch our plane to India.

Reflecting back on our short visit to the Holy Land, I realized at some point we would have to return since there was so much more to see and in less of a hurried way. Secondly, it was clearly evident that the Arab-Israeli conflict was extremely deep and was becoming a "no-win" situation for either side. I felt sad that the world had this kind of festering boil in a place which had so much spiritual value for Muslims, Christians and Jews.

We arrived at New Delhi, India, at 4:30 a.m. to be met not just by a travel agent and porters, but young boys who begged from us all the way to the hotel. We were dead tired and so immediately went to bed and slept until noon. Fortunately, we had contact with a lovely Sik couple, David and Komei Dhinsa, through Los Angeles friends, and Brijlal and Lelia Sahney through the Watamull family in Honolulu. Both couples couldn't have been nicer to us and through their efforts we were able to see a lot in the way of temples and tombs, the Red Fort and the old city. Because Brijlal Sahney held a high post in the government, we were able to attend the House of Parliament while it was in session. Apparently, large electrical generators for the capitol had been frequently breaking down, so there was often no electricity in the city. We heard Paudit Nehru give a lengthy, passionate speech about the matter.

From New Delhi we flew to Agra to see the famous Taj Mahal and then to Benares, on the Ganges River, which is the most famous religious city of Hinduism. Thousands of people were washing away their sins in the dirty but sacred river. There were funeral pyres all along the bank burning dead bodies, and we could see cinders and ashes thrown into the river when a funeral was over. We saw many lepers in the streets begging, and one naked demented man shocked me. Not far from Benares we went to the place where Gautama, the Buddha, preached his first sermon. My surface impression of

Hinduism was quite negative, especially because of the terrible poverty in the streets, while in contrast there were lavish temples of wild looking gods and goddesses. Little, if anything, seemed to be done for the poor. I knew there was a lot more to Hinduism than meets the eye, but the religious impact on the society seemed of little, if any, help. Brahman was the supreme ultimate and creator; Vishnu — the preserver; and Shiva — the destroyer (or, the energy which breaks up in order to re-create). But even with these basic gods, Hinduism, it seemed to me, did not have a clear focus on reality as we have it in Christianity. Certainly, the religion lacked compassion and a concreteness while our faith in Jesus Christ is based on sacrificial love which, in turn, provides a marvelous mercy ministry around the world.

From Benares we flew to Calcutta in order to get to Bangkok, Thailand. The city was extremely dirty, crowded, and there was an estimated 600,000 people living on the streets at night. One could understand why Mother Theresa could receive such world admiration because of her Christian devotion to the poor in that tragic city.

On arrival in Bangkok we were met by our friend Lou Nordeen, who had greeted us in Hong Kong on our way to China fifteen years before. Lou was still working for Caltex and lived in a lovely Thai house formerly owned by a Thai princess. Now we were in Theravada Buddhism country, quite different from India. "Theravada" means the "Day of the Elders." Elnora needed to rest and it was terribly hot, so I went with a nice young Australian, a big fellow who was a shot putter returning from the Asian Games, to see some temples. They were fantastically beautiful and I was intrigued with the saffron robed monks whose heads were shaven and were never to be touched by a woman. Buddha had been born in India, one hundred miles north of Benares, but the Buddhist religion had pretty much left India and been transported by monks to Burma, Thailand, Cambodia, Sri Lanka, Laos, Vietnam, China and Japan. It was interesting to note that Buddha, meaning "the enlightened one," predated Christianity by four hundred-eighty years and was now the predominate religion of the Far East.

I was also impressed with the foundations of Buddhism, the Four Noble Truths and the Eight-fold path, which are wonderful concepts but seem mainly directed into a monastically dominated spirituality built around the introspection of the individual.

We left for Hong Kong August 18th, where we were met on arrival by Andrew and Sandra Eu, whom I had married at Holy Nativity Church some years ago. Sandra's family were members of the parish and she used to babysit for Lisa. We also met, in Hong Kong, Linda Lu Parker, at one time one of our teen-agers who had wanted to do missionary work. Consequently, I had arranged for her to help out at a mission in Mindinao, Philippine Islands, for the summer. Our big Australian friend, Dick Leffler had come along with us and so he made a nice companion for Linda. The Eu's rolled out the red carpet and made our stay delightful. Andrew's family owned the famous Eucliff Castle out in Repulse Bay. My highlight in Hong Kong was to meet the Rt. Rev. R.O. Hall, one of our outstanding Anglican Bishops in the Far East and who had a great influence on the development of our mission schools and social work in Hong Kong. He also ordained the first Anglican female priest during WWII.

On August 22nd we flew to Tokyo where we were met at the airport by the Rev. Kenneth Heim. His very first words were, "John, we've found your man, Kempy Yuki."

"How did you do it?," I asked.

He explained that he had advertised and written articles, both for the English and Japanese newspapers. One example:

"Searching for Japanese Benefactor"

"A former U.S. Infantryman (incorrect — artilleryman) and now an Episcopalian minister in Hawaii is searching for an ex-Japanese Army officer who had been kind while he was a prisoner-of-war in the Philippines during the Pacific War.

Recently John J. Morrett wrote to the Japan Mission of the American Episcopal Church in Aoyama-Minanicho, Minatoku, asking for help in locating a Japanese man whom he knew only as "Yuki."

He added that the man he was searching for was either a first or second lieutenant in the former Japanese Imperial Army.

Rev. Morrett explained that he was coming to Japan shortly, during the course of a global tour, and, if possible, wanted to locate and thank "Yuki" personally for the kindnesses shown him while he was in a POW camp in Davao, Mindinao from December, 1942, to March, 1944.

Morrett is scheduled to arrive in Japan Wednesday and is staying at the Imperial Hotel until Sunday. He will leave here August 30th after touring Kansai and other parts of Japan.

Anyone having information which would lead to locating "Yuki" is asked to contact The Yomiuri Shimbun or the Japanese Mission of the American Episcopal Church."

On the day of our arrival in Tokyo the following article appeared with these headlines:

"Yuki Hopes to Meet Morrett"

Takamatsu (Kagama), August 22nd — "I know John J. Morrett," said "Yuki," the kind prison camp guard sought by a former POW who is now a priest."

This article mentioned that Yuki was fifty years old and it had been twenty years since we had seen each other.

On August 25th a lengthy article with my picture showing me on the telephone talking to Yuki came out in the Shipping and Trade News of Tokyo. The headline was:

"Think More Kindly About Past.

Former U.S. POW is Here to Meet and Thank His Ex-Captor

by: Kent Nixon

"Time has a way of making us remember only the pleasant experiences.

This was the observation Friday of a forty-five year old American clergyman who was a prisoner for two years in four Japanese prison camps during WWII.

Many of the pleasant recollections The Reverend John J. Morrett has of his days as a captive center around the humanitarianism of Kempy Yuki, an ex-lieutenant and prison official."

This was a nice long article and set a positive tone for our meeting.

After several days in Tokyo Elnora and I went to Miyanoshita way up in the mountains for some rest, then to a Japanese inn in Hakone where we slept on the floor in traditional Japanese style. We then went to beautiful Miyoko Hotel in Kyoto and I took the day to fly to Takamatsu to see Yuki. He greeted me at the airport with his two sweet daughters, who seemed as excited as he was over the meeting. Yuki's hair was grey, but he was the same gentle, kind man I knew years before. We first went to a quiet park where we talked about prison camp days. After the big escape from Dapecol by Capt. Ed Dyess and his group, he lost his command of American prisoners and I had the impression he received some kind of severe punishment. But he seemed to have no regrets. We had lunch with some of his friends at a nice restaurant and then he took me to his home to meet his wife. She spoke no English but seemed anxious to conduct a traditional tea ceremony on the floor, giving me at the end of it the tea bowl in which she had mixed the powdered green tea. I took this back with me as one of my treasured possessions of the trip.

What a strange and awesome experience this was:

Two supposed enemies peacefully talking to one another, following the most terrible war in human history. Millions of dead and wounded, military and civilian, seemed to linger in the back of my mind as we talked. Japanese and Americans had literally intended to kill one another and we ended the war with America using the atomic bomb. Yet here we were friends with complete trust and respect for one another. Had we two tricked fate— that power to supposedly make certain events inevitable? We had humanized a set of dehumanizing circumstances and God had blessed us. From the ruins of war we men still had found a pinnacle of respect and admiration and I was moved by it.

Yuki and I continued to correspond over the years, mainly at Christmas when he would send me beautiful Japanese greeting cards. When one of the daughters got married, he sent snapshots of the bride and groom. Finally, years later, one of the daughters wrote me that her father had died of cancer and noted in her letter the value he had placed on our friendship.

As I reflected on this eighty days around the world, one of its values was to see and experience other cultures back-to-back. There is a lot of learning with contrasts, and we had them from Europe to the Middle East to Southeast Asia and the Orient. In his book, *The Way of All the Earth,* John Dunne, Catholic theologian writes:

"Is religion coming to birth in our time? It could be that what seems to be occurring is a phenomenon we might call "passing over," passing from one culture to another, from one way of life to another, from one religion to another. Passing over is a shifting of standpoint, a going over to the standpoint of another culture, another way of life, another religion. It is followed by an equal and opposite process we might call "coming back," coming back with new insights to one's own culture, one's own way of life, one's own religion. The holy man of our time, it seems, is not a figure like Gautama or Jesus or Mohammed, a man who could found a world religion, but a figure like Gandhi, a man who passes over by sympathetic understanding from his own religion to other religions and comes back again with new insights to his own. Passing over and coming back, it seems, is the spiritual adventure of our times."

I had had this adventure of "passing over" and was grateful to God for it.

17

A CATHEDRAL DEAN

The Very Rev. Richard Coombs, Dean Emeritus of the Cathedral of St. John the Evangelist, Spokane, Washington, has written a history of Dean's Conferences from 1954 - 1987. He asks at the beginning of this historical record, "What is a Cathedral? What is a Dean? Every priest who has been made a Cathedral dean has asked himself these questions. He begins by being frustrated on learning there are no clear answers. But soon he realizes what that means is that, consistent with whatever local statutes may apply to his Cathedral and his position, he and his Cathedral are free to be and to become what they are called by God to be and become. In the institutional church that is freedom indeed!"

Under these circumstances I was not at all clear about my job at St. Andrews except I felt its task was far more than a parish church like Holy Nativity. I also knew it was clearly linked to the Bishop and his administration of the Missionary District, whose offices were also on the Cathedral close. At the outset Bishop Kennedy asked me to serve as the Chairman of Cathedral Chapter meetings and to be pastor of the Cathedral congregation. Dean Coombs notes in his history of the Dean's Conferences, that an American Dean sent a long questionnaire to his fellow deans asking them about their

Cathedrals. Of the fifty-seven deans who replied, only twenty-four reported the Bishop to be president or head of the governing body of their cathedrals. "The Cathedral as the Bishop's Church, therefore, is a diffuse definition," he says. At no time did Bishop Kennedy ever inject himself into Cathedral operations except in the case of one Canon who came to the attention of the police and was dismissed by me. I sincerely appreciated the freedom to develop and administer Cathedral programs as I saw fit.

It was an honor to be called to St. Andrews, not only because it was the Mother Church of the Missionary District, but also because it was the first Episcopal Church in the Hawaiian Islands. Two outstanding Hawaiians were responsible for this mission, King Kamehameha IV (1854-1863), grandson of King Kamehameha I, and his wife, Queen Emma. As a young prince the King had traveled to France and England with an advisor, Dr. Gerret P. Judd. This began his admiration for England and its state church. He was treated as royalty in England but faced prejudice in the United States, and he frowned on the institution of slavery.

Emma Rooke had been educated by an English governess and the *Book of Common Prayer* was used in the Rooke home. Her sympathies were strongly in favor of England and English institutions. When the King and Queen were married at Kawaiahao Church in 1856, the *Church of England Prayer Book* was used. The King subsequently translated the *Book of Common Prayer* into the Hawaiian language. Eventually, the King petitioned the Archbishop of Canterbury to send a missionary bishop to Hawaii, which brought the Rt. Rev. Thomas Nettleship Staley to the Islands in 1864.

The land for the Cathedral was given by the King and the cornerstone laid by King Kamehameha V in 1867. Funds for the original building were largely raised by Queen Emma, who had the architectural plans drawn up in England after the King's death on St. Andrews Day, 1863. It is a handsome French Gothic structure, unusual for Hawaii, with a marvelous, great west window. It covers the whole facade, a brilliant wall of intricately patterned stained glass. It measures fifty feet in height and twenty in width and was completed in 1958. A handsome fountain in front has a delightful bronze figure of St. Andrew in a rectangular pond surrounded by fish with water spouting from their mouths. The Cathedral can proudly refer to Queen Emma, whose name is the very first on the baptismal register, so its beauty and historicity thrilled me.

I inherited a fine Chapter (governing body), a small office staff and two canons who gave me courtesy resignations and began looking elsewhere for other jobs upon my arrival. It almost goes without comment that the Dean has the right to choose his own staff. The Cathedral, as I saw it, in general terms had two primary tasks:

1) To serve the Diocese as best it could.

2) To serve the congregation and community, the latter in a servant role depending upon needs as we saw them.

My immediate concern was over the music, since the Cathedral had a part-time organist, and music on a Sunday morning was, at best, mediocre, even though we had an excellent organ. Consequently, my first goal was to find a superior organist and choir director to make the worship experience in the Cathedral, from a musical standpoint, as fulfilling as possible. A second task was to find two canons who would cover the main areas of pastoral work and Christian education. Staffing a cathedral is generally a difficult job since most clergy are soloists and want their own churches. My first canon, whom I hired from a stack of applicants, turned out to be an alcoholic and had to be sent back to the mainland. At the invitation of the Coast Guard I had made a trip to the South Pacific to preach to men serving on bases at small atolls. When I returned I received bad news which brought on my first dismissal. Two priests were soon hired to fill the slots of Canon Pastor and Canon Educator and two additional part-time priests came on the staff to make sick calls at the large Queens Hospital just two blocks away.

One of the real pluses in being a Dean is the opportunity to attend annual Dean's Conferences at different Episcopal Cathedrals around the country. The first conference began through the initiative of the Very Rev. Francis Sayre, Dean of the Washington Cathedral and the Very Rev. James Pike, Dean of the New York Cathedral in 1954. Each conference has a specific theme relevant to the particular locale and cathedral situation.

There was no formal organization or dues and Dean Sayre served as the "Papa Dean," coordinating each conference, thereby creating a continuity for the various deans to follow. Because of my connection with Frank at seminary and then with his family in the Philippines, it was always a joy to renew our friendship each year.

The theme for the first conference I attended in March, 1963, was Foreign Affairs: "Decision and Conscience." This was just up my alley since I had been so personally involved in U.S. policy in the Philippines and China.

Twenty years earlier, as a prisoner, I had felt abandoned by our leaders and longed to be able to communicate with them. Now as a priest and free citizen I could appreciate the tremendous effort made by our government to keep us out of war, or to deal with it if necessary.

While in Washington, Paul Callaway, Cathedral organist, suggested John McCreary as a possible organist for St. Andrew's Cathedral. John and I met at the College of Preachers to discuss the possibility; he later came to Honolulu to meet with the Music Committee of the Cathedral and was subsequently hired. This was one of the best personnel choices I ever made. John came to us full of experience, talent and enthusiasm. In a short time he organized an excellent choir and gradually built up a men and boys choir using the Iolani Diocesan School as a resource for boys.

He also organized and directed a Cathedral Choral Society which performed the great masterpieces of choral work from once to twice a year, with orchestral support from members of the Honolulu Symphony. One year, using the Cathedral and Priory choirs and the Ensemble Player's Guild, he put on the *Shepherd's Playe* by John LaMontaine, as a Christmas Opera. Also, one of the most interesting and enjoyable presentations was a modern mass which he wrote himself and which was performed by St. Andrew's Priory, our large Diocesan Girls' School on the Cathedral close. I was always pleased to raise outside money for John because I knew his performances would be a real contribution to the cultural life of the city.

When I assumed my deanship there were some long-standing organizations such as the Women of St. Andrews, Iolani Guild (Hawaiian Women), Friendly Friday, Altar Guild, Ushers, Acolytes, and a Men's organization. To these I added the Aloha Calling Committee, Volunteer Receptionists, Cathedral Guides, and Library Committee. I felt that the Cathedral should have a good library for the Diocese and so enlisted the help of Mrs. Charles Bernie who established a fine small library which became pretty much self-supporting by selling a Cathedral Cook Book.

In addition to these Cathedral organizations we organized a day care center for working mothers, provided office space for WICS (Women in Community Service), National Council for Crime and Delinquency, and a task force to establish FISH, a social service organization . A very large AA group and a senior citizens club also used our facilities weekly. One last organization of which I was particularly fond was the Cathedral Players, who used our small Tenny theater to put on plays four times a year. The name was changed to "Mallory Players" so they could be completely independent of us financially, but still, I had a fine working relationship with this enthusiastic group of dramatists.

As to my own special ministry to the city, I was asked to serve on the Mayor's Advisory Council for Urban Renewal. At this time, especially with statehood in 1959, there was a tremendous amount of urban development all over the island of Oahu, as well as high rise buildings planned for downtown Honolulu and Waikiki. So, I began to focus a great deal of my attention on our urban growth. A lot of federal funding became available for low and medium income people needing good, yet inexpensive housing, so I became a board member and on-year chairman of the Hawaii Council for Housing Action. It was made up of labor, business and civic leaders with Jack Hall, President of the ILWU Labor Organization, as its first chairman. By 1970 the council had completed four projects, was in the process of constructing six others totaling 1,400 units with $32,000,000 in mortgages. One of the projects was Keola Hoonanea, a 175 unit elderly project sponsored by the Cathedral, Methodists, and the United Church of Christ. I was able to obtain the $10,000 needed for seed money from a sincere friend and member of Holy Nativity. (Happily, Aunt Maggie became one of the first residents.)

Another place where I spent a lot of time was at Kuhio Park Terrace, two giant, government twin towers which provided low cost housing. Shortly after occupancy it developed a lot of social problems. Many Hawaiians and Samoans living there were not accustomed to living in high rise buildings or using elevators.

There were problems of alcoholism, incest, and juvenile delinquency. Incest was common and particularly difficult to deal with. Consequently, a group of clergy organized into what we called the "Pastoral Counseling Service for Public Housing." I served as the chairman and hired an excellent young Chinese woman to serve as staff person who arranged for counseling sessions with volunteer clergy. With my training as a social worker at Ohio State University this became a pet project for me and whereby the Cathedral's influence could touch the poor in the downtown community.

Soon after my arrival at the Cathedral the Bishop asked me to co-chair the Episcopal Centennial Advance Fund with

Rudolph Petersen, a fine layman and President of the Bank of Hawaii. The Bishop wished to celebrate 100 years of the Episcopal Church in Hawaii. We had good cooperation from the parishes and missions, who scheduled us for fund raising speeches throughout the Islands. We were able to raise gifts and pledges amounting to $708,500. A year later the Centennial Celebration took place with Presiding Bishop Arthur Lechtenberger coming out to Honolulu to give the opening address. Other Archbishops came from Japan and the Philippines, along with numerous bishops from dioceses on the mainland. On the day we celebrated the landing of the first bishop in Hawaii, the Rt. Rev. Thomas Nettleship Staley, October 11, 1862, the Most Rev. Archbishop Lord Geoffery Fisher came to represent the Church of England and to preach at the Cathedral. This celebration was a tremendous undertaking for the Missionary District.

Besides such large events, the Cathedral was always host for the annual convocation and held a Massing of the Colors Service every year for the Disabled Veterans of Foreign Wars. I was often called to conduct large services such as the burial of Rear Admiral Richard Lynch, Commandant of Pearl Harbor who died suddenly of a heart attack, and the funeral of the famous Olympic swimmer and outstanding Hawaiian athlete, Duke Kahanamoku. Special services were held when President John F. Kennedy was assassinated and when Martin Luther King was shot. A candlelight service for Czechoslovakia was held when the Russians quelled a revolt by tanks. One of our finest services for the Police Department was to honor its officers killed on active duty. In the eight years I was at the Cathedral there were five-hundred-fifty-seven baptisms, four-hundred-twenty-two confirmations, four-hundred-forty-one marriages and two-hundred- eighty-three burials. The job of being Dean was a busy one but I enjoyed every moment of it. The dimension of the job was something I particularly appreciated.

Elnora soon became a rich part of Cathedral life, and

similar to Holy Nativity, everyone loved and admired her. In 1965, she was again chosen one of the ten best dressed women in Honolulu by "Beacon" Magazine. This was an especially nice accolade as she made many of her own dresses. Her sit-down dinner parties were well known for their charm from hospitality to decorations and table settings. She moved with confidence among the leaders of the community, winning them to her by her beautiful smile and quick wit.

In 1965, I had a furlough due and there was the Annual Dean's Conference to be held for the first time abroad in Coventry, England. The conference was just what I needed, having been Dean three years and yet still not absolutely clear what St. Andrew's should be about. The theme of the conference was "The Church of Today Prepares for the Church of Tomorrow." The new, modern Cathedral of Coventry had risen out of the ruins of the old medieval cathedral almost completely destroyed in WWII. The marvelous new structure fitted into the old ruins, symbolizing "death and resurrection" as two vital aspects of the Christian faith.

I was asked by the Provost to be the preacher at the Sunday evening service attended by many townspeople who worked during the day and could not attend the morning services. (At a gas station later on an attendant looked at me and said, "Oh, you preached at the Cathedral last Sunday night.") What really caught my attention and challenged my imagination was the way the Cathedral ministered to the life of the whole community such as shop keepers, public servants, factory workers, homemakers and those in the important areas of the theatre and the arts. I now felt I had some good ideas about the direction for St. Andrews in our particular Honolulu and statewide setting.

After my return to Honolulu, with the help of staff and a small group of visionary laity of the congregation, we developed a Planning Document for St. Andrews. Added to the staff of two canons in pastoral work and Christian education, I envisioned part-time clergy specialists:

1. A priest in charge of developing a downtown ministry to business and commerce.
2. A priest specialist to work with youth and young adults.
3. A priest in charge of promoting evangelism.
4. A priest with a specialty in theology who would direct his teaching toward the adult laity because many Episcopalians are so theologically ignorant about the Christian faith. This, of course, would include a lot of Bible study.

At least now I had a better sense of direction than before coming to the Cathedral, and I also felt I was on track when it came to my focus on urban problems, especially housing that had become critical in the Sixties in Honolulu.

Since it was my furlough time in 1965 and Elnora and I spent so much time concentrating on Cathedral life, we decided after Coventry to arrange for our children to meet us in Europe. I picked up a little Triumph auto made in Coventry and we drove south to Bournemouth, where we flew with the car to France. In Paris we met Dean Sturgis Riddle at the American Cathedral who had agreed to do a month's pulpit exchange with me in July. Then we drove south through the wine country and over into Spain and Portugal, Southern France and down into Italy where we met the children in Rome. With them we traveled through Italy, Austria, Southern Germany, Switzerland and France. Every place we went people were fascinated by two things: Our Hawaiian license plates and the boys driving the car in their bare feet. I exposed the children to as much as I could about traveling, from adding up the check at restaurants to getting hotel rooms, always inspecting the rooms first for their appearance and cleanliness. At this point they had become seasoned travelers.

At the February Convention in 1965, Bishop Kennedy appointed me Chairman of an Urban Strategy Committee for the Missionary District. I suggested to him that while I was away on furlough he begin appointing members to the committee, which he did. The people I suggested were informed leaders in community life as well as good Episcopalians. Nine guidelines were set forth as our committee formed in September, 1965. A statement of purpose was agreed upon: "Due to the rapid changes in the metropolitan scene and the dependence of the church on old strategies and structures, many of which are becoming irrelevant, the Diocesan Committee on Urban Strategy is charged with evaluating the changes taking place in our cities and to stimulate new approaches and revisions in strategy and structure to increase the relevance of the church in our society."

It wasn't long until our committee was into specific areas and programs. By this time the Rev. George Lee had come to Hawaii from the National Council of The Episcopal Church and knew a lot about the emerging urban ministry. Because I was involved in so many things, I asked the Bishop to allow him to become my staff person for the committee and he agreed. We began to take a close look at the Moiiliili area, with the cooperation of St. Mary's Mission and St. Mark's Parish, and also endorsed the proposed East-West Religious Cultural Institute at the University of Hawaii. We felt the Canterbury House facilities should be improved on the campus. On the leeward side of the island we felt all the mission facilities were inadequate and we had a lot to say about the effect of the big H-1 freeway and subdivisions under development, with new mission possibilities. We recommended that Mililani Town, a large housing development underway by Castle and Cooke, be considered as an area for a new mission. Finally, we recommended that because the problem of growing urbanization was so serious, an InterFaith Coalition be explored to focus on urban problems.

To achieve this, we planned in the Spring of 1968 a Metabagdad Conference to raise people's consciences and provide information about the urban crisis. This was held at the Holiday Inn May 17th and 18th, 1968, and had one-hundred-seventy people in attendance. The conference was given outstanding news coverage by Mr. George Chapman, Editor of the *Honolulu Advertiser* and who personally attended all the sessions. This was a full ecumenical venture, with Father Lee doing an outstanding job in it's implementation. It brought a lot of new people into a concern for the planning process of urban change, and, at the end, an Inter-Faith Urban Coalition was recommended to be formed.

In 1969 I became enamored with an Urban America Study Tour of new towns in Europe. Because of the terrible devastation of cities and towns in WWII a lot had been done to rebuild old cities and plan and develop new ones, especially in satellite communities. Most cities in the past have grown without long range planning, hence many of them have current problems of urban sprawl, traffic congestion, noise and air pollution. I was happily accepted for the trip May 14—June 8, 1969. One hundred seventy-three architects, lawyers, city planners, urban coalition executives, housing analysts, model city directors and several clergy were in the group. We left from New York where we gathered together to go to London. Our first stop was to meet London city planners and to visit the new towns of Stevanage and Harlow twenty to thirty miles from the city with ready access by mass transportation. I was amazed at the thought and skill behind these new towns with their planned civic centers, good housing at minimum cost, attractive architectural features, and bicycle paths along with good roadways and attractive landscaping.

From London we went to Stockholm, Sweden, Helsinki, Finland, Leningrad and Moscow, Russia, and Paris, France. The Russian new towns were the least attractive, purely utilitarian and poorly constructed. No wonder they fall flat with an earthquake. It seemed to me the Europeans were twenty to twenty-five years ahead of us in terms of city planning with the exception of the Russians who were doing a tremendous amount of building, but not much more could be said for their efforts. It was interesting to see Russia and its plain, unsmiling people, poorly dressed and obviously controlled by the government in about everything they do. Our visit there created an amazing contrast to Paris where there were happy faces, people well-dressed, color and style among the women, and an excitement which exists in a free country like France. Although I love to travel, I said to myself, "I never want to visit Russia again. There are too many nice places in the world to see." While on the trip I wrote two long articles for the *Honolulu Advertiser* about the new towns of Europe, which were published June 15th and 22nd.

My relationship with the Press in Honolulu, I felt, was excellent. George Chapman, Editor of the *Honolulu Advertiser*, always had time for me to visit in his office. He never allowed me to leave without giving me a new book since he must have been receiving them from publishing houses around the country. He was what our generation would call "A swell guy." He was in touch with the total life of the community and the world and so we always enjoyed some conversation, especially about the city.

Bud Smyser, Editor of the *Star Bulletin*, and I were not as close but he, too, was always ready to be helpful. However, my closest association was with Nadine Wharton, Religious Editor, whom I always felt was on my side no matter what the issue. Most of the society editors were members of the Episcopal Church and loved Elnora, who was always newsworthy from their point of view.

My relationship with the Mayor of Honolulu, Neal Blaisdell and his wife Lucy, had always been particularly close, especially since I prepared them for confirmation. They were two wonderful Christians and were frequently in our home for dinner parties. John Burns, the Governor, I did not know particularly well, although we also had them in our home and she was one of the dearest women I have ever known. He seemed a bit distant as a personality, but once you got to know him he was very pleasant, and there was no doubt in my mind about his complete dedication to the State. He appointed me to the State Ethics Commission and the Governor's Commission on the Year 2000. This opened up my interest in futurology, which became more fascinating as the years passed. When we had the American Dean's Conference in Honolulu, the Governor held a reception for us at Washington Place, the traditional home of the Governor located next door to the Cathedral.

In this regard, in 1969, the American Dean's Conference came to Honolulu: twenty-five deans and twenty-one wives. The theme for the Conference was "The U.S. Encounter with Asian Problems" — approached from a Christian viewpoint: missionary strategy, world health, economics, the population explosion, power stresses, and cultural development. It lasted six days and met mainly at the East-West Center next to the University of Hawaii. Sub-themes for three days were "The Asian Setting", "Asian Problems" and "Asian Viewpoint." We had a marvelous group of speakers, much too long to mention. Admiral Jack McCain invited us to visit CINCPAC Headquarters where he was Commander-in-Chief of all U.S. Forces in the Pacific. We were briefed on the situation in Vietnam and visited the Arizona Memorial at Pearl Harbor. On Sunday morning I celebrated the Eucharist at the Cathedral and Frank Sayre preached.

As I conclude this chapter I am sure it is quite evident a Dean of an Episcopal Cathedral is a very busy person in his broad, dimensional job. I loved it but it also brought some very real pain as I ran into conflict with the new Bishop, the Rt. Rev. Lani Hanchett. Still, it was an interesting time to be a dean with the beginning of statehood, rapid urban growth, the controversy over the Vietnam War and a time when Hawaii became a Diocese and a bishop was elected.

18

CONTROVERSY

Controversy is always confusing — who is right and who is wrong over a particular issue or issues. During the heat of controversy facts can be cloudy and confusing and this was certainly the case in the two big areas of controversy while I was Dean of St. Andrews Cathedral. The first had to do with the Vietnam War and the second with the election of a bishop to succeed Bishop Kennedy. In Hawaii, at the time, we had no serious controversy over the racial segregation issue which had heated up on the mainland. We were already integrated racially and there were not many blacks living in the Islands. Naturally, everyone was shocked at the assassination of Martin Luther King, and we held a memorial service for him. However, the Vietnam War was a matter of controversy. It was intensified because of our large military installations in the Islands. These included Camp Smith, the Headquarters of the Commander-in-Chief Pacific, Pearl Harbor Naval Base, Hickham Air Force Base, Schofield Barracks, Fort Schafter Army Depot, and the Marine Base at Kaneohe. Quite a few members of the Cathedral were in the military. Having had my military experience in WWII, I felt a strong bond with the Armed Forces and wanted to support our military personnel, especially at the time of conflict. I was also convinced Communism was not politically viable as a way of life anywhere in the world.

Soon after I arrived as Dean, the Vietnam War was beginning to escalate. Because of some controversy over it, I arranged for a military public affairs officer and an antiwar activist to debate the issue in Tenney Theater. The auditorium was filled to capacity and there was a forthright debate on the matter. It was an informative evening and seemed to have been appreciated by those present, although I doubted if any opinions were changed by the dialogue.

As time went on resistance to the war grew in intensity and by 1968 frequent demonstrations took place on the campus of the University of Hawaii, the Federal Building that housed the Selective Service offices, on streets near military installations, and three times at St. Andrew's Cathedral during Sunday morning services. I got into a public disagreement with Dr. James W. Douglas over the Selective Service System. Dr. Douglas, professor of religion at the University of Hawaii, was eventually jailed by District Magistrate Frank Takao for loitering as a result of an anti-war sit down. Articles in the papers ran the following headlines:

"Cleric in Agreement With Douglas Jailing"

"Minister Denounces Draft Resistance"

"Episcopal Dean Supports Selective Service System"

Below the above headline the article read, "Morrett made his views known in his weekly newsletter. It is important for American citizens to realize the Selective Service System is now an integral part of the military program of the country. Unless the total world picture radically changes, our nation will find it necessary to maintain a strong military force on an indefinite basis.

Morrett said that doing away with the Selective Service System, as some persons advocate, would place our nation in a seriously vulnerable position in terms of militant aggressive countries and make ineffective many of our significant international policies

The above mentioned articles, too long to print, came

out in June, 1968. By the next year our Episcopal Church leaders were taking a stand against the war and requesting President Nixon to grant amnesty to draft violators. Two local deserters went to our national convention to represent their cause.

On May 20, 1970, the Executive Council chaired by Rt. Rev. John E. Hines, Presiding Bishop, passed a resolution titled, "Crisis in American Life." The second point of the resolution stated: "Call for the total withdrawal of all American forces from Southeast Asia now, and end the war." I had no problem with the high aims of the resolution but unilateral withdrawal caused me a lot of concern. Having been in a war on a combat basis, and the POW experience when thousands of men died so tragically, I realized combat forces that are locked into each other don't lay down their arms easily, and surrender can be disastrous. If we pulled out unilaterally what would happen to the South Vietnamese loyal to their cause, what would happen to our POW's, many already languishing in prison for a number of years? Precipitous withdrawal could cost thousands of lives and add to the tragedy of this prolonged conflict.

In any case, I got in touch with Admiral John McCain, Commander-in-Chief Pacific, and asked if I could go to Vietnam and see the situation for myself. I also wrote to the Honorable S.D. Berger, Deputy Ambassador in Vietnam whom I knew personally. In response to my requests I was given orders to fly to Vietnam July 28, 1970, and return August 6th. On the orders was the purpose of travel: "To receive an orientation concerning U.S. Government activities in the Republic of Vietnam."

My visit soon involved days full of appointments with top-level people to enlisted personnel and Vietnamese, including political officials and even Buddhist priests. I received a lot of information about the Vietnamization and Pacification programs in their effort to establish peace and security and a stabilized government, and, at the same time, fighting off invasion and infiltration from the North Vietnamese. Travel by helicopter took me to I, II and IV Corps. While in Saigon, I received briefings from the U.S. Army and ARVN Headquarters, and a good deal of time was spent with embassy personnel and such people as Ambassador W.E. Colby and his assistant George D. Jacobson. My travels took me to DaNang Air Force Base, Bien Hoa POW Camp, the Twenty-fourth Corps Headquarters of the 101st Airborne Division, the city of Hue and the DMZ. Finally, I ended down south in the Mekong Delta region. I visited as many as seven fire base camps and numerous outposts in II Corps, saw rangers preparing to go on a night reconnaissance, and in I Corps, I watched a platoon of Marines going out on night patrol. I visited with Pacification teams in small villages and hamlets, talked with village chiefs, council members and elders.

Upon my return to the U.S. I wrote a lengthy paper titled: "Responsible Disengagement". It seemed only proper that I send my draft to Admiral McCain for review in order to clear it for public consumption. He responded as follows:

29 August 1970

Dear Reverend Morrett:

Your proposed letter and article have been reviewed and I am gratified that your visit provided such an impressive grasp of the situation in South Vietnam. Your thoughtfulness in providing the drafts is appreciated and they have afforded me some interesting insights into our problems there, as seen through the eyes of a non-military observer.

The substance of your letter and article provide a completely objective and accurate portrayal of our mission and the situation existing in South Vietnam. I would appreciate however, amendment of some administrative items. In the draft letter you suggest that the addressees (Presiding Bishop and Council Members) visit South Vietnam and mention I made your visit possible. This may lead some members of the Council to conclude this courtesy will be further extended, whereas the method of arranging your trip was an exception to normal procedures and the timing involved. Requests for similar visits by Council members should be arranged by the Armed Forces Chaplain's Board, which normally handles visits of religious leaders to overseas military installations.

In both drafts you mention being granted, "full security clearance," which could be incorrectly interpreted to mean that you were granted access to classified information. I would be gratified for your amendment of these portions of your draft also.

Again, I am pleased that your trip was such a success. The message projected in your proposed letter and article is inspiring and reflects an unusually effective picture of our aspirations in Vietnam.

With best wishes and warm regards.

Sincerely,
John S. McCain, Jr.
Admiral, U.S. Navy

Once the paper was cleared by Admiral McCain I sent it to the Presiding Bishop along with other materials and also passed it on to Congressman Sam Devine, Congressman from Ohio, who presented it on the floor of the House of Representatives. It went into the Congressional Record March 10, 1971.

Later, after having left the Cathedral, I wrote three other papers on Vietnam and received some interesting responses:

1) "Moral Issue of Vietnam" September 20, 1972

From the White House I received the following letter dated January 8, 1973:

Dear Rev. Morrett:

Through the thoughtfulness of Representative Devine

the President has had an opportunity to read your sermon, "The Moral Issue of Vietnam," and he wants you to know how much he appreciates the support you expressed for our national goals in the longest, most difficult war in our history. Your experience in WWII and your personal understanding of the situation in Southeast Asia give particular significance to your comments, and they are especially encouraging as we pursue our efforts for an honorable, lasting peace.

With the President's best wishes,

Sincerely,
Roland L. Elliot
Deputy Special Assistant
to the President

2) Thoughts and Prayers That Reach Across the Seas (For POW Parents and Relatives)

Admiral and Mrs. "Jack" McCain's son, John, had been a prisoner, much of the time in solitary confinement in Hanoi during the war. He writes for himself and his wife, Roberta.

31 October 1972

Dear John:

I have passed on your excellent article to the Navy Chief of Information for possible placement with the media. He has a magazine and book section which deals with publishers on a daily basis, and will, therefore, be in the best position to place your story.

Retirement is upon us and after forty-one years of active service, I can't say I am looking forward to it.

3) The Spiritual and Moral Trauma of Vietnam

This was a very long paper for the Air University Armed Forces War College dealing with the whole issue of Vietnam following the release of American prisoners of war April 1,

1973, summarizing our involvement over a lot of issues. I especially wrote about the role of the clergy and at the conclusion dealt with the problems of amnesty, broad new tasks of American policy making and the message of the prisoners of war. It was personally presented at the College April 9, 1973.

The second controversy of my Cathedral years involved church politics. It was as devastating as the defeat on Bataan, but in this case I was personally involved on a spiritual basis. I survived the war, but now would I survive in my ministerial vocation, which was at the very heart of my life? The situation was so critical for me that I lost my wonderful deanship.

At the time of the General Convention of the Episcopal Church in Seattle, Washington in 1967, a surprise selection took place. Three local churchmen; the Chancellor, Mr. Hugh Shearer; a priest, the Rev. Burton Linscott; and a layman, Mr. P.K. Liu; members of the Council of Advisors, presented three names to a special committee of the House of Bishops chaired by the Rt. Rev. Anson P. Stokes. Exactly what went on in the committee's deliberations is impossible to say since the selection of the Rev. Lani Hanchett, Rector of St. Peter's Church, Honolulu, was all done in secret. Even our clerical delegate to the Convention and the alternate did not know the selection was to take place, nor did the Board of Directors of the Missionary District. I certainly did not know, even though I was Dean of the Cathedral. When our official delegate heard indirectly that the selection of a new bishop was to take place, he went to Bishop Stokes and complained. Bishop Stokes was also surprised to learn about the secrecy of the nomination process which had its financial as well as political and ecclesiastical considerations. The Missionary District of Okinawa, only ten years old, allowed each parish and mission to have a chance to help in the selection of three names, and at the same General Convention, Bishop Edmond Browning was selected. However, the Missionary District of Honolulu which was over one hundred years old, was kept unaware of what was going on. Because of this situation the Committee of Bishops recommended that instead of a coadjutor (a bishop to succeed the Diocesan), a Suffragan be selected (an assistant bishop without right of succession). The new bishop that was selected, the Rev. E. Lani Hanchett, received from the Presiding Bishop the title, "Bishop in Charge," since Bishop Kennedy wished to be relieved of the heavy duties of administration over the Missionary District because of poor health.

Many of the people in the Church in Hawaii were thrilled that a local priest, and especially one who was part Hawaiian, had been selected; others were saddened and in some cases angered over the process as well as concerned over the ability of the new leadership. Bishop Hanchett "elect" had only two years of college and three months of formal seminary training at the Church Divinity School of the Pacific. Ordained to the deaconate in July, 1952, he had read for holy orders while serving as a lay reader and youth worker on the Island of Kauai, and later served as priest at Holy Innocents Church, Lahaina, Maui.

Since I was disturbed over the way the selection had come about, I wrote Bishop Stokes. I had known him for years, beginning as a student at Columbus, Ohio, when he was Rector of Trinity Church. I knew I could be candid about the matter of process. He replied with a long detailed letter, expressed his own disappointment and requested that I tear up the letter after I had read it. He, too, said he thought the process had been flawed, no secret selection had ever been intended and that an election for a Diocesan Bishop should come about in several years. (Even though there was no right of succession for a suffragan bishop there was much concern that this would occur because the financial burden of two bishops was great for a missionary diocese.)

In a short time the Rev. E. Lani Hanchett was consecrated Suffragan Bishop at St. Andrews Cathedral, carrying the designation "Bishop in Charge," and so he began to carry a good deal of authority. I was certain I was in for a rough time as Dean. It became clearly evident that Bishop Kennedy was turning over the administration of the Missionary District to the new bishop. In the spring, Bishop Kennedy informed me by letter that the Diocesan Urban Strategy Committee was to be dissolved even though there was no consultation about it with me. All the time and conscientious planning were abruptly ended. He indicated Bishop Hanchett wanted to handle his own strategy for the churches and the community. By the fall of 1968, the Rev. David Kennedy, who had replaced Bishop Hanchett at St. Peter's Church, informed me he was appointed Chairman of a Role Study Committee to study the Cathedral. Appointments were made without consulting me or the Cathedral Chapter. In January, 1969, Bishop Hanchett informed me by letter that he was "Bishop in Charge," and stated he was taking over the Chairmanship of the Chapter, the policy making body of the Cathedral. There was no prior discussion with me. Upon receiving the letter, I told him because of this action I would have to leave, but it would take me six months to two years to find another position. However, the Chapter unanimously requested he not serve as chairman since he was still in a temporary situation.

It wasn't long after this that another parish rector and I began working together to become, instead of a Missionary District, an "Aided Diocese" so we could have an open election locally instead of an appointment by the House of Bishops. (A new kind of battle was shaping up for this soldier-priest.)

Life in the Episcopal Church in Hawaii was beginning to get polarized into two factions: the pro-Hanchett Episcopalians and the con-Hanchett Episcopalians. At an ordination service the new Bishop-in-Charge stated that clergy could not afford the luxury of dealing with controversial issues and that seemed to refer to a number of us, including me as Dean. I felt I was a pretty good target for this criticism. It was evident to some people that a submerged battle was going on in the Episcopal Church; a battle between some of the strongest clergy in the district and the new bishop.

In September, 1969, at the General Convention in South

Bend, Indiana, the Missionary District of Honolulu became a Diocese with the right to elect its own Bishop. Two good men came to my mind who would be outstanding: The Very Rev. Francis B. Sayre, Dean of the Washington Cathedral who had strong links to the National Church and Federal Government, and the Rev. Bill Heffner, one of our first missionaries to Okinawa and now in the Overseas Department of the Episcopal Church. Bill agreed to run but then backed out, probably because he knew of the stress going on in the new Diocese. Frank Sayre said he never particularly wanted to be a bishop but somehow Hawaii challenged him with its many races and its strategic location in the middle of the Pacific Ocean. He knew the area well, having served as a Chaplain in the Navy during WWII in the Pacific, and his father had been U.S. representative to the King of Thailand and High Commissioner of the Philippine Islands. He also had been Ambassador to the Trusteeship Council of the United Nations.

So, he was my man and I pressed for his election even though few people knew him in Hawaii.

An election date was set for October 24th and 25th, 1969. Nine candidates were put on the ballot and Bishop Hines, the Presiding Bishop, was requested by Bishop Hanchett to come to Hawaii and chair the election. As a local part-Hawaiian bishop and in office for two years, and with many clergy as vicars of missions, Bishop Hanchett won handily on the first ballot. Frank Sayre came in second but did not have nearly the votes seriously to contest the winner. Many of us, particularly in the parishes, were broken-hearted but not surprised. That night, following the election, a core group met together at the Columbia Inn across the street from the *Honolulu Advertiser*. Beer, laughter and tears softened the blow, but our fears were to be realized and take form in the months to come. There was a strange mixture of exhilaration, sadness and foreboding now that the long period of uncertainty was over.

The day after the election Bishop Hanchett telephoned and asked me to come to his office for a conference. Since I had pushed for Frank Sayre, I knew the ax was about to fall. He said he was now going to take over the Chapter as Chairman, he was going to appoint all staff personnel and he would be deeply involved in all Cathedral programming.

I said, "But, Bishop, if you are in command of a fleet of ships, you have to have someone to command your flag ship."

"No," he replied, "I am not satisfied with the Cathedral operations and so I intend to take over now."

"I have made up my mind, you will do administration work only, schedule services and do the pastoral work, but I will be in charge of all programming," said the Bishop.

I had a sinking feeling about the survival of what I had built up over the past seven years. I said I could not agree about the staffing and planning of programs which I felt were my responsibility as Dean and to this he said, "Well John, there is an opening in the Philippines." I did not say it, but I felt this was a blow beneath the belt because he knew of my difficult Philippine experience, but I kept my cool.

I replied, " No Lani, I don't think I want to return to the Philippines." I was trapped in the Philippines and escaped, but now I felt trapped in Hawaii and the only answer was another escape.

In January, 1970, Bishop Hanchett asked our Senior Warden, Nat Potter, our Treasurer, Harlan Benner, and myself to meet with him over his plans for the Cathedral. We were told we would get his plans before the Annual Meeting of the Cathedral Congregation. Both of these laymen, along with other fine Chapter members, eventually resigned as he began to amalgamate Diocesan and Cathedral operations. About a week later the Bishop came to my office and said he could write some friends and help me relocate. All the tension building up seemed like a nightmare. Again, I repeated I would write my own letters and it would take six months to two years to find another job, but I would appreciate a good recommendation.

Finally, in February, the Bishop and I had a lengthy conference. Among other things regarding the merger of the

Diocese and Cathedral operations he said, "There's another serious matter. We have to talk turkey about your relocation. There is no need for a Bishop and a Dean at the Cathedral. July lst is the date for the merger operation — we need to set a date for you to move and go to another job."

I said, "But Bishop, the Cathedral Chapter is the hiring body and I have a letter of contract with them."

Then he said, "I have financial problems." I replied, "But, I don't think the Diocesan financial problems have anything to do with my tenure."

It was obvious our relationship was polarized and I had to go. Nevertheless, I went to a good lawyer and an Episcopalian and told him about the situation. He looked into the Canons of the National Church, Diocese and Cathedral and found the removal of a Rector or Dean of an Episcopal congregation was extremely difficult and the matter of my tenure would have to be decided by the Chapter. This body had been heavily padded by Hanchett supporters at the Annual Meeting. Furthermore, I did not want to get into a legal battle with the Bishop and the Diocese. At this point all I wanted to do was to go elsewhere, painful as this would be for Elnora and myself. (The soldier in me had no fight left for this kind of political battle. It was something I would have never anticipated happening in the church — war yes, but not in the church.)

I began writing letters about a job, which was a bit humbling, but had to be done. Just after Easter there was another Dean's Conference at the Cathedral in Washington, D.C., so on the way I stopped in Springfield to see my family. My sister, Janie McGregor, knowing of the situation had recently seen retired Bishop Henry Hobson and he mentioned that there was an opening for a rector at St. Albans Church, Bexley, Ohio. After a few telephone calls, I got in touch with the Senior Warden, Mr. Bill Smith, who arranged for me to meet the Search Committee upon my return from Washington. After meeting with his committee, I returned to Honolulu and told Elnora about the possibility of this job. In June we both flew to

Columbus, Ohio, where St. Albans is located in the suburb of Bexley, which is now a small municipality surrounded by the much larger city and state capital. I had known the little church and its Rector, the Rev. Bob Leake years ago. A number of the congregation had been classmates and fraternity brothers at Ohio State University.

When Elnora saw the little church and its red doors she was shocked and did not like the idea of going to Columbus after beautiful Honolulu and the handsome Cathedral. She literally wept the night we stayed at the Christopher Inn in downtown Columbus at the time of our interview. She hated leaving our beautiful home on Tantalus Drive overlooking Diamond Head, Waikiki and Pearl Harbor. Over the past twenty-one years she had made many friends and the sunny environment of Hawaii was just right for her. Still, I felt I was in a time-bind with a date to leave St. Andrews, and even if I won with the Chapter, there was the problem of raising funds for the next year's budget which I had no stomach for under the circumstances. On the other hand, St. Albans Church was in my old diocese and I would be near my family in Springfield, which was only forty-five miles away. We had been separated for a long time except for furloughs. Consequently, to Elnora's great disappointment, in June I accepted the call. Even though prayers were said, and she wanted me to stay and fight, I did not want to struggle with the Bishop any longer and such action would be a very poor witness of the church to the world.

Returning to Honolulu I wrote my letter of resignation to the Chapter asking that it be effective August 1st and it was accepted with sincere regrets. One of the society editors wrote a nice long article about Elnora July 21st which included a large picture of her on our lanai. She was called, "The Wahine of the Week" in the *Star Bulletin.* (Wahine is Hawaiian for woman). Other kind articles were printed about our work and departure from the Islands. Since we had so many good friends in Honolulu there were a lot of farewell parties ending up with a delightful banquet at the Coral Ballroom of the Hilton Hawaiian Village with seven hundred in attendance, including the Governor and Mayor. The speeches and lovely gifts, including a resolution from the City Council affirming my ministry, overwhelmed us. Lorraine Cooke, Elnora's sister, gave a beautiful party the night before our departure, inviting a tremendous number of close friends to say "Aloha". So we left Honolulu, broken-hearted yet grateful to God for so many close and dear friends who still cared for us in spite of the unhappy circumstances which caused us to leave.

I ended twenty-one years in Hawaii — without bitterness but numb. Before leaving, I ran into a prominent business executive one day on the street. We began talking about Bishop Lani Hanchett and the circumstances of the church. He said, "You know what the problem here is don't you?"

I said, "No, I'm confused about it, quite frankly. All I really want to do is to help the church and the community, and I've been asked to leave."

"But John, it's the Peter Principle at work," he said.

"What's the Peter Principle?" I asked.

He replied, "Well John, the principle is that some people function very well at one level of responsibility in an organization, but should never go any higher since they can't handle it. Lani was never cut out to be a Diocesan Bishop and run a diocese."

That, at least, was one opinion of a business executive who knew quite a bit about organizational management. Spiritually, in my opinion, Lani Hanchett was a man of God, a dedicated priest and undoubtedly a good rector of a moderately sized church like St. Peters. But when it came to running a complex diocese, let alone a big cathedral, he had neither the experience, the theological training, persona, or executive ability. After I left St. Andrews he ran into a multitude of problems, one of which was hiring a part-time dean who was also running a full-time real estate business. He tried to turn the old Diocesan House into a runaway shelter between the Priory and the Cathedral and the Sisters vigorously opposed it, thus the shelter was moved elsewhere. The effort failed. On the basis of needing money, he worked to put up a high rise building on the Cathedral grounds for income purposes and ran into trouble with the Planning Department of the city and St. Peter's Church, and, after considerable cost, the project was abandoned. He dismissed the Priory Board of Directors when they, too, opposed the high rise proposal. He was always defensive with a clergy association which had been formed before his election and who had been willing to help him. However, if there was a disagreement over something, he saw them as disloyal, which only helped to polarize things. He made drastic cuts in the music budget at St. Andrews Cathedral, destroyed the choir of men and boys and substantially cut back John McCreary's salary, which caused a lot of stress since John was extremely popular and appreciated. $10,000 was raised from the general community to keep him on the staff. The Sunday morning radio broadcast was terminated, the Cathedral library abandoned, and the Day Care Center for working mothers and the Mallory Players were discontinued. The Diocesan and Cathedral offices were amalgamated, many supporters of the Cathedral cancelled their pledges and dropped out or moved to other churches. As the bad news filtered back to me I was glad to be out of the mess with its bad morale problem, but saddened over those who struggled in what had become a very poor spiritual climate.

Amazingly, the church survived its internal problems as it has for centuries. As far back as the Old Testament, we learn of Israel's survival after periods of trauma. St. Paul mentions in First Corinthians the divisions in the early church over leadership. "When you are jealous of one another and divide up into quarreling groups, doesn't that prove you are still babies, wanting your own way? In fact, you are acting like people who don't belong to the Lord at all." I Cor.3:3. Bishop Hanchett had his loyal followers, as did I. He developed a deep pastoral relationship with some clergy during his terrible bout of cancer which brought an early death. Happily, God changed the tide of things when the Rt. Rev. Edmond Browning was elected Diocesan Bishop. He was an experienced and well-traveled leader who was able to turn things around. But for me, I had lost another big battle — first Bataan, then my beloved China, and now Hawaii. Oddly, this was much tougher than the other two, but like on the death march, I had to keep going.

The war and prison camps in large measure were physical and national defeats, but in spite of them I could continue as a soldier and a lay minister under the most challenging circumstances. But losing my job at the Cathedral was an inner, personal set back from which recovery would be difficult. Strangely, I wasn't angry at anyone, not God, not Lani Hanchett or Bishop Kennedy, who somehow seemed in the shadows of it all. Bishop Kennedy had once said to me early in my ministry in Hawaii that he hoped an Hawaiian would succeed him. In this he got his wish, but later, I sometimes wondered if he was happy with the selection of a man who was unprepared for the big job. But, I was mainly sorry for Elnora who had to be a part of this. Yet, I did not feel defeated, only cut down to face another different challenge in the ministry.

19

BACK TO THE PARISH

There had been a great many changes in my ministerial life. I had been through a process of change from an overseas missionary, to a domestic missionary, to a rector, to a dean of a Cathedral, and back to rector of a parish in twenty-three years. It would seem that I had some downward mobility, but change is often good for us. I had been in and out of the mainland U. S. since 1941, with twenty-one years in Hawaii. A few people who had known me for many years said, "Jack, at last you have come home!" With some truth to this, there seemed to be some kind of challenge ahead, although I could not see any serious one in Bexley, Ohio. I had a suspicion I had gotten myself locked into something I might not like. The Rt. Rev. Philip McNairy, Bishop of Minnesota, just two weeks after I accepted the call to go to St. Albans, wrote and asked if I would be interested in being considered Dean for his cathedral, but I had already committed myself. Also, I had made up my mind I wanted to be near my family in Springfield and in the Columbus region, which I knew something about.

Columbus was becoming the largest city in Ohio with well over a million people in the metropolitan area. The economy was stabilized by light industry, huge federal and state payrolls, central banks and insurance companies and

Ohio State University, which had 50,000 students on one campus. I was challenged by the fact that Columbus had interesting urban problems, not just in terms of rapid growth but also because of the large black population in the inner city. Across the Olentangy River there was an area called "the bottoms," where many of the poor white population lived in deteriorating dwellings.

Bexley was something else again. It was a small city located in a two-and-one-half square mile area with a population of 15,000 people. It is roughly three miles from downtown Columbus and the larger city had completely surrounded it years ago. It was separately incorporated with its own Mayor, City Council, police force and public schools. Columbus serviced its needs for water, power, sewage disposal and fire department. Bexley took great pride in its school system which was the reason it became a separate municipality. The only civic institutions were Capital University of 2,000 students, Trinity Lutheran Seminary, and Columbus School for Girls (private). These institutions were several blocks from the church. Consequently, in some sense I had gotten myself into an all white community with the exception of a few black families, who had bought homes in Bexley about the time of my arrival. In every respect it was stable, a typically American upper and middle class community with prime real estate property.

St. Alban's is located on Drexel Avenue, between the large arteries of Broad and Main Streets which go east and west through Columbus. The street is tree lined and peaceful. The small, white New England-style church with a tiny steeple is on about an acre of land with no off-street parking and no room to expand. The main building had one distinctive feature, two bright red entrance doors that open into a small nave. A red brick split level educational building is located just behind the church and beside it is a nice lawn. Inside the parish hall, attached to the main church building, is a lounge, giving the feeling of intimacy and making the church feel very much like a home. The lounge area was the original building and as a mission was called "the chicken coop."

By this description one can see how these facilities stood in sharp contrast to the Cathedral of St. Andrew's and the many accompanying buildings which surrounded the large Gothic edifice, and in contrast to Holy Nativity with its large school facilities and youth center. The Cathedral seated eight hundred and Holy Nativity four hundred fifty. At St. Albans the small nave seated around two hundred people, crowded in. Elnora was shocked when she first saw St. Albans.

We had looked at houses in Bexley when we made our initial visit to consider the job. We could not find anything we liked and there were not too many from which to choose. To the consternation of some Bexley parishioners we bought a home on Walnut Cliffs Drive, a good four miles from the church. The house was new and Elnora had no objection to it but it couldn't compare to the Deanery which was a large, beautiful home with spectacular views. However, the die was cast and we both held up our heads, as it were, thanking God for our many blessings but, it was hard!

The parish staff was made up of a young curate who had been three years in the parish, so he was ready to have his own church. Miss Betty Varney was the Christian Education Director, who had been on the staff a number of years and was loved and appreciated. She knew everyone from grandparents to parents, children, uncles and aunts, and knew a lot about the little city. She was a great help to me right from the start. Since she had been in the parish about ten years, she told me she had been considering leaving but would stay on if I wanted her to. There were three part-time people: a secretary, janitor and organist.

The parish life was largely built around the Sunday services, an active Woman's Guild, Altar Guild, a small prayer group mainly made up of elderly women, a strong children's choir, small adult choir, acolytes, and a small youth group. Shortly before my arrival, an adult forum which scheduled some excellent speakers was started on a Sunday morning. St. Edward's mission on the outskirts of eastern Columbus was started by St. Albans. It was a credit to the church's vision for outreach.

The lay leadership was long term, made up mostly of people who held executive or professional positions in the community. I think it fair to say most of them were not well versed in Scripture, but they were sensitive, intelligent people who took responsibility seriously and comfortable to be around. Most parishioners were college graduates, belonged to the Columbus Country Club, others to the Rocky Fork Hunt Club, the Columbus Club (for men only) in downtown Columbus, and the University Club. There was a great deal of interest in the Columbus Symphony, Art Gallery and the University, and some men were interested in the expansion of the larger city of Columbus.

The membership wasn't small, it ranged from six to seven hundred communicants, two hundred fifty to two hundred eighty persons in attendance at three services on a Sunday morning and fifty to sixty children in the church school. Decisions were generally made in a cooperative manner. Growth came mainly from transfers or by friendship and association in broad areas of community life. There seemed to be a real loyalty to the parish, extending through two and three generations, although church attendance and pledging in many cases did not reflect this. Most parishioners were quite busy in business and social activity. Only a few, at the time I went there, seemed interested in church related services such as a food pantry, relocation of refugees, or the serious problems of the inner city. There was no group Bible study going on, and I believe it is fair to say no real vision of what God's church could be under the powerful leadership of Jesus Christ in the Holy Spirit. It seemed to me that it was a fine operating church organization, but for the most part it was not an organism of spirit-filled Christians. God was not allowed to inspire every moment of their lives as He does in what is now commonly called "an alive church." Nevertheless, the parishioners were friendly and made a sincere effort to make us feel welcome and wanted. Coffees were organized in neighborhoods so we could get to know people on a personal basis.

Almost from the start I began spending a good deal of time alone in the church reading the Bible and praying before going to work. I had loved the spiritual classics of the past such as Thomas A. Kempis "Imitation of Christ," Evelyn Underhill's, "The House of the Soul," and, by an unknown author, "The Cloud of Unknowing." I returned to this kind of reading as well as the Bible and also started to enjoy the spiritual writings of a new Catholic author, Henri J.M. Nouwen. My growing spiritual library was one of my most precious possessions and it was a good resource now. After being so busy at the Cathedral, particularly in social action activities, I knew I needed a deeper spiritual life again, and in the process I needed to allow God to heal some of my hurts. So I relished my time with God alone, more than ever. In total self-honesty, I didn't want to be in Bexley and would have been far happier overseas someplace, but circumstances brought me to this church in a somewhat wealthy, conservative community. I didn't feel it necessary to discuss openly why I had made the change from Honolulu to Columbus, and when asked I simply said it seemed time for me to return to my old Diocese and to be near my home, and added, there seemed to be a challenge in Columbus.

It wasn't long until I was involved in the local clergy association, which was about dead, so I helped to revive it with a fine Presbyterian clergyman, the Rev. Keith Conning. At the parish we developed a music committee to support the organist and to consider the purchase of a pipe organ to replace the electronic one. A lovely older woman who was dedicated to the parish wanted to help me start a "Calling Committee" of laity who would call on our many elderly and shut-ins and take the Sunday altar flowers to those sick in the hospitals. We organized such a committee which began meeting once a month for lunch and soon became a marvelous extension of the pastoral ministry. Because the National Church was finalizing a new prayer book, a worship committee was formed to deal with this change and I began a trial "use." I also felt it necessary to set up a long-range planning committee to decide on a stated purpose for the parish and set up some long range goals. There were other functioning committees of the Vestry such as Finance, Christian Education, Building and Grounds, Stewardship, and Social Concerns which seemed to function very well.

In terms of social action, I was asked to serve on the Maryhaven Board of Directors for Alcoholic Women, which I found very interesting, and on occasion I would attend a large AA group meeting using the parish hall three nights a week as well as the Al-Anon Group on Friday mornings. Wanting to relate to the City of Columbus, the Senior Warden, Bill Smith, a lawyer, and John McCoy, President of City National Bank, helped me organize businessmen's luncheons once a month to consider urban affairs. To make a connection with the black community, I developed a sincere relationship with a black pastor, the Rev. Robert Meyers and in time became a good friend of the Metropolitan Baptist Church, located in the inner city. Some dedicated laymen began to join me in this relationship and we were able to contribute some land for expansion of the Baptist facilities. To link our church with "the bottoms" area on the west side of Columbus, a few members of the laity and I became supportive of Mr. Chrislie Fair, who ran a food pantry out of the basement of a declining Episcopal Church. So in a real sense, as a parish, we began reaching out beyond our comfortable borders of Bexley to the city of Columbus. Enthusiasm was limited, but there were Christians ready and willing to follow my lead. Some individuals were already involved in this work in their own quiet and individual way. Soon after my arrival at St. Alban's I attended a conference on "New Models of Parish Organization and Ministry," and an Institute on Futurology. These events were important to me, because, as a church, we were in the process of radical liturgical and organizational change. For the nation we were in a process of extensive sociological and scientific change. Now that I was on the mainland it seemed important for me to be in contact with people on the cutting edge of the church and the world. A person who came to my particular attention at these events was the Rev. Dr. Reuel Howe, who had left the faculty of the Virginia Seminary to found the School of Advanced Pastoral Studies at Bloomfield, Michigan and for whom I had had great admiration when I first met him at the College of Preachers. At the Futurology Conferences there were such men as Dr. Herman Kahan, Director of the Hudson Institute and who really excited me as far as the future was concerned.

At this point I was feeling that the traditional Anglican form of worship which I had known all my life with the 1928 Prayer Book, and our formal worship setting, beautiful as it is, was not meeting the spiritual needs of most people living in the twentieth century. It brought great comfort and a spiritual connection with God for some, but not all Episcopalians, and to outsiders it was a lot of ritual but lacking in free-form spirituality. A well known priest of our church, the Rev. Terry Fullam, was saying, "The Episcopal Church is a Cadillac running on a flat tire." I also sensed, at the time, some disengagement with the secular world which was moving so fast it threatened to over-run our church with its dwindling membership. About this time I read Archbishop Arthur Michael Ramsey's book, "The Sacred and the Secular" — a study in the other worldly and this worldly aspects of Christianity. He put things neatly in perspective for me.

"Sacred and secular, other worldly and this worldly, my conclusion is that Christianity is uncompromisingly both, both not in a facile Anglican or archespicopal compromise, but in a costly inter-relation. We follow Christ who, in the form of a servant, made himself utterly one with humanity and history, but was no less so, but rather drew the power to be so because he was found a great while before day alone in the desert place praying to the Father. As Christ was in the world and not of the world, so is the church called to be." (page 70)

In this time of internal struggle with the institutional church and the rapid movement of the secular world, my prayer life was my salvation. It was an anchor in a time of rapid cultural change, moving almost at breakneck speed, especially in the field of computer sciences. Yet, here I was, stuck in a church which seemed on dead center in terms of spiritual growth, and I was afraid I couldn't move it.

While I was wrestling with problems on the big mainland with its rapid advances in the secular sphere, I was struggling for a deeper faith as kind of a displaced person. Elnora took her frustration out in the secular side of things. She helped organize women's fashion shows at the Columbus Country Club, promoted a "Mad Hatter's" party in the parish hall and did a lot of entertaining to get to know the parishioners, and those on the social circuit gravitated to her. After I was asked to bless the Rocky Fork Hunt in the fall, I began riding in the hunt, jumping (with my heart in my mouth) over the high ones. Dr. Trent Smith, Master of the Hunt, loaned me a wonderful mare named, "House Call" and she took good care of me. My son Scott was now out of the Air Force, having served in Vietnam, and began attending Ohio State. Lisa attended the Columbus School for Girls, and Danny was about to finish a three year stint in the Army.

One day Elnora came into the house all excited. She had run into a parishioner who had recently married. Her new husband had left his own residence on Preston Road to live with her. His house was now up for sale, located just outside of Bexley on a lovely tree-lined street zoned as a part of Columbus. With her imagination Elnora saw all kinds of possibilities in the empty house when she went inside to look it over. I made an offer to purchase it and it was accepted. Catherine, Elnora's sister, who was doing interior decorating in Los Angeles, came to Columbus and helped Elnora select wallpaper, curtains, carpeting, etc. It seemed that Elnora had finally established herself in Columbus, Ohio! This was another culture shock for her and I felt she was heroic in facing it.

Not long after we arrived in Columbus, the Rt. Rev. Roger Blanchard, Bishop of the Diocese of Southern Ohio resigned and went to New York to help restructure the National Council offices. The Rev. Dr. John McGill Krumm was elected bishop. He had an earned doctorate, served a number of years as Chaplain of Columbia University, N.Y., and had years of experience with various churches. He was an excellent administrator, preacher and theologian, and related well with people because of his warm friendliness and delightful wit. I was thrilled to be able to work under him. He knew of my keen interest in foreign missions and so asked me to serve on a committee with the fancy title "Mutual Responsibility and Interdependence in the Body of Christ (M.R.I.). This program was a visionary brainchild of Bishop Stephen Bayne who served, at the conclusion of his career, as Executive Officer of the Anglican Consultative Council — the umbrella body of the whole Anglican Communion.

The program created companionship dioceses around the world which were to last a period of six years. Very often self-supporting dioceses were linked with missionary dioceses overseas for mutual spiritual support and in some cases material support on the part of domestic, self-supporting dioceses. Bishop Krumm appointed Bill Hoyer, one of our laymen at St. Albans, as chairman. We were fraternity brothers from university days and close friends.

In a short space of time our diocese picked up a relationship with the Diocese of Hong Kong. Because Bishop Krumm became ill, I represented him in going to Hong Kong and formally establishing a relationship in 1972. Since I had known Bishop Baker, the Diocesan, and his wife Patty in Shanghai in 1947-48, I was thrilled to be going back to the Far East and to see old missionary friends again.

Well over one million refugees had poured into the British Colony since 1949, and by now were pretty well integrated into the life of this great seaport. Elnora and I spent ten full days there visiting churches, schools and social service centers both on Victoria Island and Kowloon. There were by then 50,000 students in our Anglican day schools. Because of resettlement problems, the various churches sponsored centers for the handicapped, aged, youth, the trades, and a strong mission to seamen. While there I received an excellent briefing at the American Embassy about Hong Kong and Mainland China. God had put me in touch again with my favorite mission field.

Since we were half-way around the world at the end of our visit, we continued on to Singapore, Bombay, Cairo, Istanbul and Paris. Always interested in world politics and the fact that the U.S. had broken off formal relations with Egypt I received a good briefing about American-Arab relations from one of our diplomats now housed in the Spanish Embassy. We flew on to Istanbul, Turkey, where again I had a briefing about our relations with that Muslim country while Elnora had a grand time bargaining at the bazaars. I never ceased to be amazed at what she could get out of a merchant. You always had to bargain with the Arabs or they thought something was wrong with you. From Istanbul we flew to Paris to see our old friends, the Burton McLeans. Burt was former headmaster of Iolani School, Hawaii, and now headmaster of the American School in Paris.

By 1973, Elnora and I were well into the life of St. Albans. She had begun to feel comfortable about living in the Mid-West even though it would never be her choice of a home environment. An old friend from Beverly High School days, Beverly Clark, moved to Columbus with her husband Martin, who was also originally from California. They had been living in Florida and moved to Columbus when Martin was made President of Gold Circle Stores, an affiliate of Federated Department Stores. They had recently experienced a "Faith Alive" weekend at their parish and had become "turned on" Christians. Martin talked to me about sponsoring one at St. Albans which I felt, by now, definitely needed some sort of renewal (even though I knew some in the parish would be cool to it). However, I was beginning to realize that there was more spirituality in the parish than I had thought when I came in 1970.

At one time I had asked Mrs. Harold Stallman to give a meditation at a Wednesday morning Eucharist and I was amazed at how beautifully she presented it. Soon I began asking other women to do the same thing and suddenly realized I had discovered a gold mine of spirituality. Some women were better than others but it made no difference, the women were beginning to disclose what was going on in their inner lives and I was impressed. The seven o'clock early Eucharist began to pick up in numbers and I sensed a lovely feeling of Christian community in that early congregation. Many attending would go to breakfast afterwards and I discovered that they were pastoring each other when there was a need. This was thrilling, and there was evidence of a quiet spirituality and congregational growth.

In October, 1973, Lorraine Cooke, Elnora's other sister was coming to visit us and we were planning a nice dinner party for her on Tuesday evening, October 24th. All the twenty-four guests had been invited, the house was cleaned, a caterer was scheduled to come in to help and the house was decorated with flowers. Suddenly the day before her scheduled arrival we received a telephone call from Lorraine that her plans had been changed and she was not to arrive until late Thursday afternoon. Elnora frantically telephoned all the guests changing the date to Thursday night and reorganized for the party. Lorraine arrived at six o'clock p.m. and the party had been set for eight o'clock.

It turned out to be a lovely evening. Elnora was beautifully dressed as always and about ten-thirty p.m., when people were close to leaving, someone asked her to dance the hula. She had two favorites: "Lovely Hula Hands" and "To You Sweetheart Aloha." Her sweet smile, sparkling eyes and graceful movements charmed everyone. It was a perfect ending to the evening and the Ohioans went home thrilled with their lovely hostess. However, Elnora went to bed exhausted.

The next morning around nine o'clock Elnora, Lorraine and I were in the kitchen. As Elnora closed the refrigerator door, she turned to me and said, "Oh, John, I'm terribly dizzy." I took her into the sun room where she lay on the couch. She became nauseated and I carried her upstairs to our bedroom. I laid her on the bed and got a towel. While Lorraine watched her, I telephoned Dr. Reuben Hoover to ask him to come to the house right away. He and his wife Betty had been at the party the night before and so were aware of some of the pressure Elnora had been under with the change of date for the dinner, due to Lorraine's revised arrival.

"Reub" came to the house in about ten minutes, gave Elnora something to relax her and after making a few checks over her body said, "John, watch her closely and telephone me if necessary. She should stay in bed all day and simply rest."

He then left and Lorraine, who was with us, returned to the kitchen. Shortly, Elnora began looking gray and said, "John, sit on the bed with me," which I did.

Then she said, "Hold me," so I took her in my arms. Then she feebly said, "I love you." That was all and she went limp. I called down to Lorraine who rushed upstairs, took one look at Elnora and exclaimed, "Oh, John, she's dying!"

I immediately dashed to the telephone and called Dr. Hoover's office, but the nurse said he had not returned as yet, so I should call the emergency squad, and she gave me the number. The squad appeared very quickly and went to work on her body. They gave her an intravenous shot and put her on a stretcher to go to Grant Hospital. The siren screeched as the ambulance dashed down East Broad Street with Elnora completely unconscious and with a medical man and me in the back of the ambulance.

After she was taken into the emergency room I waited outside while the doctors worked on her body to keep her alive. Lorraine came and then Dr. Hoover appeared and told me Elnora had had a brain hemorrhage and could die. My sister appeared, having made a mad dash from Springfield after Lorraine telephoned her, and looking at Janie I literally fell apart. How could my beautiful Elnora die, and so suddenly? Then I thought of all the things I should have done for her in the tough job of being a minister's wife. I could have relieved her of so much stress over the years. I began to cry in an uncontrollable way, something I would never have imagined doing.

Finally, she was taken to a room and put on heart and lung machines to keep her body alive. At some point in the evening Bishop Krumm arrived and said a beautiful prayer for her and for me. The hospital chaplain had also been very attentive, knowing the critical situation. I was so grateful for both men.

Sometime early in the morning the nurses advised me to go home, which I did, needing to shower and shave, although sleep was impossible. Before returning to the hospital Dr. Bill Pace, a surgeon in the congregation, came to the house and said, "John, there is no hope. Blood is in her brain and spinal column, she will not live very long and there is no activity in the brain whatsoever. Will you give her up and give the kidneys away?"

There was only one answer to that and I said, "Yes. " I knew how desperately people needed kidneys and I did not want her to live like a vegetable. In a very short time she was dead. My dearest "Sparkle plenty" was gone. I was devastated, and in fact in real shock — one day she was alive and vibrant and beautiful, the next she was gone. It all seemed like a bad dream, but yet it was true, my beautiful, vibrant Elnora was dead.

Sally Pace came over to the house and helped me contact the family. Lisa flew in from Denver where she was in the Colorado College for Women, Catherine Older flew in from Los Angeles, and Scott, the last to come, flew in from Honolulu. Dan had been discharged from the Army and was with us in Columbus. The house was soon crowded with parishioners and the women took over answering telephone calls and organizing food for everyone. St. Albans was at its best as it was also trying to absorb what had happened.

On Tuesday there was a lovely memorial service at the church and then Lorraine and I flew with the urn to Honolulu, where there was another packed service at Holy Nativity. We placed her urn in the columbarium where so many other parishioners who had helped build the church were laid to rest. When I conceived of the idea, I never dreamed my own wife would be placed there before me, and so soon.

Dick and Lorraine Cooke took me to their home up in the mountains on Molokai where there was a beautiful view of the pineapple fields and in the distance the ocean. For a while it poured rain as if the skies were literally weeping, and then it suddenly stopped. I walked out on the lanai and saw a beautiful rainbow — God was saying to me, "Things will be all right."

Recovery from grief takes time. I returned to Columbus heavy-hearted and literally feeling like half a person. I had seen so much of death during the war and conducted so many funerals that I thought I knew a lot about death, but there had never been an experience like this in intensity. After several months of sheer inner pain and a kind of dull, emotional hurt which is hard to describe unless one has been through it, Elnora came to me in a dream. She looked perfectly beautiful, smiling, her lovely figure in full view and she said, "John, I'm all right." That was a great comfort, but I still missed her terribly. So much in the house, recently redecorated, spoke of her invisible presence and creativity. When I would go to the supermarket my eyes would always seem to fix on couples shopping and I yearned for that husband and wife relationship which was now no longer. I felt so utterly alone.

Christmas was a bit softened by a visit from a Chinese couple from Hong Kong but now at a seminary and visiting St. Alban's for the holidays. Lisa returned from college. In the fall before going back to the Colorado Women's College in Denver, she had said she was going to finish up her semester in

February and then attend Ohio State University to get her degree. This meant a lot to me. At O.S.U. she pledged PiPhi, her mother's sorority at U.S.C. This was good, especially since she felt she was following in the footsteps of her mother. But I was still having trouble with my grief. I told Lisa that if I were to continue in a healthy way in the ministry I needed to break out of the grief syndrome. She understood since she was feeling a lot of it, too. However, she had the new and exciting life at the university and in the fall she was runner up in the contest for campus queen.

I wrote Bishop Gilbert Baker in Hong Kong and asked if there was some supply work I could do for a month. He responded, telling me about a priest who was about to go on furlough to England. He needed someone to take his place at Christ Church, Kowloon in May. Also, it came to my attention that there was a two week course at the Ecumenical Institute in Bosey, Switzerland, sponsored by the World Council of Churches, beginning the second week in June. The theme of the course was: "The Church in Search of Community Life." I spoke to Bob Leake about supplying for two months, which he agreed to do and the vestry approved.

So, on May 5th, 1974, off I went again to the Far East, lonely but challenged, and supplied at Christ Church until June 9th. It was just what I needed. Services were all in English and there were a number of Britishers in the congregation. The M.R.I. link to Hong Kong seemed to be enhanced and I met some lovely Chinese people in the congregation whose friendships have continued over the years. I did date the Chinese English-speaking secretary several times and she was a lovely person, but I knew nothing could ever develop out of the relationship. Since there was a two week period between the work at Christ Church, Hong Kong and the course at Bosey, Switzerland, I traveled to Kathmandu, Nepal; Teheran, Isfahan and Sheraz in Iran and then to Geneva, Switzerland. Nepal and Iran were fascinating. It was interesting to see the syncretism of Hinduism and Buddhism in Nepal and to fly over Mt.

Everest. The crown jewels of the Shah of Iran, the gigantic mosques of Isfahan and the ruins of Persepolis, the ancient capital of Persia at Sheraz were also extremely interesting. I was amazed at the beauty of the Persian culture, but still there was someone missing with whom to share these marvelous sights — Elnora. How she would have loved them! "Life is to be shared" was a phrase that kept running over and over in my mind.

The Ecumenical Institute as a part of the World Council of Churches drew Christians from many nations. The theme for the two week period, "The Church in Search of Community Life," was based around hundreds of small Christian communities that have surfaced in Europe, chiefly outside the organized church. Some were monastic in nature, but many were made up of sincere Christians who simply lived and worked together in order to have a sense of close Christian community life. The groups scheduled time for the study of Scripture, prayer, discussion, work details and, in many cases, worked at secular jobs to help support the little community. It was evident these people were realizing an authentic spirituality which they did not seem to find in the organized church. The key to the existence of these communities was sincere relationships in Christ on a daily basis rather than simply coming together with like-minded Christians on a Sunday morning. In any case, this experience intensified my concern for St. Alban's as a Christian community, above and beyond the institutional church structure.

20

RENEWAL

As I returned to Columbus I made up my mind I wasn't going through life alone; I was going to re-marry because I hated being single. Elnora and I had developed a lovely companionship, especially when traveling and I desperately wanted that again — someone to eat and sleep with, someone to talk intimately to and to share my hurts and joys . . almost next to talking with God. I felt there was a need of renewal in my own life as strong as a need for renewal in the church.

Not long after I arrived back a friend, Eloise Shropshire, telephoned and suggested I bring Joani Germanson to a dinner party at her home on Friday night. Joani, I discovered later, was twenty years younger, an inactive Episcopalian who had one daughter, age twelve named Christa. She had an older daughter, "Alex," who had died suddenly of a brain hemorrhage in 1971. Eloise informed me that Joani was attractive, taught ballet classes for a living and had been divorced about six years. She was living in a garage apartment back of her grandmother's house, one block away from my own home on Preston Road.

Joani and I went to the party together and had a nice time, but when taking her home I said to myself, "She's not for me — much too young since I'm fifty-eight and she is thirty-eight." Also, it seemed apparent that she had no interest in the organized church, having dropped out of St. Paul's Episcopal Church where she had been a member years before. Nevertheless, several weeks later, going through my usual lonely evening when Lisa was out on a date, I noticed a movie advertised in the newspaper titled, *That's Entertainment*. Apparently there was a lot of dancing in it, so I telephoned Joani suggesting she might like to see it with me. It included some of the old dance stars like Fred Astaire, Ginger Rogers and Gene Kelley, who danced his famous routine, "Singing in the Rain." On returning home we passed the Ohio State Fair Grounds which was to open the next week, and since I had never seen a fair, I suggested we go, especially to see the horse show. It wasn't long until I was talking to Lisa about my dates with Joani and she would tell me about her dates with Ohio State men. We had fun together laughing and giggling throughout these conversations. Soon I was using the term, "back alley romance," since I would walk out of my backyard and down the alley to Joani's garage apartment. It wasn't long until I kissed her, and soon proposed marriage. Despite twenty years difference in age, we seemed compatible; she liked adventure and was prepared to travel with me any place in the world. Since her father, a flyer, had been killed in Ceylon (Sri Lanka) during an air raid by the Japanese in WWII, I promised her we would visit his grave some day. I did not know exactly when but of one thing I was certain, my traveling days were not over.

Just prior to our marriage Joani gave me three of her religious books which she had loved, one being on "The Mind of Christ." At this point I realized there was a beautiful inner spirituality in her which would bring into our relationship a depth I needed in my life. She obviously knew God intimately and not by hearsay. She was seeking the relevancy of God in life above and beyond the immediacy of her human existence. I sensed that now I was to have not just a wife and homemaker, but a spiritual companion as well — and that was exciting!

Our short but lovely romance was carried on with few people at St. Alban's Church knowing about it. I realized there was a spiritual side to Joani, but she, for her own reasons, did not want to attend Sunday services until after we were married. Several weeks prior to our marriage, Joani's grandmother, Mrs. Lester Bush, known by everyone as "Dearie," gave a reception at her home announcing the engagement and the coming event. On November 3, 1974, we were married at St. Alban's Church by the Rev. Robert Leake, with only our families in attendance. Following the ceremony there was a lovely reception at "Dearie's" home. We went to Hawaii for our honeymoon and life, for me, was once again in balance.

As to the renewal of the church, the theme of the institute at Bosey, "The Church in Search of Community Life," seemed to be related to the "Faith Alive" program which had now become prominent in the Episcopal Church. It's central focus on the Person of Christ was absolutely clear. I worked closely with Martin Clark, who helped get a Faith Alive program organized for the following year. It took place in February, 1975, with Delevan Baldwin, a layman in the Savings and Loan business in Jacksonville, Florida, coming to Columbus at his own expense as coordinator. Martin carefully chose visitors made up of business and professional people who would fit into our congregation. I liked Delevan as soon as I met him. I knew he would give excellent low key addresses and that his fine lay witnesses would be honest, open and enthusiastic Christians.

Some people in the congregation were apprehensive, but the Vestry had approved the program even though no one knew exactly what to expect. The visitors traveled at their own expense so the financial outlay was minimal. The critics were asked to withhold judgment until the event was over.

Lay visitors poured into the church February 2nd from various parts of the country. The Friday evening program went well and there were excellent coffees the next morning at parishioner's homes, followed by lunches for men, women and youth. I had never seen a group of so many outstanding lay persons who told their stories of conversion to Christ in such beautiful ways. Sunday morning the church was electric with anticipation for the final address. I realized then that the Holy Spirit was taking hold of St. Alban's and would move it to deeper levels of Christian commitment and community life. I said to myself, "We need more of this!"

Enthusiasm was still high after Faith Alive was over, so to keep the momentum going, we planned an Advent Mission in 1976 in a effort to create a strong Christian focus on Christmas. The Rev. Robert Hall, author of a good book on renewal entitled, *There's More*, came as spiritual director for three days.

By this time we had developed a strong inner core of committed people, turned on by an ever deepening faith in Jesus Christ. They were not charismatic, nor speaking in tongues, nor turning toward a fundamentalist view of the Bible, although Bible study and prayer groups were readily accepted as a part of their lives. Some of our people began going to Faith Alive Weekends as lay visitors and others went to St. Paul's Church, Darien, Connecticut to attend seminars conducted by the Rev. Terry Fullam — now a strong leader in the renewal movement and an outstanding teacher of the Bible. In 1979 we had the Rev. Dr. John Guest, Rector of St. Stephen's Church, Swickley, Pennsylvania, come for a four day preaching mission. On the last night, approximately one hundred traditional Episcopalians re-committed themselves to Jesus Christ by signing commitment cards and taking them to the altar.

Finally in 1981, just prior to my retirement, the Rev. Donald Hulstrand, then Executive Director of the Anglican Fellowship of Prayer and author of *The Praying Church*, led a splendid all-parish program on prayer. We had now reached the very center of our Christian religion — a human being's deep, personal relationship with God through Jesus Christ in prayer. Those who attended the renewal programs grew in Spirit because they allowed the third person of the Trinity, the Holy Spirit, to touch them. Those who stood on the sidelines went untouched, but in my opinion, in the words of Jesus, they missed "the pearl of great price." Maybe the time was not right for some, but those of us involved were grateful for what God was doing in our lives now.

Over the six year period of renewal at St. Alban's Church what were some of the fallouts? One thing was evident, certain Christians became excited about their faith and could now be lay witnesses in public with ease and assurance. They wanted more in-depth Bible study in order to learn of God's word in Scripture; they appreciated more than ever the value of personal and corporate prayer life and could pray extemporaneously rather than needing a prayer book to guide them in their communication with God. I was amazed at the way the laity volunteered for all-night prayer vigils on Good Friday and their willingness to join in small Christian cell groups, often interdenominational. Joani's mother, Amelia Dewey helped start a library of books and tapes with a display table out every Sunday. It was gratifying to see how our people were taking advantage of this new material.

Joani and I started a "Care and Share" group on a Sunday evening at the Rectory for those who wanted to conclude the Sabbath in a caring and sharing way. A small evangelistic team was organized to reach out and visit the new people who attended a church service. To receive special training for this project, participants went to some sessions at the College Hill Presbyterian Church, Cincinnati, Ohio. Bibles were now placed in all the pews along with the Prayer Books and Hymnals. The choir director was praying with the choir before services. To my joy I began hearing our lay persons tell about how they were talking about their Christian faith within the framework of their secular positions.

After a number of our lay persons had attended the Terry Fullam seminars at St. Paul's Church, Darien, Joani and I attended a clergy-spouse seminar. We knew we had to keep pace with our people and identify with their enthusiasm and spiritual growth. Upon our return, we felt we had been powerfully recharged, spiritually, and that we had focused clearly on the renewal movement in the Episcopal Church. The story about "The Miracle of Darien," by Bob Slosser became our guidebook on where to place the parish emphasis: "To Know Christ (personally) and to Make Him Known." This became the overall purpose of the parish. We were going to emphasize the Lordship of Christ in personal life and Jesus was the Head of the Church — not the Rector, not the Vestry, not the Bishop, not the Diocese. I came to the realization that most Episcopalians over the years had become institutionalized Christians but not evangelized Christians, and for survival in the modern age, simple love and loyalty to the institution was not enough. What I felt deeply during those final years of ministry at St. Alban's was that the Holy Spirit had touched me and the parish in a wonderful way. Our sense of renewal was coupled with social action and became a part of our personal spirituality.

Without any difficulty, we brought to St. Alban's five Vietnamese refugee men and one large Laotian family for resettlement in Columbus. More of our people became active in supporting the food pantry and Central Buying Center in "the bottoms" on the west side. Out of our parish budget went funds to support "The Place to Be," an outreach program of Trinity Church in downtown Columbus. Our businessmen's luncheons took on new depth. For example, Reuben Peterson, from Battelle Institute, talked about nuclear waste disposal in the context of our Christian concern. Our youth program under the Rev. Henry Galganowicz, the curate, became an alive group of young Christians who continued their faith on college campuses.

One of the lovely fallouts from the John Guest preaching mission was the arrival of the Rev. Robert "Chip" Nix as my associate, replacing "Hank" Galganowicz who ended four years of curacy in 1978. "Chip" had been an active member of St. Stephen's Church, Swickley, Pennsylvania, and had been highly influenced by John Guest. He was a natural evangelist and marvelous pastor. We took to each other immediately and found we could develop an excellent team ministry. "Chip" and his wife Carol brought to the parish fine skills in Bible study and Biblical preaching along with warm personalities. With them on board, we began to get the reputation of being an "alive church."

There was one social-action event which had personal ramifications. A pornographic magazine called, *The Hustler* began to be published in Columbus and a sign went up at the airport, "Columbus, the Home of the Hustler." Larry Flynt, the publisher, bought a large home in Bexley, three blocks from the church. The whole community began talking about Larry Flynt and his magazine, which had national circulation. One afternoon when I was taking communion to an elderly woman in her eighties, she asked me if I had seen Hustler magazine. This was just at the time I was setting up the communion vessels on a small table in front of her. She said, "John, do you know what I am sitting on?"

I replied, "No Mina, I haven't the slightest idea."

"Well," she said, "Under the cushion is a recent copy of Hustler magazine; would you like to look at it?"

Smiling, I said, "No Mina, not now, but I would be interested in looking at it later on."

Before leaving she put the porno magazine in a brown paper bag and I took it home to look at the contents. One of the most offensive colored pictures was of a high-rise building under construction. A buxom blonde was standing on a large steel beam being hoisted up by a crane. She was urinating on a priest on the sidewalk in a clerical collar. Naturally, I was offended.

The Hustler magazine was readily available in drug stores and supermarkets where children could be seen looking at them. The porno magazines were showing up in children's bedrooms hidden under mattresses. Larry Flynt was frequently in the newspapers and could be seen around Bexley in a large stretchout sedan.

I went to the Mayor of Columbus with some copies of the Hustler which had offensive pictures and articles relating to the clergy and religion and proposed that the city council do something to stem the growing tide in pornography. If nothing else, it seemed appropriate that the sign, "Columbus, the Home of the Hustler" come down. The Mayor's response was, "Rev. Morrett, pornography has been around for a long time and there isn't anything we can do about it."

I did not say to him that I had seen it in ivory in Peking, in carved images in a wooden temple in Kathmandu, and in magazines on the streets of Hong Kong. It was, and has been, a world problem, but it seemed to me we didn't have to have it flaunted in our faces in Columbus, Ohio. After leaving the Mayor's office it occurred to me that Christians should go public on this offensive matter.

A committee called "Citizens for Public Morality" was formed and $4,000 quickly raised to print full page ads in the morning and evening papers stating that there were citizens who rejected the publicity. How much influence this had on the sign coming down and Larry Flynt moving his operation to California is impossible to say, but at least some Christians reacted by responding to this offensive advertising.

Turning to the Diocese, I shied away from a lot of involvement which would take me away from important pastoral counseling and making calls in the parish. There was always a parish address list with me in the car, and beside each name I recorded the date of a call. I endeavored to call on parishioners at work or in the home each week in a continuing effort to get to know people on a "one-on-one" basis. This was one of the joys of my ministry. Visiting a person at home or at the work place brought a personal relationship which went beyond the Sunday morning contact. Parishioners generally called me "John" rather than "Father" or the incorrect personal address, "Reverend". Although most Bexley people were secure economically there were many who had personal and family problems. My pastoral work was relatively heavy, visiting the sick in hospitals and counseling those in grief following a death in the family. Because of Elnora's untimely death, I had become extremely aware of the grief process people have to go through when a member of the family dies.

In 1973 I became involved with the Diocese as a member of a committee having to do with "Tomorrow's Church", and in 1974 I served as Regional Chairman to help raise two million dollars for the Diocesan Advance Fund.

My contacts with Hong Kong continued as a part of a six-year relationship which we completed in 1977 when the Rev. Leroy Hall went to our overseas companion to round off the relationship. Engraved chalices were exchanged and the Diocese of Southern Ohio made a gift of $20,000 from the Centenary Fund toward the Anglican work in Hong Kong. Along with Bishop Baker, one of it's women priests, the Rev. Jane Huang, visited us. We developed a sincere appreciation of the benefits of women in the priesthood as a result of her visit. She was an outstanding example of this at a time when there was a great deal of interest in our church in the ordination of women. If qualified women like Jane Huang could be in the priesthood I was all for it. All in all, I felt good about what had happened in this MRI relationship and was grateful to Bishop Krumm for having used me on this Diocesan Committee.

After the Hong Kong project was completed, I was asked by Bishop Krumm to chair the Diocesan Commission on National and World Mission. This was formed to find another companion diocese overseas. The complex title, "Mutual Responsibility and Interdependence in the Body of Christ" was changed to P.I.M., "Partners in Mission." The change in name largely came about through the Rt. Rev. John W.A. Howe, Secretary of the Anglican Consultative Council, who proposed that a province to province companionship be developed. Never before in the history of our Anglican world-wide communion had such a challenge been undertaken. The aim of this multi-national endeavor was to create spiritually and mutually supportive links between diverse national, social and cultural groupings within provinces or clusters of dioceses in our communion.

At a meeting of the provincial bishops, Bishop Krumm was designated to develop a formal relationship with the new Province of Nigeria made up of sixteen dioceses under the administration of the Most Rev. T.O. Olufosoye, Archbishop and Bishop of the Diocese of Ibadan. Bishop Krumm, the Rev. Lorentho Wooden (who was a Diocesan staff officer), and I flew to London on November 16, 1979, to meet with Bishop John Howe. From London we flew to Lagos, Nigeria, Africa. Our task was to set up official relations between the two large provinces, and for the Diocese of Southern Ohio we were to set up official relations with the Dioceses of Lagos and Ijebu. Lagos was an urban diocese and Ijebu a rural diocese, adjacent to each other. For eight days Bishop Krumm led our small group of emissaries to the Nigerian Church. Because of the pressure of business Bishop Krumm returned to Cincinnati. Lorentho Wooden, along with a young woman deacon (who had been in Mawali) and I, traveled through the rest of the Nigerian dioceses working on the Partners in Mission project and beginning to set up a communications network.

Traveling through West Africa was a fascinating experience. However, there were many problems. Infrastructure was always breaking down: electricity, water, traffic control, telephones, etc. Oil resources had brought Nigeria a great deal of wealth but efforts toward modernization were difficult. The major cities were crowded as thousands of tribal people migrated to the cities to find jobs and a better lifestyle. As we approached Lagos by plane, I asked a Britisher who lived in the country about things of interest. She said, "Oh, just wait until you get there and you will find out."

"But, can't you tell me just one thing about Nigeria?" I asked.

"Oh, yes," she said, "Nothing works."

That was about as simple a description of the country as one could offer. I had never seen so many wrecks on the highways, such congestion, such problems of sewage and trash, and so many electrical outages in all my life!

But the Anglican Church was alive with many new converts! I watched one baptismal service for at least eighty babies and children, confirmations frequently numbered over five hundred, and Sunday services were crowded and full of excitement with the sound of drums and dancing up and down the aisles of the churches. I loved the experience and wrote a long report for the province expressing many ideas and opportunities for mutual support.

On our way back to the U. S. we made stopovers in Freetown, Sierra Leone, and Dakar Senegal, all of which were interesting places to visit. Some years later, the Nigerian Bishops, along with a number of clergy and laity from Lagos and Ijebu, visited Southern Ohio. We were now starting another challenging overseas relationship. In contrast to Africa, the Episcopal Church in America was in a decline, hence the need for renewal programs such as Faith Alive and Cursillo if we were to stay alive. I began to wonder, "Was there something fundamentally wrong with the way the Episcopal Church was operating?"

By this time, the new and accepted revised *Prayer Book* was causing all kinds of negative reactions: Bishop Krumm was shut out of an old conservative parish, St. Paul's Episcopal Church in Columbus, by its Rector who was opposed to the revised *Prayer Book* and the ordination of women. For two reasons we had no trouble at St. Alban's: I used the Tudor English called "Rite I" at the early service, and the modern English called "Rite II" at the nine-thirty and eleven o'clock a.m. services; and we had prepared the congregation for the revision through the work of the Worship Committee. Still there was tension and difference of opinion between those who liked the beauty and power of the words of the 1928 prayer book and those who enjoyed the flexibility and contemporary language of the revision of 1976.

Of importance, it seemed to me at the time, was a cultural issue which an organization called the Associated Parishes in Washington, D.C., was trying to address in various ways. Also, the Rev. Loren Mead, Director of the Alban Institute, began going into parishes as a consultant trying to deal with church fights because congregations seemed to be undergoing a lot of stress. Church attendance was on the decline except in the renewal and charismatic congregations. A few people at St. Alban's insisted on having a questionnaire to get reactions on what was going on in the church, but this survey was not particularly helpful nor did it expose any serious problems of parish life.

The prayer book was useful as a guide in corporate worship and the language was Scriptural, but there existed a rigidity in our style of worship that did not relate to the new age of free expression and open enthusiasm over our faith. In our services we were addressing matters of the mind rather than of the heart or the spirit. Had we moved into a post rational culture which was not so much based on a structural form of worship, logical and orderly, but now toward one which was intuitive, emotional and calling for a spontaneous response. Religion which involves our relationship with God is expressed by the whole person body, mind and spirit. The Nigerian Anglicans could dance and sing and move about enthusiastically while we American Episcopalians were locked in pews with books in our hands as if we were at school. Besides, one who is unfamiliar with the books and service leaflets gets lost and confused as the service progresses. We have a great deal of dignity in our worship service and I have loved it since childhood, but I began asking myself — is this form of worship right for the new age?

I had always felt the need to keep growing in the ministry, which naturally involved continuing education. But this was intensified after marrying Joani because it seemed important that we should develop a "team ministry." I was never after acquiring advanced degrees, but I did want to keep close to "the cutting edge of spiritual evolution." Consequently, we enrolled in the School of Advanced Pastoral Studies conducted by the Rev. Reuel Howe within a year of our marriage.

This was an excellent experience for both of us, so much so that we talked all the way back from Bloomfield, Michigan, to Columbus, Ohio, about what we had received at the school. There was open and free forms of worship without breaking from our Anglican traditions. Sharing such courses soon touched the heart of our marriage and our Christian life together.

In 1976, Joani and I took our vacation time to go to Salamanica, Spain, to attend an Ecumenical Institute having to do with "Catholic and Protestant Relations."

In 1977, we attended St. George's College, Jerusalem, taking a fascinating course on "The Bible and the Holy Land Today." This experience placed us at the very center of the Arab-Israeli conflict and how it relates to Biblical history.

Finally in 1980, we went to St. Andrew's University, St. Andrew's Scotland, to take a course on "The Clergy in the Eighties." When we returned from these trips we enjoyed showing our slides and told about the experience, which seemed to be appreciated by the congregation.

A year before my 65th birthday I gave the parish notice that I would retire on September 21, 1981. I was now approaching thirty-four years of full-time ministry in the church, plus (I always liked to add, in my mind), five years of a kind of lay ministry during World War II. There, as a layman, I had conducted services under the most severe, war-time conditions.

We experienced a farewell event at St. Alban's with appreciation speeches and thoughtful gifts. We had made wonderful friends, and I felt the parish had moved into the church of the future. It had been a slow, gradual process during which time I, too, grew spiritually along with my congregation. I rejoiced in the way the laity blossomed; and I was sad that some had not. Through my ministry in little Bexley, God had still used me in many broader dimensions such as Hong Kong and West Africa that seemed to follow my original calling to become an overseas missionary. I was blessed with an understanding bishop who was theologically well grounded, and a Christian leader with an appreciation of the worldwide mission of the church. There were lovely times with my dear family in Springfield, Ohio, only forty-five miles away. They were always supportive of me and I tried to be supportive of them. The loss of Elnora had been devastating and without her life was at a low ebb. Finding Joani brought "renewal" of a personal nature in my life and, again, a fulfillment that came from a dedicated co-worker.

There were some added dividends such as a parishioner, John Loehnert, who recruited me to become chaplain of the local Navy League of Columbus and I ended up becoming National Chaplain to the Navy League of the United States. This outstanding organization took me to national meetings in Washington, D.C. and New Orleans, Louisiana. Another dividend was to be a rare chaplain of the Rocky Fork Hunt Club, which never caught any foxes, but the chase was always a thrill and I survived the jumping without any broken bones.

It was a good feeling to know I had come to the end of my full-time ministry with a sense of fulfillment, knowing that God in Christ had been with me the whole way — in good times and in bad. Sallman's portrait of Jesus had always hung in my office, and I left this lovely portrait as a gift to St. Alban's. In leaving this most cherished painting, I hoped to leave another picture in the minds of my parishioners — the picture of the living Christ I had helped to paint during my years of ministry at St. Alban's parish.

I came in sorrow, I left in joy with Jesus as the way, the truth and the life. Jesus said, "Let not your heart be troubled; ye believe in God, believe also in me. In my Father's house are many mansions: if it were not so, I would have told you. I go to prepare a place for you. And if I go to prepare a place for you, I will come again, and receive you unto myself; that where I am, there you may be also." (St. John 14).

21

RETIREMENT — NOT YET!

About three months before my stated date of retirement on my 65th birthday, September 21, 1981, I wrote the Rev. Canon Samuel Van Culin, an executive in the Overseas Department of the Episcopal Church, asking if I might again serve the church overseas. He suggested chaplaincies in Cyprus and Saudi Arabia. At the same time I wrote the Rt. Rev. Edmond L. Browning, Bishop of Hawaii, about any needs of a priest for interim work, and he replied by telephone upon receiving my letter of inquiry. He said there was an urgent need for a priest at St. George's Church, Pearl Harbor, a parish I had known quite well. The parish had reverted to mission status and was declining rapidly. Since I knew quite a bit about the church and always liked the Navy, I accepted the call. The day following my last service at St. Alban's, Joani and I were on the airplane to Honolulu.

The people at St. George's Church welcomed us enthusiastically. Some had been reading about Terry Fullam and the "Miracle of Darian". Despite difficulties, the parish was ripe for renewal of some sort. The vicarage was barely furnished, but Joani and I went to a "swap meet" not far from the Navy base and bought what was needed of cast off furniture from sailors, on the move to other posts. At our new home we created a good feeling of hospitality built around Bible Study and discussion groups. Most people sat on the floor for hours, talking. The service men and their wives were alive, committed Christians simply waiting for a clergyman to come along and give leadership even though it was a revolving door situation since military personnel are frequently on the move.

John Guest passed through Honolulu on his way to an evangelism conference in Australia and gave a marvelous talk to the parish. Martin Clark and his wife Beverly led a "Faith Alive Weekend." So within a year the congregation was back on its feet and ready for a permanent Vicar.

One incident stands out in my mind worth remembering. At the Diocesan Convention, Bishop Browning gave a strong address on the urgency for peace and demilitarization which came to the attention of Admiral Robert Long, then Commander-in-Chief Pacific. At a social function Admiral Long told me of his interest in the address. It seemed important that these men discuss the matter, so I arranged a meeting. It began in the briefing room at CINCPAC Fleet Headquarters to describe the military situation in the Pacific Basin. Then at lunch with the Bishop, Admiral Long, the Admiral's Intelligence officer (a Major General in the Army) and I discussed the defense situation. There were some differences in point of view and some agreements. At the end I suggested we hold hands and said a prayer for the defense of the country and world peace. I found myself in the interesting role of soldier-priest, instigating a dialogue which I think was helpful.

After the interim at St. George's was over Joani and I made a trip to Mainland China with Scott, Dan and Lisa. We departed Honolulu October 1, 1982, for Tokyo, Japan, and then spent three weeks traveling to Beijing and eight other cities.

At the end we spent five final days in Hong Kong, which was a lovely time together by ourselves. On the last evening at the handsome Regent Hotel, with a great view of Victoria Island across the harbor, we discussed our travels. It was interesting to hear the impressions and to project what was going to happen to China in the years to come. One of the fallouts of this trip was to help one of our lovely tour guides in Shanghai, Wei Li Qian, come to the United States for study. Danny was deeply involved in a long discussion with her about freedom in our country, little knowing the influence it would have on her life at the time.

Following Hong Kong and our emotional farewells, Joani and I traveled on to Thailand, Burma, Sri Lanka, India, Egypt and Portugal. Burma, for some unknown reason at the time, seemed a pull which later took shape in 1984. It was a socialist country with stiff regulations about travel. For quite a few years it had been closed to foreigners and now could only be entered through Bangkok, with visits limited to six days.

When we reached Colombo, Sri Lanka, we visited the grave of Joani's father, Jack Lisle, who had been killed in the only Japanese raid on the island. We found his grave without difficulty in the British Military Cemetery. His marker read: John B. Lisle, Killed April 20, 1942. Flight Pilot, Sergeant, Royal Canadian Air Force. Standing by his grave both Joani and I felt a deep emotion and wanted to cry. Jack Lisle seemed to be right there with us in a spiritual presence impossible to fully describe. I tried to say a prayer but it was difficult and I could hear Joani mumbling a few words to God. A native caretaker standing by brought us some flowers and we took pictures.

Later we drove to Kandy, an ancient city high up in the mountains and venerated for its Temple of the Tooth, supposedly a tooth of the Buddha. We occupied a small guest house on a tea plantation overlooking a picturesque Buddhist monastery located in a valley below and surrounded by heavy foliage. We would frequently hear the bells of the monks ring during their incantations. This created a mystical feeling for me, sensing it was a time when the religions of the Far East were reaching out to God. In the mornings we would wake up actually in the clouds which wouldn't be burned off until around nine o'clock. At the guest house I wrote these remarks in my travel diary:

November 13, 1982
Guest House
Kandy, Sri Lanka

"Yesterday in the late afternoon we were leaving the market at Kandy and an old beggar woman approached me in the backseat of the car with dirty hands pleading for money. It was always a shock for me when I look into such pleading eyes. I reached into my pocket for some coins and gave her several. Almost immediately a younger woman with a child in her arms appeared and I wondered if she was the daughter of the old lady. I gave her a rupee. The old lady looked at the coin with questioning eyes, I guess wondering at the size of the gift and the younger woman asked for more and when I refused she walked away. Since the car was held up by traffic, still another beggar woman appeared with a child in her arms and so I gave her the rest of the coins in my pocket. Then I closed the window and as I did so a beggar boy started knocking on the car window pleading for money. Then the traffic cleared and we drove away.

How do you handle the many beggars in Asia? You give to one and others come like flies to honey. How much do you give, and ask yourself, "Am I supporting a sub-strata of society that the government should be doing something about?"

We returned to the guest house on the top of the mountain, which seemed like a palace because we knew the beggars would sleep in the street that night. We listened to Montovani's "Golden Hits" on our tape recorder and were soothed by the romantic sound, ate a simple but plentiful dinner with food left over and felt guilty. Joani and I discussed how to handle the beggars. I told her India would be much worse. She suggested we simply carry with us some small amount of money in our pockets and respond as best we could without getting inundated, as I once was in Calcutta and had to make a forced retreat back into the hotel.

As I went to sleep, my mind went to Gautama Buddha and St. Francis of Assisi who were both moved by beggars, so much so that their lives were completely altered and they gave up their wealth in order to make a spiritual contribution to the world. They were shocked as I was yesterday, but they renounced all wealth and gave their lives to the poor, their minds fully in the spiritual life. I know quite honestly I am unprepared to do this and so inside of me carry an accommodation to my guilt feelings. I am sure most of the world does this — (at least the Christian world). But there are a few like Mother Theresa of Calcutta who do not make the accommodation, and she gained the Nobel Peace Prize. So few of us, even deeply religious people, can make the ultimate sacrifice as did also our Lord Jesus Christ."

We flew from Colombo, Sri Lanka to Madras, India, and there by train went to Vellore where we visited Dr. B.J. and Meana Prashanthan who operate a Christian Counseling Centre and an Institute for Human Relations, Counseling and Psychotherapy — the only one in all of India. We had met them at Capital University, Columbus, Ohio, when B.J. was working on his doctorate and they became active members of St. Alban's parish. The Prashanthans lived in a large two-hundred-year old building constructed by the East India Trading Company and then later occupied by Dr. Ida Scudder who founded the twelve-hundred-bed hospital and Christian Medical College in Vellore. She was a leader in birth control for India. Beside the centre we visited a fine institute for destitute and delinquent boys (three-hundred-eighty-two) from the ages of eight to sixteen years, mostly picked up from the streets of Madras and Vellore. This was a fine witness of compassion in a non-Christian country.

We returned to Madras by automobile through the kindness of B.J. At Bombay we had an unfortunate layover of several days which threw us off schedule. We then flew on to Cairo, Egypt, where we were now limited to a day and a half.

I wrote the following in my travel diary:

November 26, 1982
Tivoli Hotel
Lisbon, Portugal

"Yesterday we left Cairo via Rome and Madrid for Lisbon. But still the experience in Egypt holds on to me, even though we were only there a day and a half. The short time in Cairo was perfect. We saw the sound and light program at the pyramids the evening of our arrival which is a one hour spectacular event before these great tombs of the ancient Pharaohs. The next morning we went to see them in daylight, so seeing them at night and then by day made for an interesting contrast. Prime Minister Mitterand of France was due to visit the largest pyramid at noon so we could only go into the smaller ones, although they are gigantic, too. Since I visited the big one in 1962, I have now gone into the burial chambers of all three. An amusing coincidence was that the camel driver who took Elnora and myself to the pyramids twenty years ago was the same one on this excursion using the same American slang and comical remarks. He took our pictures on the camels with our camera just as he had done before. I could hardly believe this — considering all the changes in my life since then! It was lovely to see how much Joani was now enjoying this experience.

After visiting the tombs we went to a restaurant and sat looking out on the Sphinx with the three pyramids in the background. I felt very calm and silently said to myself some memorized morning prayers. The dead Pharaohs honored so many centuries ago by these vast structures in a sense are not dead, since these burial markers bring millions of people to them year after year. The past of BC and AD were linked by these living monuments which I will cherish for the rest of my life. They made possible this beautiful scene, the crystal clear sky, the vast Sahara Desert of bare sand and rock, the intriguing simple triangles and the weathered face of an Egyptian King forever cutting into time.

We then went to see how papyrus paper is made and this was an education in itself. After lunch we went to the Cairo Museum, and instead of hiring a guide we wandered around by ourselves taking plenty of time to look at the artifacts of one of the truly great civilizations of the world. I could take time to look carefully at the sculptured faces of the pharaohs and their wives and children. They were all so handsome in the eyes of the artist who preserved their features in gold, enamel, ivory, jewels and stone. Joani and I were glad to just look at this marvelous collection of antiquities alone. We could share our impressions and wonderment by ourselves.

When the museum was closed at 4:00 p.m. we walked to the nearby Hilton Hotel and, low and behold, the second floor dining room overlooking the Nile River was serving an honest to goodness American Thanksgiving dinner. It was a holiday we had forgotten. Practically no one was in the dining room at this early hour. So the two of us had our turkey, dressing and all the other traditional food including cranberry sauce. We sat quietly together in almost regal splendor. We watched the traffic through the big window in front of us, even horses and carriages passed by along with trucks and automobiles. A gorgeous red sun finally went down over the horizon and the lights of the city came on. The string of lights along a nearby bridge reflected in the quiet river. We had planned to go to one of the old bazaars but I suggested we return to the hotel room rather than break the spell of the day by Arab bargainers hacking their wares. Also, we had packing to do for we were to be up at 4:30 a.m. and off to the airport by 5:30 a.m."

November 27, 1982
Hotel Tivoli
Lisbon, Portugal

I definitely picked the right place for our re-entry into

the Western world. Lisbon is a lovely old city with many 17th, 18th and 19th Century buildings, fascinating stone carved facades and some lovely new buildings, especially hotels constructed in good taste. It was a rainy day but we didn't mind. The best thing to do was to take a bus tour of the city which was interesting. Even though raining, I took a picture of Joani before the monument to Henry the Navigator. We even got out of our bus for a snapshot at the gigantic statue of Christ the King which dominates the harbor. Back at the hotel we had hot toddies and a warm bath followed by a delicious dinner beautifully served in the hotel dining room.

November 30, 1982
Hotel Tivoli
Lisbon, Portugal

I have a sad feeling as our trip today comes to an end. Two months around the world seemed such a long time and now it seems so short. The question now is, what does it all add up to? Did the considerable amount of money spent bring the desired results? How successful was the planning? Is all that we did a hodge-podge of memories or does the experience fit into a larger life to come? I so love traveling that in some ways I hate this kind of adventure to stop, but we must. There is a limit to our dollars, the use of our time this way and the practical matters of everyday normal living. I know the time has come to cease daily adjusting, of coming to the limit of our absorption and to return to family, friends and consistent day-by-day living. I must adjust to a new type of retired living which will be different than I have ever had before. But there will always be the desire to go on — see more of the world.

Back in Columbus, Ohio, I was now out of the ecclesiastical harness which I had been in for thirty-four years plus my first interim church job. I felt strange and a bit restless. I was now in the pew instead of back of the altar as celebrant of the Eucharist or in the pulpit preaching. The reins I had held for eleven years at St. Alban's were now in the hands of the Rev. Timothy Carberry, so I was feeling something like a boat floating around without an engine or an anchor.

But I knew this was right, my resources were not what they use to be mentally or physically and it was right that a younger man take my place as Rector of the parish, with his own style and persona. Also, our home seemed not quite the place where we should be. Our year in Hawaii and traveling for several months seemed to have cut some roots to this place, the environment and the church community. Joani felt the same way, so we prayed for guidance. We knew the house was bigger than we needed, the upkeep too expensive and there was the hard reality that the new priest didn't need another retired rector in the wings, although Bob Leake had been very helpful during my tenure. So it seemed clear we should eventually move, and probably back to Hawaii. The sunshine, the outdoor activity all year long, being nearer my children appeared to be a long-range plan for us.

Joani, during the interim at St. George's, had found almost a new role as a clergyman's wife. Her spiritual growth was clearly evident when she moved out of Elnora's turf and went to a struggling congregation, making do with cast-off furniture, but it was her home and she was by my side in helping to rejuvenate a dying congregation.

It was only a matter of weeks after our return that some churches began calling me for help and one in particular, St. Paul's Church on East Broad Street where Bishop Krumm had been locked out at the time of an Episcopal visitation. Now the congregation was in more difficulty, compounded by their location between Trinity Church downtown Columbus and St. Alban's in Bexley. Although at one time St. Paul's was a strong parish, the neighborhood had changed from all white middle and upper-income residents to low income poor black and white residents. Most of the lovely old houses had run down although there was a serious effort by some residents, mainly young married couples, to renew the neighborhood. A conflict had developed between the rector and many in the congregation, so he was asked to leave. It had become again, in a few years, a divided congregation with the pros and cons for the rector, but in time he was asked to leave by a majority on the vestry. Fortunately, the church had a sizable endowment which kept the parish in the black.

On my first Sunday as a supply priest I felt the mixed vibrations coming up from the congregation. The church edifice was lovely. Its marvelous rose window above the altar, the handsomely carved choir stalls, and excellent pipe organ, a rather large well cared for nave with a dear side chapel, made St. Paul's a fine house for Christian worship, but the spiritual environment was hurting. I felt there was only one major strategy that had to be followed besides holding services and that was house-calling. A priest of the church had to hear the people out — their tales of woe over the liturgical changes and pastoral neglect. I made over two hundred house-calls in approximately a year and three months and up to the time a new rector arrived. The loyalty of the laity was amazing and most were theologically well grounded, but they simply needed a lot of attention like a sick child. People can forgive a priest for many weaknesses, but the ministry is like a love affair and real love needs to be shown on both sides or the relationship will die.And relationships happen with personal contact and expressions of genuine caring.

So, back into many homes I went, and because I naturally like people and enjoy them mainly on a one-on-one basis, the parish began to come alive. However, I did something at St. Paul's I had never done before. The devil loves sick parishes and will begin to manipulate people and circumstances in order to break down the church. So late one afternoon I went alone into the church and read aloud certain New Testament references when Jesus drove out demons. Then, after prayer, I shouted, "Satan, in the name of Jesus, get out of this place! You have no business here. These are God's people who worship here and this is God's House of Prayer. Get out! You are not to be here any longer!"

The next Sunday I felt a difference in the worship services at St. Paul's Church. The congregation seemed peaceful and united once again. Our romance with each other and God was moving along beautifully and within six months the parish had a new priest — a mature man in the ministry quite capable of handling the situation.

Joani and I knew it was now time for us to leave Columbus and go to Hawaii, so our house was sold and packers came in to box and store our household effects for a year or so. In the midst of organizing to leave I received a telephone call from my former associate at St. Alban's, "Chip" Nix.

After preliminary hellos he said, "John, I've just heard there is a desperate need for a priest to go to Bangkok, Thailand, to serve as interim Vicar of Christ Church. Carol said to me, 'John and Joani Morrett will go.' What do you think about it?"

"Well, Chip, you know me, I'm always ready for adventure," I said. "I'll talk it over with Joani and will pray about it and then call you in the morning."

Chip had received information about the need of an interim priest from Dr. John Rogers, Dean of Trinity School for Ministry at Ambridge, Pennsylvania. I telephoned John and within a short time I was in contact with the Senior Warden of Christ Church, John Higgins.

By July 10th we were in Bangkok, presumably for a three month's interim while the Vicar, the Rev. Ian Bull, was in England for medical treatment. He had been having seizures and confused states of mind, but doctors in Bangkok could not come to a diagnosis. The Far East was not finished with me — retirement — not yet!

22

THAILAND
THE BEAUTIFUL AND THE UGLY

Joani and I arrived in Bangkok, Thailand, in the early evening of July 10th tired but excited. It was raining since the country was in the monsoon season and the traffic was heavy. We were met by John Higgins, the Vicar's Warden and his attractive Chinese wife Ping; both seemed relieved to see us. On the way into the city on a super highway jammed with traffic, big trucks and buses, civilian cars and motorcycles, we were told of the problems of the congregation. The Vicar, the Rev. Ian Bull, was in England for medical treatment and observation since he had been having seizures, even falling down unexpectedly. He had also divided the congregation between Britishers who wished to continue to use the 1662 *Book of Common Prayer* on a Sunday morning and those who liked a modern English service which he had introduced. He had changed the floor plan of the church by moving the altar from the sanctuary at the back of the church to the crossing between the nave and the choir. He had angry spells which annoyed some people who then left to go to the International Church. There were those who liked the Vicar's wife but criticized her for being involved in the production of the movie, *The Killing Fields*, which was about Cambodia.

Consequently, some felt she spent too much time away from parish activities. Nevertheless, John assured me the situation was temporary and we probably would not be needed longer than three months. As an interim priest I would simply conduct Sunday services, take care of emergencies and we would be free to do all the sightseeing we wanted.

Accepting the call as quickly as we did, we had no orientation to the country or the culture, let alone the circumstances of the Anglican Church in Thailand. Fortunately I had been to Bangkok several times and Joani once, but we were there as tourists then. We knew Thailand was an all Buddhist country, the only one left in the world, although there were Muslims (4%) and Christians (.06%). We also knew Thailand had a king and a queen since we had visited the beautiful royal palace in 1982. We knew the royal couple were highly respected since pictures of them were hung everywhere — in government buildings, banks, shops, businesses and homes. John Higgins made it clear that our ministry would be mainly with expatriates, although there were some fifty English speaking Thais in the congregation. Both Joani and I realized we had a lot to learn in a short space of time.

When we arrived at the vicarage we were taken to the second floor of a pleasant new building which had on the first floor a chapel, offices, a storeroom and rooms for servants. A circular stairway in the center took us up to a square balcony with rooms all around it, including a living room, dining room, Vicar's study, kitchen, pantry, and five bedrooms, one of which was used by the cook. This fat, smiling Thai named Et greeted us. Also present was her niece, Nitnoy, who lived with her. We were dead tired and so went to sleep on a very hard mattress in the master bedroom.

The next morning I learned from Et about our staff. She was assisted by Sian who cleaned and did the laundry. This middle-aged Thai, with a number of teeth missing, lived on the first floor with her husband and two very nice children. He was out of work so he fixed things around the property. Jit was a young Thai woman who lived in a little house in back of the building and was married to the son of the Vicar's driver. She mainly took care of the offices, chapel, and church and helped in the kitchen when there was entertaining.

Except for Et, we found out Jit was the hardest working of the lot. We soon learned there was a clear distinction of work duties between the house women and the head gardener named Pang, who lived downstairs, and Gordon Baltimore, his assistant. Gordon was a black who had been in the American Army in Vietnam and drifted into the church for help some months ago. Pang's wife had been caught stealing so was sent away to her village. Gordon was very verbal, spoke fluent Thai and seemed to know about everything, but no one, especially the Thais, seemed to trust him. He lived in a small room in the old teakwood vicarage between the church and new vicarage. The old vicarage was now used as a parish hall. Tang, the driver of an old Ford sedan and a relatively new mini van, lived away from the church with his wife (who was more toothless than Sian) and seldom made an appearance. Varuni, the church secretary, was a nice young Thai who also lived away from the compound, spoke fair English and was a mediocre typist. In time, I had to encourage Varuni to seek another job and replaced her with Orawan, a lovely, Thai middle-aged woman who had worked for a British company and spoke excellent English.

I felt I was back in China with all this staff, who were paid a minimum wage but seemed to like their jobs in the cleanliness and security of a Christian compound. It seemed that Gordon was the only Christian, but Orawan had gone to a Catholic girls school and in time I discovered she had some fine Christian values. I felt she was absolutely loyal to me and could be trusted. Joani and I became dependent upon these people and came to love them.

Once we were up and about the next day following our arrival, we discovered we were in a busy part of the city on the corner of a large double highway, Sathorn Road and the less traveled Convent Road. The only time the noise of heavy traffic quieted down was between three and five in the morning. Bangkok was unbelievably hot and humid since we arrived in the middle of the rainy season. We learned the winter months could be quite comfortable, but from now on it would rain almost every day. Fortunately, there were a number of big old trees on the compound which provided shielding from the hot sun. Along one side of the vicarage was a wall five feet high surrounding a memorial garden with a large stone cross in the middle of it. The wall was used for burial urns, so scattered around the wall were plaques with names and dates on them. Obviously, we were living next to a cemetery.

The church was distinctly Anglican in style, seating around three hundred people. There was the sanctuary with an impressive stained glass window of the Crucifixion, the pipe organ in the choir with carved seats and high prayer desks, a handsome intricately carved pulpit, typical brass lectern, simple altar at the center of the crossing and cane seated chairs in the nave. The interior was very nice, with other large stained glass windows in the nave and big doors which opened both at the back and along the sides. The outside of the building had simple, Gothic lines and a big squarish bell tower without the bell. It was a typical old English church with a nice reverence about it.

I read in a short history of the parish that King Mongkut in 1853 granted a piece of land to the Protestant foreign community for use as a burial ground along the Chaophraya River, running through Bangkok into the sea. In 1861, further demonstrating his religious tolerance since he was an enlightened King, he gave Christian foreigners a site for a church along the river. Because of periodic flooding this site was later sold with the King's permission and his successor, King Chulalongkorn granted a new site. The proceeds from the sale of the original church property to the Borneo Company allowed funds to build a new church away from the river. This building was dedicated April 30, 1905, and a new pipe organ was purchased the same year. It is still used and has the distinction of being the only pipe organ in Thailand. Going back a few more years, it was in 1892 that the English-speaking services used the rites of the Church of England largely because a number of British people were attending Sunday services. In time, it was logical that the Vicar of the parish started serving as the Chaplain to the British Embassy. Nevertheless, the church for many years also directed its ministry to the general Protestant community.

Along with finding out about the church, I learned that Bangkok was a city of six million people and still growing rapidly. It once had many beautiful canals called "klongs" and tree lined streets, but most of the klongs were now filled in, trees cut down, and Western construction, including a large number of high rise buildings, replaced the many teak houses and shops.

Beautiful Buddhist temples called "Wats" were scattered all over the city and saffron-robed monks could be seen everywhere. Much of the elaborate Thai architecture was being crowded out by modern Western style structures, generally stained with mildew and cheapened by corrugated iron roofs. Not all construction was bad and there were numerous old residences left, some handsome high-rise apartment houses, banks and beautiful hotels. But there was clearly an ugly side to Bangkok, with its many dirty little shops and alleys, which took away from its exotic atmosphere.

It wasn't long until Joani and I were out on the streets taking a look at our immediate neighborhood. Not more than two blocks from Christ Church was the famous Pat Pong, a world renowned red light district with its glaring neon lights, cheap bars and many young Thai girls doing the bumps and the grinds on tops of bars backed by a long series of mirrors. Across from Christ Church on Sathorn Road was a large massage parlor with probably seventy beautiful young Thai women on display behind a long plate glass window. Out of curiosity, at some point much later after our arrival, Joani and I went in to see what the place was like. A male dressed like a woman came up and seated us in front of this long array of prostitutes. Joani and I pretended to be dumb tourists passing through the city. All these young women were divided into three groups, one dressed in similar white evening gowns, another in yellow and a third in blue. They sat on tiers as a kind of sexual smorgasbord and customers paid different prices for what they wanted. We were deeply saddened but amazed by this situation. Once I went into Pat Pong with an evangelistic group from Singapore and began asking the girls if they liked what they were doing, all of them said "no," but we knew they were trying to help their poor families living in poverty in northeast Thailand.

We soon discovered that Thailand was a peaceful country literally surrounded by warring nations and tribes. Burma on the west and north was in a state of revolution, with minor tribes such as the Karens, Kereni, Kachins, Mons and Shans fighting the central government. In the so called "Golden Triangle" in the north where Thailand connects with Burma and Laos, various warlords, mainly from China, were trafficking in drugs and frequently fighting each other and the Thais, who were trying to stop the drugs coming into the country. Communist Laos on the northwest border was fighting the Thais over border villages. Communist Kampuchea (Cambodia) on the east now occupied by the Vietnamese, was resisting three dissident groups, one being the Khmer Rouge of *Killing Fields* fame. The Gulf of Thailand had many Vietnamese boat people trying to escape their homeland and they were often attacked by pirates who raided them for booty and raped the women. On August 1st, a conference on Indo-Chinese refugees was held at the Royal Orchid Hotel, and it filled me in on the refugee problems the Thais and the United Nations were dealing with.

John Higgins and I began to have frequent conferences about the church and people who needed attention. The congregation numbered around two hundred fifty adults, mainly from foreign countries, although about fifty were local

Thais. Others were Chinese, Japanese, Indians, Sri Lankans, Filipinos, Burmese, Danes, South Africans, Australians, New Zealanders, Canadians, Americans, and we even had one Iranian. We were really a melting pot of people. In time we also included quite a few Romanian refugees. I liked this diverse body of people since I had traveled through most of their countries and knew something of their cultural backgrounds.

The Thais came into the church mainly through two mission schools, one for boys and one for girls, sponsored by a British missionary society. They were closed down at the time Thailand was occupied by the Japanese and were never opened again. The women graduates continued to meet several times a year for lunch and called themselves "The Old Girls." They were a delightful group of upper-class Thai women, some who became Christians when they were students.

One Thai woman who was not a member of this group was Winnie Liauburindre, who spoke excellent English and was a volunteer in the office several days a week. She immediately became invaluable to me as she had been to numerous former vicars and served as a link between the English speaking expatriate members of the parish and the Thai world. She had been a secretary for many years at the Borneo Company and her husband had been an executive there until his retirement. Winnie taught me the phrase "mai pen rai" which means "never mind." Thais by nature do not want any confrontation and will do everything in their power to escape it. Consequently, if anything difficult develops, the escape route is simply to say "mai pen rai." That is to say, the situation is not important and we will do the next best thing.

Thais, I discovered, are quiet in manner even though possibly seething inside, and if under tremendous pressure can explode in some kind of violence. Once I heard Et break out of her smiling composure and it was pretty shocking as she railed at Pang. Winnie taught me to 'wai', which is an action of respect by putting the two hands together and bowing the head rather than shaking hands, which is generally not done. There is a height rule and in any social encounter the social inferior takes a physically inferior position and the social superior assumes a posture of physical superiority. It was strange to see in the newspaper a picture of the Prime Minister crawling toward the feet of the Queen even though he had gotten out of a sick bed to greet her. We were soon to get a book titled, *Culture Shock Thailand* by Robert and Nonthropa Cooper, which gave us many guides to Thai behavior. But still, Winnie was my constant resource, especially with the servants who had their clashes. On several occasions I had them all into my office to talk about things, especially salaries since Sian was always asking for more money.

Neither Joani nor I tried to learn the language because of its complexity and presumably the shortness of our stay, but in a matter of weeks, we began to pick up words of greeting and appreciation. Since Thai is a tonal language like Chinese, I knew it could be disastrous if I used the wrong tone for a certain word.

At the very beginning of our work in Thailand street people came to the office daily for food, clothing and transportation funds, and a variety of personal problems came to my attention by foreigners. Fortunately, Ian Bull had left a rather sizable discretionary fund which received baht (the Thai currency), from the United Kingdom fund for Thai Charities. This fund raised money each year by sponsoring a large fair on the British compound involving the whole British community. The Vicar of Christ Church was on the distribution committee so he pled his cause for the never-ending street people who came to Christ Church for help. Varuni, the church secretary became my translator, so I heard many stories about how the poor Thai was trying to survive in what was now a vibrant urban center but with crushing social problems. It was estimated there were around one million slum dwellers and street people in Bangkok alone.

Within the first week Winnie took me to the Bangkok Nursing Home and Hospital to meet Miss Edith Stewart,

Matron, who spoke with an excellent Scottish accent. I wouldn't say she ran the hospital with an iron hand, but there was no question that she was in the command position and wouldn't put up with any nonsense, even from the Vicar of Christ Church. We liked to spar a little bit with each other as she gave me names of people to visit. We reached the hospital next door to the church compound by crossing a little footbridge over an old klong separating the two properties. Many prominent foreigners were there for treatment, coming from not only Thailand but Burma, Laos, Vietnam, Napal, Bangladesh and India. The little hospital had an excellent reputation for treating tropical diseases. Consequently, I began enjoying talking to the patients about what was going on in their various countries. Travelers were also regularly hospitalized which often meant serious pastoral work since they were sometimes frightened at being so far from home, and in the case of Britishers, terribly concerned about medical costs, normally taken care of by their government.

In regard to the Buddhist culture all around us, we couldn't have felt more like foreigners. It was clearly evident that the Buddhist religion had deeply influenced every aspect of Thai life. There were small spirit houses by every house and near every building looking like tiny Buddhist Wats, often draped with snow white jasmine flowers and inside sticks of incense and white Lotus buds. Tiny doll figures represented attendants who served the spirits. This strong sense of spirit existence, where people lived and worked, comfortably existed with the Buddhist faith amply represented by beautiful yellow and green roofed Wats with a large gold figure of the Buddha inside. The central Buddha was usually surrounded by many other Buddhas. Saffron robed monks twice a day with begging bowl in their hands roamed the streets asking for food.

Within several weeks I went to see the British Ambassador, Mr. Justin Staples. John Higgins said I would probably be asked to serve as Embassy Chaplain even though I was an American. The Ambassador received me in his office in a friendly manner but indicated early on in our conversation that his wife was the Anglican in the family while he was a Roman Catholic. Still he said he enjoyed and appreciated the relationship of the Embassy with Christ Church. I gave him my resumé which he said he would forward to the Foreign Office in London for approval. He also wanted me to meet his consul who would brief me on the work of the chaplain, which in the main was to provide pastoral aid to incarcerated British prisoners who were held in two large Thai prisons not far out of the city. He informed me that the chaplain was also called to officiate at a memorial service at the Victoria Monument on the Embassy Grounds on November 9th called, "Remembrance Day." It was held yearly in memory of men and women who died defending the Empire. On that occasion many ambassadors would be present to place wreaths at the foot of the monument. Another duty of the chaplain was to travel to Hanoi, Vietnam, generally around Christmas and Easter, but the details of the visit would be worked out with the British Ambassador in Vietnam if I were to stay in the position after three months.

After my interview with Ambassador Staples, he took me to the office of his Consul, Mr. Bert Jakeman, who briefed me on the "Brits" in prison. Most had been caught smuggling narcotics and had been given long sentences of between twenty-five and thirty-two years by the Thai government. It was interesting to get the facts on each man, which later helped me in my pastoral relationship. The British along with other governments, were in the process of negotiating with the Thais to get the prisoners released to their own countries after eight years. Once back with their own countries, the sentences could be reduced. Twenty-five to thirty-two years was a long time for anyone to languish in a prison in Thailand. Mr. Bert Jakeman also informed me that both of us served on the Protestant Cemetery Committee along with an executive from the Borneo Company since they held the burial records.

A final duty of the Embassy Chaplain was to accompany

the military attaché to Kanchancburi on the border of Thailand and Burma where the infamous bridge was built to span the River Kwai.

It was made famous by the story of prisoners of war in WWII who were forced to construct the bridge and, because of their terrible treatment by the Japanese, were written about in the novel by Pierre Boulle, "Bridge on the River Kwai". Having been a POW myself I began making trips there, especially with war widows, to two large cemeteries numbering eight thousand in one and two-thousand in another. The camp and prison hospital had long disappeared. This was always a moving experience for me. I repeated on occasion the poem I had memorized at the O'Donnell Camp in the Philippines, "The Vanquished Speak."

Not long after I called on the British Ambassador, I paid a call on the American Ambassador, Mr. John Gunther Dean, who was the last ambassador out of Phnon Penh, Cambodia in 1975. We seemed to get along well but he had one complaint—there had been no Thanksgiving Day service for Americans in the past year. I told him if I was still in Bangkok in November I would correct the situation, which I later did. He also remarked about the respect foreigners should show when visiting a Buddhist Wat. He referred to a problem he encountered recently when two young Mormon missionaries had taken photos in a Wat with one of them sitting on the lap of the Buddhist statue. Apparently the photographic shop reported the incident to the police who took up the matter with the American Embassy. They emphatically requested the Ambassador to send the young men out of the country immediately. This situation created an embarrassment for Ambassador Dean.

Because of what appeared to be a short interim, Joani and I followed the advice of John Higgins and began doing some pleasant sightseeing along with continuing the Bible Class, visiting in the hospital and in homes and seeing three to four street people a day. Intrigued by the refugee situation, with the help of a parishioner I made a trip to Aranyaprathet on the Thai/Kampuchian border to visit Khao I Dang, the main Khmer refugee camp. The thousands of people there were in a large enclosure completely surrounded by barbed wire fencing and under Thai military control. They were housed and fed by the United Nations, better known as UNHCR (United Nations High Commissioner for Refugees). The Thais felt the confinement was necessary so that the refugees would not infiltrate into Thailand, since it had already too many poor people. The pathetic scene took me immediately back to the POW days in the Philippines where people were housed in bamboo shacks, water and food were scarce and there was little to do. Schools were organized for the children and Christian workers from a variety of countries maintained handicraft shops, but for the most part it was a matter of bare survival.

In an amputee ward in the Kao I Dang Hospital two men showed interest in becoming Christians and being baptised. I did not know when I would be coming back. So I asked them questions about their faith in Jesus and then said, "Would you like to be baptized now?"

"Yes," they said they would.

It was pouring rain outside so I asked someone to fill up a glass of water and then in the most simple of circumstances I baptized them with the rain water. We prayed together and later, after returning to Bangkok, I sent them Khmer Bibles, crosses and the prayer for peace attributed to St. Francis of Assisi. I realized here on the border one had to live constantly in the now and do the critical religious thing at the moment for a refugee, because one may never see that person again.

Refugees were not only on the borders of Thailand, but right in Bangkok. I was soon signing checks for thirteen Burmese political refugees who came to Christ Church each month for housing and food allowances provided by U.N.H.C.R. The arrangement had been made with the Rev. John Taylor, Vicar before Ian Bull, and who had developed a large refugee program at Christ Church until the United Nations got involved in 1979. I would often hear their political viewpoints which were always strong, giving one an appreciation for how deeply people feel about personal freedom.

In late August the Rev. Ian Bull died of a brain tumor and that immediately changed our situation. Instead of "interim priest" I became "Acting vicar" with full responsibility for the parish. This meant getting volunteer teachers to staff the church school due to open in the fall, helping to organize fund raising for the 1985 operations, chairing Vestry meetings and committees, and going to the annual synod in Singapore to represent Christ Church in Thailand. We were an appendage church of the Diocese, along with an Anglican Church in Jakarta under the Rt. Rev. Moses Tay whose main jurisdiction was in another country, Singapore. Out of the woodwork of parish life came a series of responsibilities I had never intended to assume, and they would last for over two years.

About this time I received a surprise telephone call from London informing me about the arrival of Bishop Bruce Rosier and his wife Faith who were passing through Bangkok enroute to Australia. They apparently had seen Ian Bull before he died and he had suggested they stay at the vicarage for a few days. The Rosiers arrived with sad news about the Vicar and his great concern over Karen refugees prior to his death. Ian had been able to see the Rev. Canon Samuel Van Culin, now Secretary to the Anglican Consultative Council, urging him to get some kind of Episcopal oversight over the two thousand Anglican Karens who had fled Burma within the past year. Now Canon Van Culin wanted the Australian bishop to made a trip north to see them. Our Singapore bishop, who was ecclesiastically in charge of all Anglicans in Thailand, would not make a visitation because of the sensitive political situation. When getting my briefing from John Higgins, he only alluded to the Karens since he knew very little about them. Ian Bull had apparently made one trip to see these people and had immediately shown great concern over their welfare. He had taken his file with him to England so I had nothing in the office to inform me about what was happening. Bishop Rosier's time was short so we decided to pray about the matter and the next day come to some decision. After a good night's rest we decided that I would first visit the Karens and report back to him. Then I could intelligently advise how he could help with the possibility of making an Episcopal visitation before the end of the year.

The following Sunday morning I discussed what was going on in Burma, and particularly in reference to the Karens fleeing into Thailand, with Capt. Griffin Herring, Attache' U.S. Navy. "Griff" told me there was a Baptist clergyman in Chiang Mai whose name was Ed Hudspeth. He apparently worked with the Thai/Karen people and spoke Karen fluently. He thought there was a good possibility this contact could help me.

The next day I was on the telephone with Ed Hudspeth who said he was coming to Bangkok for a meeting in several days, at which time we could talk about this tribe which was opposing the central government of Burma. Possibly, we could visit the refugees together. Several days later at the vicarage where we had breakfast before his meeting, he told me about the many years he worked with the Karens and what was going on in his mission to support them. He said the situation in Burma was a complicated matter and some of the Baptist leaders had doubts about his contacts with the revolutionaries. Nevertheless, we discussed the arrangements that had to be made for our trip, setting a date of September 3rd to meet at the border town of Mae Sot. By now I was fully moving into the refugee problem in Thailand.

23

REFUGEES, A COUP, HANOI, A FLOOD

Life began to take on bizarre events almost immediately upon word of the death of Ian Bull in England. On that very day the first thing was the tragic death of a British alcoholic whom Ian had allowed to live in the old vicarage before my arrival. He died in a little second-floor room alone with his scattered, dirty rags and bundles. I had never seen a more emaciated body except in prison camp. The police came, wrapped him in a sheet and one of them threw him over his shoulder and carried him out. Sadly, he was the son of a Methodist clergyman and was an educated man.

A memorial service for Ian Bull was held on August 30th at Christ Church on the same day he was buried in England. I was sure many parishioners felt badly about all that had happened during his brief two year tenure as Vicar. Undoubtedly, he would have worked through his difficulties had he lived; the problems with the *English Prayer Book,* the relationship with the people in the church, and the work to be done with the Karen refugees. In talking with a lot of people, I gained a good impression of the man, but I also came to realize Christ Church, Bangkok, was a very complex parish situation. It was not a mission but a self-supporting parish in a Buddhist country and with a bishop who lived in another country miles away.

As planned with Bishop Rosier, on September 3rd, I flew to the town of Mae Sot to see what the refugee situation was all about on the northwest border. Up at 4:30 a.m. and at the airport at 6:00 a.m., I flew to a town called Phitsaniouk in the center of the country; from there transferring to a small plane which took me to the border town. As I flew over the miles and miles of rice fields I kept thinking about the strange life I had lived. For months I, too, had planted rice like an oriental peasant in southern Mindinao, but born in Mid-America. Now I was going back to a world of guerrillas, refugees, and bamboo houses.

There would be people chewing beedlenut, dressed in strange tribal clothing and struggling on the bare edge of survival. This new adventure in a strange land filled me with anticipation.

Ed Hudspeth was at the Mae Sot Airport to meet me with a Major Ganemy, who was serving in the Karen Army and would be my interpreter. We piled into an old pickup truck and headed north on a terrible gravel road to Mae-la where we were to have lunch. I wrote in my travel diary:

"Went to Mae Sot Monday, September 3, 1984, to visit Karen Refugee Camps — people driven into Thailand by the Burmese Army who burned their villages with incendiary bombs, raped their women and forced farmers into becoming portages while taking their rice and livestock. The June figure of refugees now across the border is nine-thousand-seventy-one. Five other villages are seriously considering coming over to the Thai side. Off and on there have been as many as twelve thousand among whom are an estimated two thousand Anglicans."

At Mai La Village we stopped at a small roadside restaurant for lunch. Across the Moei River we could hear a lot of artillery, machine gun and small arms fire. As we sat down for lunch I asked if any shells fell on the Thai side. Ganemy said,

"Look up! " Above our heads was a hole in the roof where a stray shell had recently come through. So, I was back into another war, of sorts.

All the way north, which took about five hours to a refugee camp, Ganemy filled me in on the current situation. He told me he had been an Anglican seminary student and, like me, had left his seminary training to go into the Karen Army where he had seen a lot of combat.

He said the Karen were an indigenous hill tribe who for centuries had lived in Burma but had originally migrated from western China. When the British colonized Burma they used many Karens for military and civilian jobs instead of the Burmese, whom they did not trust. This in itself created tension between the two peoples. Like himself, many Karens attended mission schools, particularly those sponsored by Anglicans and Baptists, and in the process of education were converted to Christianity. In WWII the Karen stayed loyal to the British government and cooperated with the Allied Forces, fighting with the British during their withdrawal into India. Then, at the time the "Brits" returned into Burma, they continued to give them support. The Burmese on the other hand had sided with the Japanese and cooperated with them as they took over the country for several years.

After Burma won independence from the British Empire in 1948, the Karen tried to create their own independent state of Kawthoolei within a Burmese Federation of states and tribes. However, the Burmese thought differently. The new central government established after the British left, and strongly Buddhist, was intent on forcing the thirteen minority tribes into a socialized serfdom and wanted to imprint the Buddhist culture on them. Karen, for example, were not given voting power in the new government even though they numbered three million people. The long-standing animosity between the Burmese and Karens grew into a war situation in 1948 as the Karen, and particularly those living in the Dana Mountains along the eastern Burmese border, fought for an independent state. The rest of the Karen, scattered throughout southern and central Burma lived a peaceful but subservient existence. However, a limited number of plains people, many with college educations, joined the tribe living in the mountains. In the process of Burmanization, the sixty-thousand Anglican Karen lost their many mission institutions, especially primary and secondary schools, to the central government.

When we arrived at the Maes Rit refugee camp in the afternoon we came to some four-hundred bamboo houses scattered throughout the thick jungle with an estimated three thousand people. Fifty of the houses belonged to Anglicans who had built a bamboo chapel for themselves and which was operated by the Rev. David Kharo, age twenty-seven. He had graduated from St. Peter's Bible School at Toungoo and then attended the Holy Cross Theological College, Rangoon in 1980-81. Helping him were five catechists (Bible teachers). Not able to meet with us at the time was the Rev. Pha Eh, age fifty-three, who had received his training from different Bible schools in Burma. He was away at the time performing a marriage ceremony in another refugee camp. The two ordained clergy, I was told, were operating four chapels in the various camps and had over one hundred persons waiting for confirmation.

Father Kharo asked me through Ed Hudspeth to celebrate the Eucharist and preach. This came as a surprise; to use an Anglican rite I was unfamiliar with and to suddenly preach a sermon through an interpreter to people whose culture and circumstances I knew nothing about. But I agreed and a congregation of around sixty people arrived and sat down crosslegged on the bamboo floor, women and girls on one side, men and boys on the other. Babies were breast feeding from their mothers, chickens and pigs could be heard underneath the flimsy building and a slight drizzle of rain began to fall. Father Kharo loaned me his surplice and stole and I quickly organized the service so that the Karens read the Psalm, lessons, creed and intercessions in their own language. They sang familiar Christian hymns in Karen with enthusiasm.

Ed Hudspeth translated what I had to say with, I hoped, a few embellishments of his own since he knew the Karen people and culture quite well. The good thing about using an interpreter is that you do have time to think before each sentence. We used rice cakes and a sticky mixture of grape juice for bread and wine.

After the service we took snapshots and then I was taken to people's homes, simple but clean, and prayed for the sick. There was only one chalice and one patten for two priests so it was obvious to me they needed ecclestical equipment. Consequently, I made a list of the needs included besides another chalice and patten, communion wine, wafers, altar vestments, Karen Bibles, teaching aids for church school and evangelism material. Also, they were short on rice, blankets, mosquito nets, school supplies and medicine, especially for malaria.

Two groups seemed particularly strong among them, the Mother's Union and Youth Organization. Many of the men were fighting in Burma. Later on I organized a Chapter of the Brotherhood of St. Andrew which was joined with enthusiasm. Even though it wasn't China, I now felt I was where God wanted me to be — back in the Orient.

When I returned to Bangkok, I was excited and wanted to do all I could to help the Karen, who were carrying on their Christian faith under such difficult circumstances. They had lost their homes, live-stock, land, church and schools, but they had not lost their Christian faith and love of their culture. Without delay, I sent an application to the Presiding Bishops' Fund for World Relief U.S.A. asking for funds to buy rice, blankets, mosquito nets and some of the basic ecclesiastical supplies. Happily, there was a positive response. I made arrangements with the Karens to return in October and November on my own with ecclesiastical supplies I could get in Bangkok and began preparing for Bishop Rosier's visitation from Australia the first week of December.

I soon learned that the Thai government did not wish to acknowledge publicly the existence of the revolutionary Karens in their country and were opposed to the United Nations' assistance since they wanted the refugees to return to Burma as soon as possible. Nevertheless, they were not about to drive them back into the arms of the Burmese because they knew they would be slaughtered. Also, the seven Karen refugee camps were in the mountains where few Thais lived and, in fact, Karens in small groups had been crossing over into Thailand for years.

Knowing we were now to stay a while in Thailand, Joani became involved in helping to organize the church school for the fall and led chapel services for the children. She started a Women's Guild with the help of a fine Christian Danish woman, Anette Lemonius, began an ecumenical prayer group and somewhat later a woman's morning Bible class. She joined the American Women's Club, the International Women's Club and was made an honorary member of the British Women's Club. We also started to do some entertaining which Et seemed to enjoy, particularly since she always had Sian and Jit to help her. We always gave them tips which added to their enthusiasm. I was pleased the way Joani took to the challenge and began to make a substantial contribution to the life of the parish.

Anette assumed the Presidency of the Women's Guild and began helping me coordinate our work at the Immigration Jail where some six hundred people were held because of passport violations. It was a miserable place with severe crowding and terrible food. Soon Anette had five volunteers to help her, which allowed me time to concentrate on the big prisons.

An influential parishioner got us a membership in the British Club which had a large swimming pool and four tennis courts. Consequently, our days and nights were full of activity and we quickly became a part of the Bangkok scene.

In October I flew to Singapore to attend the Diocesan Synod, which took me back to China days where Mandarin was used in the Anglican services. The Diocese was to a large degree charismatic, so it was interesting to hear a roomful of

Chinese clergy speaking in tongues. In November Bishop Moses Tay came to Bangkok for his annual visitation to the parish and to confirm a lovely Japanese woman. Although he was very friendly there developed some tension between us over the support of the refugees on both borders, which he felt was humanly compassionate but politically not expedient, at least for his diocese. Consequently, he was frank to say he did not wish to be involved except to approve of aid if it came from elsewhere than the Diocese of Singapore.

By now life had become extremely busy and intriguing because we were no longer temporary residents. Major things came up on our calendar such as celebrating the 120th anniversary of the church which in a Thai calendar is an important date, the Remembrance Day Service for the British community with the Gurkas from Napal proudly carrying the British and Thai flags before the Queen Victoria Monument, the St. Andrew's Ball at the Dusit Thai Hotel and the famous elephant round-up at Surin. At this border town near Laos there were well over one hundred elephants that danced, ran races, demonstrated their obedience, played soccer, did a tug-o-war with several hundred soldiers and performed a mock battle between Thailand and Burma.

My days became packed with meetings, interviews, counseling, pastoral calling and various church activities, especially with the large Scout program held for many years at Christ Church.

The St. Andrews' Ball, a gala affair at which I gave the opening invocation in Scottish dialect, was a challenge. Miss Edith Stewart, matron at the nursing home became my tutor:

"Grace be here, an' grace be there,
An' grace be roon the table;
Let ilka one take' up their spoon
An' eat as mickle's they're able.

Bagpipers and drummers from the 1st Battalion Scots

Guard were flown in from Scotland for the big event and some people danced all night. The hardiest ones went to the British Club for breakfast Sunday morning.

Bishop Bruce Rosier from his Diocese in South Australia returned to Bangkok December 2nd. Early in the morning we flew north to visit the refugee camps and to hold a confirmation service at St. Gabriel's Church in the Thai/Karen village of Noe Bo, which could only be reached by fantail boat up the Moei River dividing Thailand and Burma. The Bishop was enthusiastically received by some two-thousand refugees and Thai/Karen coming to the event from nearby villages. His natural and humble way of meeting them was lovely to see.

The Bishop consecrated the little teakwood church and performed nineteen baptisms, two marriages, confirmed one-hundred-forty-two persons, and installed a large number of women into the Mother's Union. The Bishop returned to Australia tired, but still smiling and with a shopping list of needs which the Australian Church would try to fill.

He did not seem to mind the pill boxes and the presence of Karen soldiers here and there in uniform. No guns were ever in evidence. He made two other yearly trips while I was in Thailand, and the last year he ordained two of the young catechists to the deaconate. Now with two priests, two deacons and four catechists we worked out missionary strategy and in time had seven churches operating. We began evangelizing in the Thai/Karen villages as well as in the refugee camps.

Also, while making monthly visits to the Karen's I was able to start an orphanage with the support of a Major Lamoo who was in charge of the seven refugee camps. I was saddened over the eighteen children whose parents were killed or died of disease. In some respects I became their "papa" for a while. Major Lamoo was an Anglican who helped me in every way possible, but I never saw him without a chew of beetlenut in his cheek.

Joani and Anette Lemonius began going with me each

month to the camps where fighting had subsided on the border. On almost our last trip north Joani and I made two long elephant treks, seven hours each way with a stop-over for lunch. It wasn't too bad, sitting in a basket which was attached to the elephant's belly like a saddle. We traveled through the jungles, bamboo groves and over mountain paths. I was amazed at the use of the elephant language by our "oozie" or elephant rider who gave orders by kicks and scratches with his bare feet behind the elephant's ears. He could make the big beast sit and kneel on command. We loved the trip!

At Noe Bo there were eight elephants in the village and two were owned by our host. He owned a great bull elephant, whose tusks had been sawed off by robbers, and a small female. The oozie stays with his elephant for life, usually beginning training with the elephant as a small boy and so becomes a constant companion. During my travels with a Karen army man I was sorry to see a big bull elephant with a foot missing, probably injured stepping on a land mine, but amazingly still working hauling timber with a limp.

On a special trip up the big Salween River Joani and I met the President and Prime Minister of the Kawthoolei Government, both Baptists, who asked me to preach at one of their evening services. On some occasions and without Joani, I traveled into the battle areas in Burma, but stopped this when I was told by a Thai official that if caught I would be put in prison for two years, fined $5,000 and sent out of the country. But, it was evident the soldier was still in me.

Needless to say, my first priority was to take to the refugee camps each month 400 bags of rice, medicine, blankets, mosquito nets, books, school materials, and ecclestical supplies — all financed by the Presiding Bishop's Fund for World Relief. On these trips which amounted to three days each month, we were definitely roughing it — sleeping in the little bamboo houses on the floor, eating the Karen food and bathing in the streams. I was always exhilarated by these trips, thanking God that he had allowed me this experience in my final years of ministry.

Assistance to the Burmese, Khmer and Karen, however, was only part of my refugee work. One day I was surprised to have some Rumanians come into my office in 1985, in this case not so much for help but for what they might give. Some forty of them had gotten visas (apparently in Bucharest) into Thailand, but once there, they could not get visas to go elsewhere. Also, they could not get work because they were foreigners and the Thais would not give them work permits. After three months their visas expired so they became illegal aliens. They reported their presence to the United Nations office for refugees and were given recognition as political refugees, which provided them with some funds for accommodations and food. As the months passed they became bored. Since some were Orthodox Christians they started attending our Sunday services and, with time on their hands, volunteered to help in some way. I suggested that the four who came to see me paint the old vicarage, so members of the congregation contributed to a fund to purchase paint and brushes and they went to work. I had also noticed that some of our beautiful stained glass windows needed repair but no one in Thailand could do this. So, I asked the Rumanians about it and Sergio, with his artistic talent, did the repair work free of charge. In time we developed a close relationship with the Rumanians, both men and women, learned of the oppressive conditions in their country, and worked with the United Nations to get them into other countries.

Unfortunately, some landed in jail for one reason or another. We worked with the police to get them out and with the cooperation of the United Nations all the Rumanians went to Sweden, France, Canada, Australia and Denmark. What a joy it was to take them to the airport and say goodbye as they flew off to freedom after so much oppression under communism. This was one thrill Joani and I and others at Christ Church would never forget.

By the Spring of 1985 I was well into the job as 'Acting

Vicar' with no idea of how long we would be in Thailand. My nice middle-aged Thai secretary, Orawan, became a dear friend and co-worker. However, I discovered our black American war veteran was stealing us blind and he had to be fired. The organist who was playing the piano at Pat Pong on Saturday nights sometimes failed to make the early morning service, also forgot a wedding and a funeral, so he too had to be fired. Et, the cook and Pang the gardener got into some kind of a scrap which Winnie had to sort out for me. The young gardener we hired in place of our American black started having young women in his room at night, which I had to put a stop to. Tong, the driver, seemed to have little fits while driving and had an accident, so he had to be replaced by Sian's husband who at one time had been a taxi driver, but he spoke no English. One of the Burmese political refugees began going insane, screaming for me late at night or early in the morning, so he had to be taken away by the police and put in a mental hospital.

With all the parish activities, foreign visitors, and a busy social life, there was never a dull moment. I began losing sleep, so often I was on my knees beside the bed in the middle of the night praying for strength to meet the demands of the next day.

As time went on one of my most interesting jobs was to see the British prisoners at the big Thai prisons once a month. At first they were suspicious of me and would hardly talk. But I told them of my own prison experience and the value of prayer life as a spiritual escape from where they were. Finally, we established a good relationship and high level of trust. This was further helped by my writing letters to their families who were anxious about their welfare. They always asked me about negotiations over their release back to England since the thought of being incarcerated for between twenty-five to thirty-two years was terribly depressing. My guess was that most of them were still on drugs and they looked thin and gaunt. So, I started taking them a lot of fruit as well as soap and razors, vitamin pills and cigarettes. In time they began to gain some weight and to appreciate my prayers and personal interest. Others from various places like Kenya, Scotland and Sri Lanka became involved in my ministry which developed into two groups. I baptized the Scot in the prison yard in a lovely, simple ceremony. These were obviously tough, high-risk men, but underneath they, too, were human and sensitive. They were like trapped animals desperately in need of spiritual help. One had been a boxer with a quick temper and so sometimes would appear in leg irons, having blown off at one of the guards.

Anette Lemonius, who carried the pastoral load at the immigration jail, mentioned to me that there was a Lebanese interested in becoming a Christian. This began some contacts, so again I baptized a prisoner using Joani and Anette as witnesses in the jailer's office. We gave him a Lebanese Bible which he read at all hours of night and day in the middle of a packed jail situation where several hundred men simply slept on the floor together. With some extra funds I was able to get him released after a year of confinement.

One memorable incident happened on September 9, 1985. Early in the morning I received a telephone call from the People's Warden "Rob" Brewitt. (A People's Warden is elected by the congregation, the Vicar's Warden is selected by the Vicar to be his advisor.) He said, "John, there is a rumor that we are about to have a coup, I advise you to stay close to the compound. By ten o'clock the city got very quiet. The Thai staff had a radio on in the kitchen, listening intently to the broadcast. Then there was an announcement that the coup was taking place at the government buildings across the city. Tanks were involved and in the fire-fight five people were killed, fifty-nine were wounded. Two of those killed were a well known Australian correspondent and cameraman, Neil Davis, and an American soundman, Bill Latch. As soon as I heard about their deaths I telephoned Neil's office and offered my services. The two men were killed while filming rebel tanks firing at the First Division Headquarters not far from the capital. The *Bangkok World* ran a headline September 13, 1 985, "NBC Chief Newsman deliberately shot." The government replied that it was not responsible because the tanks were under rebel control. This incident created some real tension between the foreign correspondents and the Thai community.

With members of the press corps, I organized a service to be held at Christ Church. The nave was packed at the funeral service and there were so many floral wreaths we covered every wall with them. Three prominent foreign correspondents gave eulogies. Some of their remarks made me feel like slipping down behind the prayer desk, they were so critical of the government. In front of me were Thai generals and important members of the Thai community. NBC General Manager for Asia, Bruce MacDonald said, "What we have before us is a pretty good case that murder was done here." This statement was later reported in the *Bangkok World*.

Gary Burns of *Vis-News*, a London based company, was near Bill Latch when he was shot. On a positive note, he said Bill showed grace under pressure, courage under extreme fire, retaining his composure when he stared death in the face." Both Davis and Latch were admired among their colleagues who were often on the firing line when there was trouble. So, quite naturally they were upset. What hurt most is that these men had survived difficult assignments during the Vietnam War. It was Neil Davis who filmed the lead North Vietnamese tank crashing through the then South Vietnamese Government Palace in 1975.

To dramatize the tragedy I had Neil's camera and Gary's sound equipment sitting on the altar as a focal point for the service and behind them the congregation could see the crucified Christ in the stained glass window. It was a deeply moving occasion. My role as soldier-priest never seemed to end.

I made several trips to Hanoi, Vietnam in 1985, where I stayed with Ambassador and Mrs. Richard Tallboys who were living in a nice embassy, but which had formerly been a French brothel. They would always entertain me beautifully and I conducted services in their living room.

On my second trip, it had been arranged that I would go to Bai Bang, a Swedish financed paper mill around one hundred kilometers north of Hanoi, for a service since this community was isolated and not far from the Chinese border. On arrival in Hanoi the British Consul took my passport so he could arrange for my departure back to Bangkok in several days. A large Swede met me and we went to his station wagon parked at the airport. Things like eggs and canned goods were loaded in from Bangkok and then we made a three hour trip to the paper mill. When we arrived, I was surprised to see that the Swedes were living behind a ten foot high cement wall. There was good housing inside with a recreation club and swimming pool; yet living conditions outside were terrible. The installation had aroused a lot of controversy in Sweden. Conservatives had reported that young women (seventeen thousand) were taken from their homes, forced into work brigades and prevented from leaving by armed guards. Sanitary facilities were reported as being very poor. These young women were cutting down thousands of trees to be used in the mill.

The service in the evening went well. The next morning I met the manager of the mill and asked him if I could see the installation before returning to Hanoi. He agreed, so we simply drove around outside the mill and then he took me back into the compound. I briefly saw their commissary and then he put me in a company car with a Vietnamese driver to return to Hanoi. Just at the gate of the compound we were stopped by a little man in uniform and two men in civilian clothes who spoke broken English. Through one of the interpreters, the Chief of Police of Bai Bang, as he identified himself, said he wanted to know why I had not reported to him on arrival. Then he asked to see my traveling document but I had none, not even my precious passport. This, however, might have gotten me in deeper difficulty since our U.S. Government has no official relationship with Vietnam. I was then taken to a little house by the gate and for an hour was questioned through the interpreters. Finally, they said I must apologize to the Vietnamese

Government and sign a document of confession:

1. I confessed to not reporting to the police on arriving in Bai Bang.
2. I had come there with no traveling document. (A mistake by the Swedes)
3. I had not asked the police for permission to see the paper mill.

This incident in Vietnam was in some ways amusing and showed me the rigidity of the Communist system there. But it was also threatening since I had a Christmas service to be held at the British Embassy that night and Christmas services in Bangkok a few days after my return to Thailand. But I had faced so many threatening things in my life already that I refused to get nervous. From their point of view they were right, so I simply smiled and signed the confession, shook hands and was released. But the trip was good, to experience the Vietnamese government in action beyond the cool reception at the primitive airport and to see what was going on in the villages and countryside. I could see how terribly poor the country was at first hand. Had we won the war and had it not been dragged out by America, Vietnam would be a different place today. Like all Communist countries, it was trapped by its own system of control over every aspect of human life.

The main event in 1986 was the flooding of the church during May of the monsoon season. One morning about three o'clock Et came knocking on the door. It was pouring rain outside. With a worried look on her face she took me to the porch where I could see the whole compound covered with water. Then I looked down the stairwell and could see water covering the first floor of the vicarage. By this time Jit, Sian, and their children appeared, absolutely soaked. I was very concerned about the office records and equipment, so while the rest of the staff brought up their household effects to the second floor, Jit and I began wading through the offices bringing up church records and equipment such as typewriters and our mailing machine.

After bringing up as much as we could, I made it to the church with Et, Jit and Nit Noy. Pang was there, too, not knowing what to do since the power was still on. I foolishly waded into the church and pulled the main switch even though I could have been electrocuted! By this time, it was daylight so we could see kneeling cushions, prayer books, hymnals, and boxes floating around in the muddy water. I had just received a number of boxes of the American Hymnal 1940 edition which would supplement the British one. Our beautiful altar hangings which were in a large box in the back of the church had fallen over and were obviously ruined. There must have been three feet of water in the church and four feet in the compound. Things were a mess. The poor chapel was practically destroyed since plaster on the walls cracked and carpeting was absolutely ruined with silt.

The whole city was inundated, causing businesses to shut down. Streets were rushing rivers for several days. Nevertheless, we held a Sunday Service in our dining room; I celebrated in short pants. It took weeks for everything to dry out. Once again, I appealed to the Presiding Bishop's Fund for World Relief to help and Bishop Browning sent us a $10,000 emergency check without delay. Young people belonging to Youth With A Mission, an International Christian organization came over to the church to hose out the building and clean up the choir stalls, chairs and nave. What a help these young people were!

By the Spring of 1986, the search for my replacement was fully underway. We thought we had an American priest who was eager to come and had a great interest in refugees, but we could not get him approved by Bishop Tay.

By September the whole Vestry gave me a 70th birthday party with skits which brought on many laughs. Inwardly, Joani and I felt definitely on the way out, although our days were packed with things to do. Two Britishers were brought to Bangkok for interviews, but a former parishioner, the Rev. Dr. Monty Morris, an Australian, was finally chosen because of his familiarity with both the parish and the culture of Thailand. In my opinion it was an excellent choice, although I stayed out of the decision-making process.

Joani and I made a final trip with Bishop Rosier to see the Karen refugees, now numbering 20,000. They gave us a touching farewell at the Sho Glo Camp of over 6,000. I had made twenty-four trips to see them, close to every month while in Thailand, so we had made many close friends who were keeping their faith alive under trying circumstances. There were times when I would imagine how we Americans might feel if we lost everything we owned and members of our families were either killed or in flight. Each story of a Karen or a Cambodian or a Vietnamese was filled with pathos and tragedy. No relationship in my life had gone any deeper. Also, I felt Joani and I had deepened our relationship because of the way she stood beside me in this special ministry. The women belonging to the Mother's Union loved her and she turned into an excellent teacher, using flannel graphs as teaching aids, and above all she was powerful in her prayers. She didn't mind bathing in streams, eating strange food, and teaching the basic Bible stories to many people who couldn't even read or write. So, her ministry became closely coupled to mine and this created an even deeper spiritual bond between us. We turned the leadership of the parish over to Barbara and Monty Morris on December 14, 1986; after almost two years and a half since our arrival on July 10, 1984. It was an experience neither of us would have wanted to miss!

CONCLUSION

In December, 1986, Joani and I left Thailand with a sense of thanksgiving to God and a feeling of accomplishment. We had helped revive one more struggling church and had learned about refugee work in a troubled world now filled with millions of refugees.

Upon returning to the United States we had a beautiful Christmas with our children. For the next three months we rested except for some traveling which I did for the Presiding Bishop's Fund for World Relief. I was so grateful for the help given the Karens, and, to a limited extent, the Cambodians, that I felt compelled to tell others about it.

In the spring of 1987, we went to Kona, Hawaii, where we enrolled in a Crossroads course, a discipleship training course in Christianity for people over thirty-five years of age. It was sponsored by "Youth With a Mission" located at the Pacific and Asia Christian University. (The name has since been changed to the University of the Nations). This outstanding organization was started by Loren Cunningham in 1960.

At the end of the course in Kona we went to Makapala, an annex of the University on the northwest side of the island of Hawaii. We enrolled in other courses and I served briefly on the staff. However, much of my time was spent on building a pole house (Japanese in style) on the northwest tip of the Big Island of Hawaii. It is in this lovely setting that I completed my life story. Along with developing the manuscript there have been two more interims, Holy Apostle's Church, Hilo, and St. Augustine's Church, Kapaau, where I am now serving.

The theme of my life has been clear — a combination of

being a soldier and a priest. I make no apologies for having been a soldier who served in the military in honorable defense of the Philippine Islands and for the virtues of justice and freedom in the world. War is terribly wrong, but as long as the world produces men like Adolph Hitler and Saddam Hussein there will be armies of defense. There are times when tribal people like the Karens fall prey to the Burmese and military action will take place.

As a priest I have never doubted my calling. There may seem to be a dichotomy between the soldier and the priest — one focused on defending and killing, the other focused on loving and giving. But this division is simplistic. Life is extremely complex, a strong mixture of good and evil, of truth and lies. Because of this situation we desperately need a saviour, whom as Christians we know is Jesus the Christ.

I wish to end this life's story with one final incident when I was wrestling over the possibility of America's involvement in WWII. I was home for the summer of 1940 and spent a night at the International House in Columbus, Ohio. It was a restless time for me. I remember asking God to speak to me through the Scriptures. Opening my Bible, I turned to Galatians 2:20 and read, "I have been crucified with Christ; it is no longer I who live in the flesh. I live by faith in the Son of God, who loved me and gave himself for me." Needless to say, St. Paul had a very difficult ministry. One can read all about his trials in II Corinthians 11:21 where he writes about terrible ordeals as a Christian. He was beaten, stoned, ship wrecked, starved, in perils by the heathen in the city, in the wilderness, in the sea, among false brethren. Besides these things, he said there was the daily care of all the churches. He also expressed his own weakness, something one might conjecture as a personal limitation.

I have been able to identify with a lot of his struggles, having been knocked down by a fist in the face, starved, ship wrecked, accused falsely, cold, thirsty, and naked. And, as did St. Paul, I had the care of churches. But St. Paul had no regrets and I have none. And why? Because it is the Christ within who has made it all worth while.

I have today a quiet sense of fulfillment with never a single doubt that the ordained ministry was a calling and I could do no other. Although the military seemed to be a pull because of its adventure, national need, and the world situation in 1939 - 1945, it was secondary to the priesthood. But for both vocations my life is filled with thanksgiving.

ADDENDUM

In 1990, my successor at Christ Church, the Reverend Dr. Monty Morris, wrote to me with the suggestion that I return to Thailand for a visit. He commented that Karen refugees needed a lot of encouragement because of the declining situation in Burma. Hopes to return to their homeland had been recently shattered.

A Burmese woman named Aung Sun Suu Kyi, had been openly opposing the central Burmese government, beginning with speaking tours in 1989. She was finally put under house arrest in Rangoon. Her rigorous call for freedom and reform helped to bring about an open election in May, 1990, at which time the Burmese opposition party won 80% of the seats in parliament, but they were never allowed to meet. The success of the election had built up hopes for the Karen to return home, but these were soon shattered. A military junta took over, hundreds of people were killed, especially the new political leaders, and thousands of people fled into Thailand. It is estimated there are now 180,000 illegal Burmese nationals in the country. Mrs. Aung Sun Suu Kyi was given the Nobel Peace Prize in 1991 but has never been able to officially receive it.

On October 17, 1991, following the family celebration of my 75th birthday September 21st, Joani and I flew to Bangkok. I was unsure about the situation although reports of the activities at Christ Church, the ministry to the Karens and newspaper articles about the turmoil in Burma, gave me a fair picture of the situation.

We were greeted warmly at the Bangkok new international airport and after a few days rest made our way to Noe Bo on the Thai/Karen border. We were greeted enthusiastically and I felt like a hero returning home after a five year absence.

A new high school had been started at St. Gabriel's church, plans for new buildings were underway and an orphanage I had started with a Major Lamoo, had expanded into a school for 460 children. He had named it "St. John's School and orphanage" which was located at a nearby refugee camp named "Gray Tha."

But the military situation was still bad. After a few days meeting with clergy, lay leaders and school teachers, I went alone to Manerplaw to the Karen National Union Headquarters inside Burma. There I had meetings with General Bo Mya, head of the Karen army, Mr. Ba Thein, Prime Minister of the Kawthoolei government and Dr. Em Marta, Foreign secretary, who had just returned from the United Nations Headquarters in New York. I also visited with Burmese leaders of the National Goverment of the Union of Burma and young Buddhist monks who were opposed to the military junta. As I talked with these men who were revolutionaries, I suddenly became conscious of my own revolutionary heritage. My ancestors first came to America in 1663. They were simple farmers not unlike the Karens who grow rice instead of corn and care for their livestock. They were fighting for their freedom as intensely as my forefathers did. As I identified with their situation and the human indignities they were undergoing, my mind turned to the plan of God in the Garden of Eden, when mankind was given the freedom of choice. The Karens were fighting for this basic freedom as my ancestors did several hundred years ago. I felt deeply allied to their struggle as both soldier and priest.

APPENDIX

copy

18 Catherine Street
S. Glens Falls, New York,
23 Feb. 1945

The Rt. Rev. Henry Hobson
Bishop of So. Ohio
Cincinnati, Ohio

Deer Bishop Hobson:

For some time I have been intending to write you about one of the members of your diocese, Capt. John J. Morrett. I was a prisoner with John for a couple of years; and, knowing John's inherent modesty, I thought I would tell you about his work with us, because I know he won't speak for himself.

I'm sorry to say that the Protestant Chaplains with us were not very forceful men and when the only Episcopal Chaplain died, John assumed the responsibility of conducting services for the Episcopalians. Unlike the other Chaplains who had official status, John had to continue the daily labor for the Japanese and prepare for his services in his spare time.

We didn't get a great deal of food, of course, and at the end of our day's work most of us were ready to go to bed. Many nights, however, I found John perched up on someone's bunk under a dim light working on his next week's sermon. At one time he was really not well, but in spite of our protests and admonitions he insisted on carrying on his work.

Despite a lack of reference books, John's sermons were always either instructive or helpful and inspiring. He saved all his sermons, I think, primarily to show to you. It is a great pity that they were lost with the ship as I know you would have found them interesting.

At Christmas 1943 he organized a midnight candle service which was the most beautiful service I ever attended. I'm sure no rector ever had a more temperamental bunch of personalities to work with but he finally assembled and trained a creditable choir. How he ever managed to beg, borrow or steal enough candles for the service I'll never know but he planned and worked on that service for weeks. I know that his efforts were worthwhile as far as I was concerned, at least, in that the service helped me over the most trying day of our imprisonment.

In addition to his assumed duties as chaplain, John also was secretary and sparkplug of the Ohio Club, which was the only one of several state clubs which survived after the initial enthusiasm. This alone was no small job and took a lot of his time.

I hope that some of the other former prisoners will write you; but, if they do not, I think I can speak for all of them when I say that no one more deserved to be spared when our ship was sunk. Those who may not have known his worth before that incident came to know him because he nearly worked himself to exhaustion as adjutant to Maj. Fischer, and later Col. McGee who organized and helped all of us who survived.

During my time in prison camp I hoped that I would someday get back to tell you about John's work and now I am glad that I've been able to make my report of a job well done.

Sincerely yours,

Robert B. Blakeslee
Major, Ord. Dept.

Dedicated to those who died at O'Donnell Prisoner of War Enclosure — Philippine Islands

The Vanquished Speak

Here on this sun-scorched hill we laid us down
In silence deep as is the silence of defeat.
Upon our wasted brow you placed no laurel crown.
But neither did you sound the trumpet for retreat.
Mourn not for us for here defeat and victory are one:
We cannot feel humanity's insidious harm:
The strife with famine. pain and pestilence are done.
Our compromise with death laid by that mortal storm.
Though chastened. well we know our mission is not dead.
Nor are the dreams of victory we dreamed in vain.
For lo. the dawn is in the east: The night is fled
Before an August day which will be ours again.
So rest we here. dear comrades. on this foreign hill.
This alien clay made somehow richer by our dust.
Provides us with a transitory couch. until the
Loving hills of home enfold us in maternal trust.
We are assured brave hearts across the sea will not
Forget the humble sacrifice we laid on Freedom's sacred
Shrine. and hold that righteousness will be triumphant
Yet. and o'er the Earth again His Star of Peace will Shine.

by Fred W. Koenig. 1st Lt.. U.S.A.

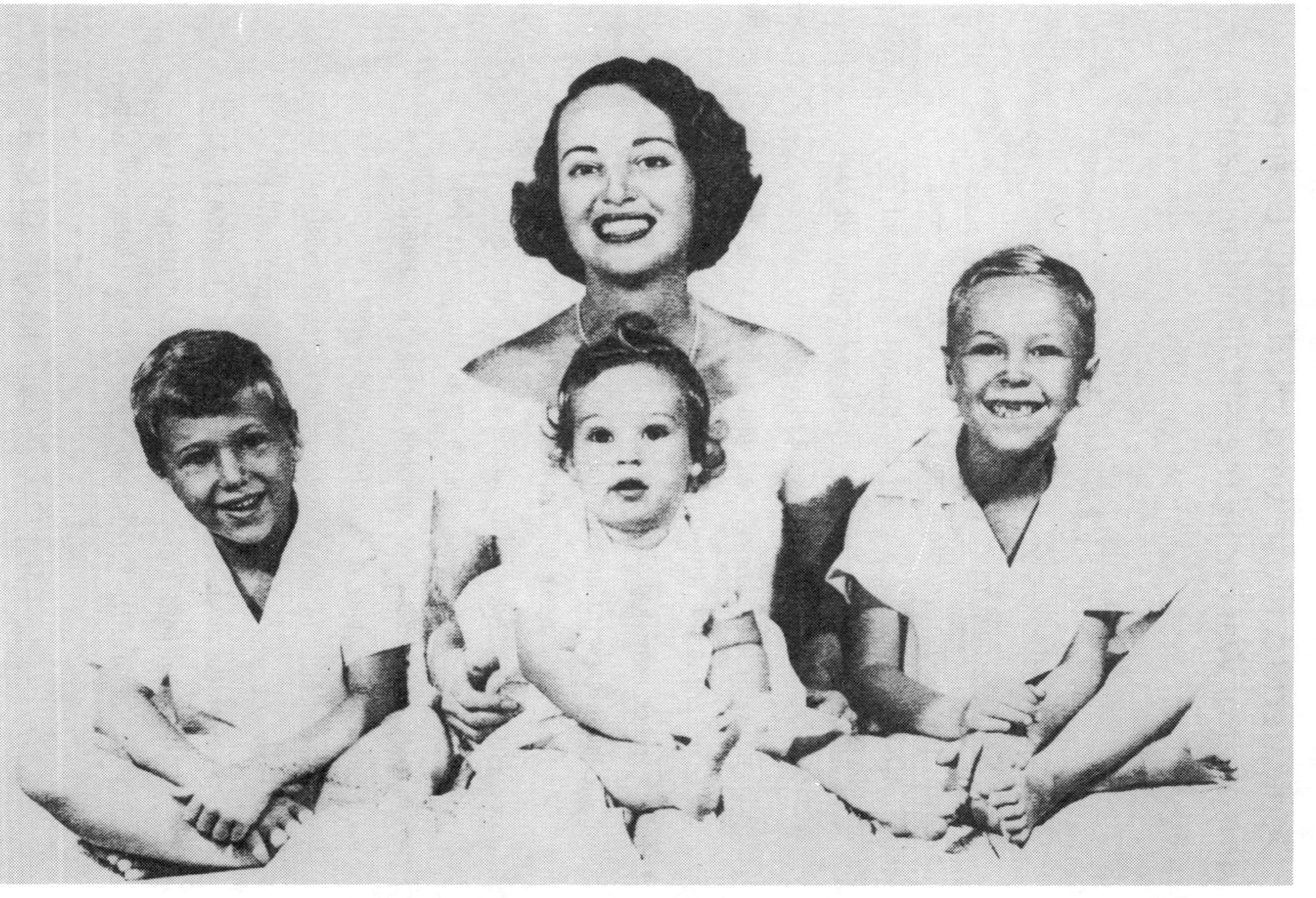

Elnora and Dan, Lisa and Scott at Holy Nativity

Marriage to Joan Lisle Germanson, November 3, 1974. Lisa and Christa were the bridesmaids. Ceremony took place at St. Alban's Church, Columbus, Ohio

ROTC — Spring Parade 1939, Ohio State University

On 75th birthday serving as Interium Vicar of
St. Augustine's Church, Kapaau, Hawaii. September 21, 1992

Seven hour elephant trek through the Jungle and over mountains to an isolated refugee camp 1986. The Khmers walked. We rode the elephant.

On Jantail boat going up the Selworm River in Burma,

Marriage to Elnora Edith Day — All Saints Church,
Beverly Hills, California June 12, 1945

"The poles of the heavy baskets would cut into our bare shoulders"

"Little Ceasar wasa judo expert, and loved to work on the prisoners"

"We worked side by side, bending over and sticking the rice seedlings into the muck"

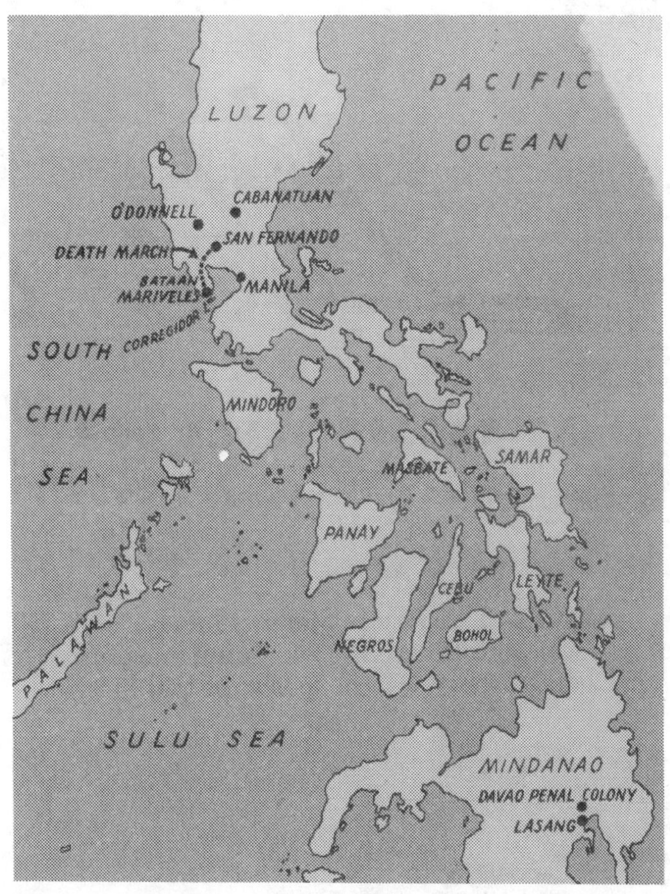

Drawings by Lt. Murray Sneddon at the Dzuzo Puzl Colony 1942-43.
From "We Lived Tto Tell"

Mary Jane, "Jack" and "Pik" Morrett, July, 30, 1921

John Joseph and George Pixley Morrett, Christ Episcopal Church Boys Choir, Springfield, Ohio — 10 and 12 years old.

"Jack" Morrett Boy Scout Troop 3, Age 14

Our maneuvers

Philippine Scouts Battery C

With a truck convoy

Missionary Staff at St. James Church and Hospital —
Ankung, China 1947.

Holy Nativity Children's Choir — Arna Hania, 1950.

Banquet for the most Rev. Geffry Fischer, Archbishop of Canterbery.
Our Hundredth Anniversary of the Cathedral, 1964.

ROBINSON

WE LIVED TO TELL
COLLIER'S
THE NATIONAL WEEKLY
FOR MARCH 3, 1945
BY CAPTAIN GENE DALE • CAPTAIN JOHN MORRETT • CAPTAIN BERT SCHWARZ

Pledge Class Beta Theta Pi Fraternity — O.S.O. 1935.
John 3rd from the right, second row.

Faculty and students. Episcopal Theological School, Cambridge, Massachussetts — 1940. First row right cud.